Appalachian Trail Guide
SHENANDOAH NATIONAL PARK
With Side Trails

1977
Eighth Edition

THE POTOMAC APPALACHIAN TRAIL CLUB
1718 N Street, N.W.
Washington, D.C. 20036

Eighth Edition
Edited
by
Molly Taber Denton

Floral Photos by Molly Denton, others by Dede Bauer

Printing History

The area covered in this GUIDE was originally part of a more
comprehensive publication known as the *Guide to Paths in the Blue
Ridge.* The first version was issued in 1931 and referred to Virginia only.
In a second edition in 1934, the area covered was extended to include
Pennsylvania and Maryland; supplements were issued in 1935 and 1937.
The third edition was published in 1941 and the fourth in 1950. In 1959,
the comprehensive Guidebook was divided into three sections, one of
which covered the area represented by this GUIDE. The fifth edition was
followed by the sixth in 1967, the seventh in 1973.

This edition, the eighth, marks the first major revision of the Guide
since its inception. All of the trail described were personally checked by
the author and information rewritten in order to bring the descriptions
completely up-to-date.

Copyright © 1977 by the Potomac Appalachian Trail Club

The Potomac Appalachian Trail Club
1718 N Street, N.W.
Washington, D.C. 20036

Library of Congress Catalog Number 76-17452

ISSN 0-915746-07-7

In a GUIDE this size it is inevitable that errors, both
typographical and factual, will occur. Please report any
you find to the editor, in care of PATC Headquarters, so
that they may be corrected in future editions.

INTRODUCTION AND ACKNOWLEDGMENTS

The eighth edition of the GUIDE represents a complete revision with a change in format which it is hoped will make the GUIDE more readable and convenient to use. For the first time a number of photographs are included. Chap. 3 has been expanded to include separate sections on the geology, flora, fauna, and history of the Park. Every trail description has been rewritten to eliminate out-of-date descriptive material; also brief descriptions are given of most of the fire foot trails and fire roads of the Park. To keep the size of the GUIDE from becoming too bulky, side trail descriptions are given in one direction only. The principal mileage measurements are placed at the beginning of paragraphs in bold face type. Distances are generally given in tenths of a mile. (For the *AT* itself and all blue-blazed trails an accuracy of ±0.06 miles may be assumed. For all other trails and roads one may rely on an accuracy of ±0.1 mile.) Overall distances are shown in kilometers as well as in miles. A strong effort has been made to correlate the GUIDE with the PATC hiking maps of the Shenandoah National Park.

Acknowledgement should be made of the cooperation of Shenandoah Park personnel in the preparation of this edition; especially appreciated was the rangers' detailed tabulation of needed changes in the old GUIDE. A number of PATC members are to be thanked for checking the manuscript for factual errors. Special thanks go to Jack Reeder, Egbert Walker and Jim Denton for their efforts in this regard, and to Alice Ruddiman for the indexing. The author is especially indebted to husband Jim for his assistance in trail checking; not only has he tramped hundreds of miles of Park trails with her but he constructed a badly needed measuring wheel and did much of the "rolling" of it.

Trail guide books, like science textbooks, are often out-of-date before they ever reach the user. As this GUIDE goes to press the SNP personnel are conducting a program of freshly blazing many of the fire foot trails to make them of more use to hikers and backcountry campers. Certain trails are scheduled to be rerouted, reopened or newly constructed.

M.T.D. Front Royal, Va. Jan. 1977

Columnar Basalt, Compton Mountain, Shenandoah National Park

PREFACE

This eighth edition to our Club's Guide to the Appalachian Trail and Side Trails in Shenandoah National Park is, in effect, a commemorative edition. It is fifty years since our Club was founded by a small group of men whose objective was to build the Trail between the Susquehannah River in Pennsylvania and the James River in Virginia. National Forests to the south and other clubs to the north were working in their areas. It was up to PATC to create the middle section.

SHENANDOAH NATIONAL PARK existed only on paper. The Act of May 22, 1926 (44 Stat. 616) had just been enacted to provide for its establishment. It was July 3, 1936 before President Franklin D. Roosevelt dedicated the Park, which consisted of lands procured by the Commonwealth of Virginia and deeded to the United States.

During this same period PATC was busy negotiating with land owners and local citizenry, building the Trail and building cabins to use as a base for its hiking expeditions. They were truly "expedition." In those days automobiles and mountain roads were not yet quite as compatible as fifty years later! We pay tribute to our founders who established hiking and trails as a joint PATC/SNP venture from the earliest days of both organizations.

Construction of Skyline Drive and other visitor facilities for the Park forced the relocation of parts of the Trail. Much of this was done by the Civilian Conservation Corps (CCC) during the depression years. As Federal property, the primary responsibility for the trails rested with the Park Service. But PATC's volunteers have been continuing partners in the enterprise. Our Guidebooks and our maps, which supplement each other, provide the public with its chief source of information for enjoying Shenandoah National Park.

Raymond H. Fadner, *President*

ABBREVIATIONS

AT or Trail .... Appalachian Trail
ATC or Conference .... Appalachian Trail Conference
FFT .... Fire Foot Trail
km .... kilometers
m. or mi .... miles
NPS .... National Park Service
Quad .... quadrangle map with contours
PATC .... Potomac Appalachian Trail Club
SNP or Park .... Shenandoah National Park
SDMP .... Skyline Drive milepost
USGS .... United States Geological Survey

USE OF MILEAGE NUMBERS

In Chap. 4, under detailed Trail data, mileages are given in bold face type.

In Chap. 5, wherever two series of mileages are given (Example 0.0-9.2), the lefthand figures are the mileages in the direction as described, the figures to the right are the mileages in the reverse direction.

"Remote for detachment, narrow for chosen company, winding for leisure, lonely for contemplation, the Trail leads not merely north and south but upward to the body, mind and soul of man."

—Harold Allen

"Leave nothing but footprints, take nothing but pictures, kill nothing but time."

—Author unknown.

TABLE OF CONTENTS

GUIDE TO THE APPALACHIAN TRAIL
AND SIDE TRAILS IN
THE SHENANDOAH NATIONAL PARK

Turkey Beard

Molly Denton

CHAPTER 1
USE OF THE GUIDE AND THE TRAIL

This GUIDE is one of a series of guidebooks covering the entire Appalachian Trail (*AT*) from Maine to Georgia. The Potomac Appalachian Trail Club is responsible for preparing this GUIDE plus a separate one for the area extending north from the Shenandoah National Park to the Susquehanna River in Pennsylvania. A complete list of *AT* guidebooks is provided in Chapter 2.

Format of Guidebook

The format of this GUIDE is suggested by the Table of Contents. A distinctive feature is that *AT* information is given in both directions, north to south, and south to north (though for certain short sections the respective directions may be more westerly or easterly).

The Trail data are broken down by the three major sections of the Park: VI north, VII central and VIII southern. Within each section the *AT* descriptions are divided into subsections demarcated by Blue Ridge gaps.

For each section, both general information and detailed Trail data are provided.

• The general information includes a brief description of the overall route and notes features of particular scenic or historic interest; it also lists side trails, accommodations in the form of shelters and cabins, and appropriate PATC or U.S. Geological Survey Maps.

• The detailed data are designated for on-the-Trail use by hikers. They briefly describe the beginning and end of each Trail section, outline geographical features and mileages which would be useful in following it, and note the precise location of accommodations (shelters and cabins), water, and side trails.

The Trails

This GUIDE provides information on 106.1 miles (170.7 kilometers) of the Appalachian Trail and over 400 miles of side trails of various types. Of the total *AT* mileage, 95.1 is within the

Park and 11.0 is outside (3.6 miles at the north end and 7.4 miles at the southern end).

Types of Trails

In addition to the Appalachian Trail, several major types of side trails are described in this GUIDE.

• Blue-blazed side trails are maintained by the Potomac Appalachian Trail Club.

• The Park Service maintains a number of graded but un-blazed side trails including several self-guiding nature trails. Other trails include Park Service fire foot trails, fire roads, and former fire roads demoted to "trail" status, and a few trails constructed especially for horse travel. Finally there are "abandoned" trials no longer maintained but kept open by use alone. The total length of these trails described in this Guide is about 330 miles. Fire foot trails (FFT) are intended for the use of Park officials but in some cases are suitable for hikers' use. However many of the fire foot trails receive only casual maintenance so should be used only by the experienced hiker who is prepared to bushwhack.

Trail Markings

The Park Service has erected concrete posts at key points along the Appalachian Trail and major side trails which provide trail information. The data are stamped on metal bands ringing the posts.

The Appalachian Trail itself is marked by white paint blazes, each about 2″ by 6″. A double blaze (two blazes, one placed above the other) is placed as a warning sign. It may indicate an obscure turn or a change in direction which otherwise might not be noticed.

Blue-blazed side trails are marked as the name indicates.

Park Service graded trails are not blazed as such but are marked by concrete posts. They are easily followed.

Fire foot trails are marked by yellow blazes, but are often inadequately marked for use by other than Park Rangers.

Trail Use

Those using the *AT* or side trails should, of course, be very careful not to damage property or to litter. Park regulations forbid the use of any motorized vehicle on trails. Fire and camping regulations are listed in detail. Cutting of any standing tree, dead or alive, is prohibited. Flowers should not be picked. All forms of wildlife are protected and firearms are prohibited.

Two sections of the *AT* are, as noted earlier, outside the Park and on private property. Many of the side trails end up outside the Park on private land. Owners can and sometimes do order trails off their property—usually after some unfortunate event. It is, therefore, *extremely important that private property rights be respected.*

Trail Maps

Three detailed maps of trails in the Shenandoah National Park are available in the Park or from the Potomac Appalachian Trail Club. It is recommended that they be used in conjunction with the GUIDE. The maps correspond to the three major sections of the Park: VI northern, VII central, and VIII southern. They are numbered, respectively, 9, 10, and 11.

The maps have been prepared by the Maps Committee of the Potomac Appalachian Trail Club and are based on U.S. Geological Survey quadrangles. They indicate the route of the *AT* (in contrasting color), side trails, cabins, highways, the Park boundary, Park facilities, overlooks on the Skyline Drive, and other major features. Relief is shown by contour lines and by separate elevation profiles for both the *AT* and the Drive. Insert maps of the major facilities are also included.

The maps, like the GUIDE, are periodically revised. Maps 9 and 11 were redone in 1973, map 10 in 1975.

Appropriate U.S. Geological Survey quadrangle maps are noted at the beginning of each section. These quadrangles, as of 1975, may be purchased for 75¢ each from the USGS office at 1200 South Eads St. Arlington, Virginia 22202.

Shelters and Cabins

Both shelters and cabins are located along the Appalachian Trail in the Park. Altogether there are 20 shelters and 6 cabins.

The shelters are three-sided structures. They may be used as overnight camping spots only during periods of severely inclement weather. The shelters are scattered at approximately seven-mile intervals along or near the *AT*; there are 5 in the northern section, 6 in the central and 5 in the southern. In addition, 4 shelters are located some distance from the *AT* on side trails. There is a stone fireplace outside each shelter.

The cabins are locked structures and must be reserved in advance by contacting PATC Headquarters. Each cabin is provided with sufficient equipment so that the user need bring only personal gear, bedding (usually a sleeping bag), and food. A spring or other source of water is nearby. The toilet facilities are privies. Lanterns and the kerosene to fuel them are provided. There are 4 cabins located in the central section and 1 each in the northern and southern sections of the Park.

(See chart opposite.)

The visitor centers are strongly recommended (only the Big Meadows Center, however, is located close to the Appalachian Trail). They provide publications, displays, and a very attractive 10-minute color-slide program. Ranger-naturalists are on hand.

The waysides, lodges and restaurants are operated by a concessioner, ARA Virginia Sky-Line Co. Inc. Reservations for the lodges may be made by writing this firm at P.O. Box 191, Luray, Virginia, 22835.

Fire and Camping Regulations

1. Camping permits are not required for use of public campgrounds. To camp in any place other than a public campground a camping permit is required. See next section: Backcountry Camping Regulations.

2. At public campgrounds the regular fireplaces constructed for the convenience of visitors must be used. Firewood is sold during the summer travel season at these campgrounds.

ACCOMMODATIONS IN SHENANDOAH NATIONAL PARK

(excluding shelters and cabins)

Facility	Northern Section	Central Section	Southern Section
Picnic Areas	Dickey Ridge Elkwallow	Pinnacle Big Meadows Lewis Mountain South River	Loft Mountain Dundo (winter only)
Campgrounds	Matthews Arm	Big Meadows (open all year) Lewis Mountain	Loft Mountain Dundo (group camping, summer)
Waysides[1]	Elkwallow (June-Oct.)	Big Meadows (open all year)	Loft Mountain (April thru Oct.)
Visitor Centers	Dickey Ridge	Big Meadows (open all year)	—
Lodges (hotel-cottage)	—	Skyland (400) (April-early Nov.) Big Meadows (250) (open all year) Lewis Mountain (24) (June-mid Oct.)	—
Restaurants[2]	—	Panorama (mid-March thru Nov.)	

[1]Provide refreshments and limited food supplies: Loft Mountain and Lewis Mountain have campers stores.
[2]In addition to seasonal food facilities at waysides and lodges. Located between northern and central sections.

3. No lighted cigarette, cigar, pipe heel, match or other burning material shall be thrown from any vehicle or saddle horse, or dropped into any grass, leaves, twigs, tree mold, or other combustible or inflammable material. Smoking within the Park may be prohibited or limited by the superintendent when, in his judgement, a current fire hazard makes such action expedient.

4. The use of fireworks or firecrackers in the Park is prohibited.

5. No person, party or organization shall be permitted to camp in any public camping area in the Park for more than 14 days in any calendar year.

6. The installation of permanent camping facilities by visitors is prohibited. The digging or leveling of the ground in· any camp site is prohibited.

7. Campers shall not leave their camps unattended for more than 48 hours without special permission of the superintendent, obtained in advance. Camping equipment left unattended in any public camping area for 48 hours or more is subject to removal by order of the superintendent, the expense of such removal to be paid by the person or persons leaving such equipment.

8. The superintendent may, with the approval of the Director of the National Park Service, establish hours during which quiet must be maintained at any camp, and prohibit the running of motors at or near a camp during such hours.

9. Dogs are not permitted in the Park except on leash. They are prohibited on certain trails which are posted by appropriate signs.

10. At all campsites, food or similar organic material must be either: (1) Completely sealed in a vehicle or camping unit that is constructed of solid, nonpliable material; or (2) suspended at least ten (10) feet above the ground and four (4) feet horizontally from any post, tree trunk or branch. This restriction does not apply to food that is in the process of being transported, being eaten, or being prepared for eating.

Backcountry Camping Regulations

Definition of Terms

For purposes of clarification at Shenandoah National Park, "backcountry camping" is defined as any use of portable shelter or sleeping equipment in the backcountry. "Backcountry" is defined as those areas of the Park which are more than 250 yards from a paved road, and more than one-half mile from any Park facilities other than trails, unpaved roads and trail shelters.

A person or group of persons may camp overnight at any backcountry location within the Park, except:

Permit Required

No person or group of persons travelling together may camp without a valid backcountry camping permit. The issuance of this permit may be denied when such action is necessary to protect Park resources or Park visitors, or to regulate levels of visitor use in legislatively-designated wilderness areas. Permits are available without charge at Park Headquarters, all Entrance Stations, all Visitor Centers, or from any Ranger. Requests for permits by mail must be accompanied by the camper's name, address, number in party, and the location and date of each overnight camp.

Group Size

No person may camp in or with a group of more than nine (9) other persons.

Location of Camp

No person or group may backcountry camp:

(i) within 250 yards or in view from any paved Park road or the Park boundary;

(ii) within one-half mile or in view from any automobile campground, lodge, restaurant, visitor center, picnic area, ranger station, administrative or maintenance area, or other Park development or facility except a trail, an unpaved road or a trail shelter;

(iii) on or in view from any trail or unpaved road, or within sight of any sign which has been posted by Park authorities to designate a no camping area;

(iv) within view of another camping party, or inside or within view from a trail shelter: Provided, however, that backcountry campers may seek shelter and sleep within or adjacent to a trail shelter with other camping groups, during periods of severely unseasonable weather when the protection and amenities of such shelter are deemed essential;

(v) within 25 feet of any stream.

Duration of Stay

No person shall backcountry camp more than two (2) consecutive nights at a single location. The term "location" shall mean that particular campsite and the surrounding area within a two hundred fifty (250) yard radius of that campsite.

Fires

No open wood or charcoal fires may be kindled in backcountry areas except in fireplaces provided at trailside shelters. The use of small gasoline, propane or solid fuel camping stoves is recommended.

Sanitation

The possession of food or beverage in discardable glass containers is prohibited in the backcountry. All other discardable material must be packed out. Do not bury such material in the backcountry.

Except in comfort facilities provided therefor, no person in the backcountry shall urinate or defecate within ten (10) yards of any stream, trail, unpaved road or Park facility. Fecal material must be placed in a hole and be covered with not less than three (3) inches of soil.

Dogs

Dogs are prohibited on certain trails which are posted by appropriate signs. Dogs must be on a leash at all times.

Bears

At all campsites, food or similar organic material must be suspended at least 10 feet above the ground and 4 feet horizontally from any post, tree trunk or branch. This restriction does not apply to food that is in the process of being transported, being eaten, or being prepared for eating.

Washing—Bathing

Campers and others shall not wash clothing or cooking utensils in, or pollute in any other manner, the waters of the park. Bathing in any of the streams near the regularly travelled thoroughfares in the park is not permitted without suitable bathing clothes.

Other

The cutting of green boughs for beds is prohibited.

The digging or leveling of the ground in any camp site without a ranger's permission is prohibited.

Any article likely to frighten horses shall not be hung near a road or trail used by horses.

Hunting or possession of fire-arms is prohibited. No camp may be established in the park and used as a base for hunting outside the park.

Saddle, pack, or draft animals shall not be kept in or near any camping area.

Clothing and Equipment

Hikers should keep in mind that temperatures are often much lower along the Blue Ridge crest than at low elevations, especially in winter. Snow accumulates sooner and lasts much longer in the Park than it does in the Washington area. In addition, when hiking along exposed ridges in windy weather, one must consider the chill factor as well as the actual temperature.

Long pants offer considerable protection from snakes, poison ivy, and nettles. In rainy weather water repellent jackets or ponchos are advisable and it is wise to have a set of dry clothes to change into.

Good shoes or boots are important if one is hiking very far. Special attention should be given to obtaining comfortable shoes with non-slip soles and heels. For detailed advice on selecting Trail footwear, see the articles on boots in the PATC BULLETIN for July-September and October-December 1969.

The amount of equipment needed will, naturally, vary with the length of hike. But in general it is good advice to carry at least a compass, a first aid kit, a whistle and a small canteen. The latter is particularly useful in hot, dry weather when springs are apt to go dry. During such periods it is also desirable to carry an insect repellent of some sort.

For a more detailed discussion of clothing and equipment for trail travel, including descriptions of specific items and where to buy them, see LIGHTWEIGHT EQUIPMENT FOR HIKING, CAMPING AND MOUNTAINEERING, published by the Potomac Appalachian Trail Club. Price $1.00.

Poison Ivy and Snakes

Poison Ivy

Poison Ivy is found along the Trail. Poisoning is largely preventable if one knows how to identify the plants. They are usually vines but in full sunlight may grow as low shrubs. The leaves always consist of three leaflets. Only one three-part leaf leads off from each node on the stem.

The skin irritant of poison ivy is found in all parts of the plant including roots and fruit. But the danger of poisoning is greatest in spring and summer when sap is abundant.

While poisoning usually is caused by contact with some part of the plant, it may also be caused by contact with some intermediate object which has touched a plant, such as clothing, dogs and cats, etc.

The time between contamination and first symptoms varies greatly with individuals. They may appear in a few hours or even after 5 days or more. There is no absolute quick cure for all individuals. Prompt washing with a strong soap may help and certain lotions can reduce irritation.

Poisonous Snakes

Two types of poisonous snake inhabit the area covered by this GUIDE: the copperhead and the timber rattlesnake. *Copperheads* are rarely more than 3 ft. long; they have a coppery-to-dull brown head and a pale pinkish- or reddish-brown body marked with large cross bands of chestnut brown resembling dumbbells or hourglasses; the tail is tapered. The *timber rattlesnake* is usually 2.5 to 3.5 feet long; it may be yellow or tan with chevron-shaped cross bands of black or dull brown, but they are often so dull as to appear entirely black; the tail either is blunt or carries the characteristic rattles. Both snakes have heads that are rather flat on top and have wide jaws; immediately behind the jaw the neck is much smaller. The body tends to be fat and heavy. Neither is aggressive. They are dangerous only if cornered or surprised.

Although both snakes are among the least venomous and cases of snakebite are relatively uncommon, they are serious enough to warrant care on the part of the hiker to avoid them. The most important precaution is not to put your hands or feet in places you cannot see clearly. In particular, avoid piles of rock, wood, or brush. Do not sit on rock walls. Wear high-topped boots. Stay on trails, rather than plunging through underbrush. During cool spells and at night, watch the trail for snakes that may be too sluggish to get out of the way. Do not hike alone.

In case of snake bite, the most important thing is to get medical attention to the victim (or vice versa, if necessary) as soon and with as little excitement and exertion by the victim as possible. Antivenin (snakebite serum) is useful even if given hours after the bite. Because antivenin may have side effects, it is important to know definitely whether a bite is from a poisonous snake, and it is desirable to know which species is involved.

Distress Signal

An emergency call for distress consists of three short calls, audible or visible, repeated at regular intervals. A whistle is particularly good for audible signals. Visible signals may include: daytime, light flashed with a mirror or smoke puffs; at night, a flashlight or three small bright fires.

Anyone recognizing such a signal should acknowledge it by a signal of two calls—if possible by the same method of signaling. Then, obviously, he should go to the distressed and determine the nature of the emergency. If more competent aid is needed, he should try to arrange for it.

Doyle River Falls

CHAPTER 2

THE APPALACHIAN TRAIL

The Appalachian Trail is a continuous, marked foothpath extending from Mt. Katahdin, in the central Maine wilderness, some 2,000 miles south to Springer Mountain in Georgia. It is a skyline route along the crest of the ranges generally referred to as Appalachian; hence the name of the Trail.

Early History

The Appalachian Trail was originally proposed in 1921 by Benton MacKaye, forester and regional planner of Shirley Center, Massachusetts. From his early wanderings in the New England forests, he had conceived the vision of a trail which would be the backbone of mountain recreation in the East. He wrote up his plan in an article, "The Appalachian Trail, An Experiment in Regional Planning," in the October 1921 issue of the *Journal of the American Institute of Architects.*

There was some interest in the New York-New Jersey area; a section was constructed near Bear Mountain in the Palisades Interstate Park. But it was not until 1926, when Arthur Perkins of Hartford, Connecticut, revived the endless footpath idea, that enthusiasm among outdoor groups initiated the inclusion of sections of trail already in use as portions of the Appalachian Trail.

The existing sections included the Appalachian Mountain Club's trails in New England, the Long Trail of the Green Mountain Club in Vermont, and the Dartmouth Outing Club's trail system between the Green Mountains of Vermont and the White Mountains of New Hampshire. With the Bear Mountain and Harriman sections of Palisades Interstate Park in New York, existing trails made up a total of about 350 miles out of the planned 2000 miles from Maine to Georgia.

In the south, trails in National Forests were developed. Some time later two National Parks, the Great Smoky Mountains and Shenandoah, each contributed some of the most used hiking trails. This was all on publicly owned lands.

The connecting trails, however, would have to be on private land. The trail pioneers worked out routes, mostly along

mountain tops, for some of the best scenery in the East. Their
enthusiasm persuaded land owners to become hosts to the Trail.
Generally it was oral permission, quite adequate in the early
1930's. Owners really didn't expect too many folks to want to
walk in their mountains.

New clubs were formed to build and maintain the Trail. The
U.S. Forest Service and the National Park Service, state parks
and forests translated their interest into real assistance.

The Trail Route

The Appalachian Trail traverses fourteen states. From
Katahdin in Maine the route leads in a general southwesterly
direction across Maine and New Hampshire and into Vermont,
where it turns south on the Long Trail along the crest of the
Green Mountains to the Massachusetts line. It then follows the
highlands in western Massachusetts, has a rather circuitous
course in western Connecticut, crosses the Hudson River at
Bear Mountain Bridge, and follows close to the New York-New
Jersey Line to the base of the Kittatinny Range, which it follows
to the Delaware Water Gap. West of the Water Gap it follows
the crest of Blue Mountain to Swatara Gap where, to avoid the
Edward Martin Military Reservation, it turns northwest. After
crossing several ridges and traversing the beautiful St.
Anthony's Wilderness, it descends from Peters Mountain to
cross the Susquehanna on the Clarks Ferry Bridge.

From the Susquehanna River south, the Trail follows Cove
Mountain to Grier Point, crosses the Cumberland Valley by
secondary roads, and then traverses South Mountain through
Michaux State Forest in Pennsylvania to Pen Mar. It leads
across Maryland to the Potomac River at Weverton, follows
the towpath of the Chesapeake and Ohio Canal to Sandy Hook
Bridge, a mile east of Harpers Ferry. From the Potomac the
Trail in general follows the crest of the Blue Ridge, continuing
south through the Shenandoah National Park.

At Rockfish Gap the section maintained by the Potomac
Appalachian Trail Club ends. Beyond, the route leads through
the George Washington National Forest and the Jefferson
National Forest, west of Roanoke. It follows the western rim of

the Blue Ridge into Tennessee and North Carolina passing through the Cherokee and Pisgah National Forests and the Great Smoky Mountains National Park. From here it cuts through the Nantahala Mountains in the Nantahala National Forest and in Georgia traverses the Chattahoochee National Forest to Springer Mountain.

The Appalachian Trail Conference

The Appalachian Trail Conference is the parent organization for the overall Trail. It coordinates efforts of trail clubs, National and State governments, and individuals in trail building, marking and maintenance. The Conference is headquartered at Box 236, Harpers Ferry, W. Va. 25425. Office hours are 9-5 weekdays. Phone: (304) 535-6331.

The Trail route is divided into six districts with three representatives from each serving on the Board of Managers, the governing body of the Appalachian Trail Conference. Sessions of the Trail Conference are held every second or third year.

The membership consists of organizations which maintain the Trail or contribute to the Trail project, individuals who in either personal or an official capacity are responsible for the maintenance of sections of the Trail, and individual duespaying members.

ATC membership is currently $12.50 for the first year and $10.00 a year thereafter. Membership includes a subscription to the quarterly, Appalachian Trailway News, published in January, March, May, August and November. (Subscriptions are $5.00 per year for non-members.) Each year in the May issue the "Trail Reports" shows when each section of *AT* was last cleared and painted, its general condition, and any new developments. The Conference also issues a newsletter, bulletins, and guidebooks.

More detailed information on the Appalachian Trail is contained in the following bulletins:

The Appalachian Trail, Publication No. 5
Suggestions for Appalachian Trail Users, Publication No. 15
Both are available from the Conference and the PATC.

Guidebooks issued by the Conference and/or available through it include:

Guide to The Appalachian Trail in Maine (Vol. I) (Published by Maine Appalachian Trail Club.)

Guide to The Appalachian Trail in Maine, Katahdin Section (Vol. II)

Guide to The Appalachian Trail in New Hampshire and Vermont (ATC Publication No. 22)

Guide to The Appalachian Trail in Massachusetts and Connecticut (ATC Publication No. 21)

Guide to The Appalachian Trail in New York and New Jersey (issued by the New York-New Jersey Trail Conference)

Guide to The Appalachian Trail in Pennsylvania (issued by the Keystone Trails Association)

Guide to The Appalachian Trail from the Susquehanna River to the Shenandoah National Park (issued by the Potomac Appalachian Trail Club)

Guide to the Appalachian Trail in Central and Southwestern Virginia (ATC Publication #25.)

Guide to The Appalachian Trail in Tennessee and North Carolina: Cherokee, Pisgah and Great Smokies' (ATC Publication #24).

Guide to The Appalachian Trail in the Great Smokies, the Nantahalas and Georgia, ATC Publication #23).

A complete list of publications, with current prices, is available from the Conference.

Legislative Developments

The first meeting of the Conference was held in March 1925. In the early years, the primary responsibility of the group was to guide the construction and maintenance of the Trail. Since completion of the Trail in 1937, the Conference has been concerned with maintenance, preserving the continuity of the route, and providing information for those using the Trail.

In 1938 the Conference was instrumental in negotiating the signing of the Appalachian Trailway Agreement by the National Park Service, the U.S. Forest Service, and most of the states through which the Trail runs. It meant that on land under the jurisdiction of Federal agencies, no incompatible development would be permitted within a zone of one mile on either side of the Appalachian Trail. (The states subscribed to ¼-mile zone because of smaller holdings).

Events of the postwar years presaged the need for protecting the Trail and its environment. Representative Daniel Hoch, an ardent hiker from the Blue Mountain Eagle Climbing Club in Pennsylvania, introduced a bill in 1945 for the National System of Foot Trails as an amendment to the Highway Act. Because it had only a preliminary hearing, it was reintroduced in the next Congress, only to fail again.

But the emphasis was now on perservation of the Trail. It was clear that some kind of help from the Federal Government was essential if an unbroken Trail was to be maintained. In 1964 Senator Gaylord Nelson of Wisconsin introduced a bill to protect and promote the *A T.* Officers of the Conference worked with the legislators to draft the bill. Although it did not pass, it demonstrated the strong backing such legislation had from outdoor people generally.

Work continued behind the scenes. In 1968, a broader bill received both strong administration and broad bipartisan support in Congress. The work of years was culminated in its passage.

National Trails System Act

On October 2, 1968, President Johnson signed Public Law 90-543, the National Trails System Act. The Act established a national system of recreation and scenic trails and designated the Appalachian Trail and the Pacific Crest Trail as the first components of the system.

The Act states that the Appalachian Trail shall be administered primarily as a footpath by the Secretary of the Interior, in consultation with the Secretary of Agriculture. The Secretary is required to establish an Advisory Council of not more than 35 persons to work with the Department on Trail matters.

The first Advisory Council met several times, but at the end of the five year term provided for in the Act it was not reappointed. By mid-1974 the clubs supported the need for a new Council with a far more effective role. In June 1975 the second National Scenic Trail Advisory Council was formally appointed. Out of their first meeting came a number of resolutions for getting the National Park Service into more active participation in securing the trail. Three months after the meeting, the NPS had made every effort to comply. The five million dollars authorized in the 1968 Act was never appropriated. The Act also provided two years for individual states to acquire protection to the *AT*. Even though it allowed the Park Service to step in to continue the program of securing the route, the states having a positive program were encouraged to continue. Both Maryland and Virginia in this area are carrying on effective but different programs under state legislation. It is turning out that acquisition of land or rights to cross land is a slow process when it is a permanent route which is essential. Under the dynamic present Advisory Council, the active participation by the National Park Service, the various state programs, and the intense interest of the constituent clubs of the Appalachian Trail Conference, it looks as if the Appalachian Trail project is moving toward a secure route.

The present procedures for maintaining the Appalachian Trail are to be continued. The role of the Conference will also be essentially the same.

Potomac Appalachian Trail Club

The Potomac Appalachian Trail Club, founded in November 1927, is one of the 32 organizations which maintains the Appalachian Trail under the Conference. It is also the third largest in number of members (over 2500) being surpassed only by the Appalachian Mountain Club in Boston and the Green Mountain Club in Vermont, both older organizations.

Altogether, the PATC is responsible for the maintenance of about 230 miles of the Appalachian Trail and approximately 260 miles of blue-blazed side trails. The *AT* is largely divided between the area reported in this GUIDE and the portion north of the Park (see the GUIDE TO THE APPALACHIAN TRAIL FROM THE SUSQUEHANNA RIVER TO THE SHENANDOAH NATIONAL PARK). In addition, PATC maintains side trails in George Washington National Forest and is currently developing an extended side trail known as the "Big Blue" (see Chapter 5, "Side Trails"). As noted earlier, PATC also maintains a network of shelters and cabins.

The Club issues a number of publications prepared by members. These include the maps and guides cited in Chapter 1 as well as two periodicals which are sent to members: a monthly newsletter, *Potomac Appalachian,* and an occasional special issue in magazine form. A complete list of publications, with prices, may be obtained from PATC Headquarters.

The Club has an active Mountaineering Section, which offers assistance and training in rock climbing techniques to beginners, as well as more difficult climbing opportunities for the advanced climber. Information on their weekly activities is contained in UP ROPE, a monthly publication of the Section, available from PATC Headquarters.

PATC owns its own headquarters building which houses its many activities and provides an office to serve the public.

New Challenges

Today, as more and more people turn toward the mountains to find respite from city life, there is a growing threat to the future of the Appalachian Trail. Despite the passage of the National Trails System Act, additional efforts are necessary to preserve enough acreage to protect shelters and springs as well as the actual Trail route. Also, with the rapid pace of new commercial developments in the mountains of southern Pennsylvania, Maryland, and northern Virginia, the inevitable delays in procurement of land under the Trails Act may mean the loss of certain areas to the *AT* for good.

In the summer of 1969, the PATC made the first commitment for trail lands by purchasing 15 acres of land in northern Virginia containing 1/3 mile of the *AT* and a shelter. To finance future such acquisitions of endangered sections of trail lands, the PATC has established a Land Acquisition Fund and continues to solicit contributions from members and other persons who have an interest in the Trail and a desire to protect it for future generations of hikers.

To date over fifty additional acres have been purchased using this fund. The club members administering the money foresee a far greater role to be taken by the PATC in the future. No matter how much acquisition and protection is through federal and state auspices, it is the timely action by the club which could save an endangered piece of trail land or provide a connecting tract between assured trail land in a state program.

The Appalachian Trail Conference has established a similar fund for land acquisition.

An added dimension of the activities of the PATC is trying to answer requests for assistance in building and maintaining trails in other areas, including a Massanutten Trail System and a network of trails in the Allegheny Front Area of West Virginia.

In branching out, the Club is beginning to fulfill Benton MacKaye's dream of a network of foot trails with the Appalachian Trail as the backbone.

The Potomac Appalachian Trail Club expressly denies any liability for any accident or injury to persons using the Trail.

CHAPTER 3

THE SHENANDOAH NATIONAL PARK

The Shenandoah National Park extends for 80 miles along the Blue Ridge Mountains between Front Royal on the north and Waynesboro on the South. It contains over 300 square miles. There are 60 peaks ranging in elevation from 3,000 to 4,000 feet.

The Park is divided into three main sections by two U.S. highways: the north, extending from Front Royal south to Thornton Gap and U.S. Route 211; the central, from Thornton Gap to Swift Run Gap and U.S. Route 33; and the southern, from Swift Run Gap to Jarmans Gap.

The Skyline Drive extends the full length of the Park. It runs 105.4 miles from Front Royal to Rockfish Gap. Parking overlooks are provided at 75 points along the Drive. A single-entry fee is charged for those not carrying Golden Eagle passes.

History of The Park

Shenandoah National Park was established through a remarkable combination of efforts at the Federal, State, and local level. In 1923 the National Park Service recommended the establishment of a park in the Appalachian Range. The following year Congress passed a bill setting up a Southern Appalachian National Park Commission. A site in the Blue Ridge Mountains was recommended and a bill introduced in Congress providing for the acquisition of land. It was signed by President Coolidge in February 1925.

The next problem was the familiar one of financing. No Federal funds were available. A Shenandoah Park Association was formed to raise money. In the course of nine months, $1,249,000 was raised from private sources. The Virginia Assembly, at the request of then Governor Harry F. Byrd, voted an additional $1 million. Congress passed a bill in May 1926 to establish the Park when title to the lands had passed to the Federal Government.

Land purchases were begun by the State in 1926 and went on for eight years. Some land was not given up willingly. Altogether, 3,870 private tracts were acquired. Approximately

300 families still living in the Park were settled nearby. The Park was formally established with the deeding of the land—176,430 acres—to the Federal Government in December 1935. President Roosevelt dedicated the Park at Big Meadows on July 3, 1936.

The Civilian Conservation Corps moved in in 1933 and soon a thousand individuals were at work on fire protection and recreational developments. To provide other facilities, the Interior Department conceived the idea of awarding the entire Park to one concessioner; the first bid was received in March 1936.

The retreat on the Rapidan River which Herbert Hoover used while President of the United States was donated to the Federal Government by him at the close of his term in office. The property, known of today as the Hoover Camp, is now within the Shenandoah Park and is administered by the Park Service.

A Skyline Drive was visualized at the outset as one of the major attractions. Construction was started in July 1931. The central section was completed in September 1934. The northern section was opened in October 1936 and the southern section in 1939. Construction costs were paid out of Federal funds. They are reported to have averaged $47,000 per mile, of nearly $5 million for the total length.

Clearing of the original Appalachian Trail route in the Park was done by the Potomac Appalachian Trail Club in the late 1920's and early 1930's. The northern section was opened in 1929-30. Many sections subsequently had to be relocated with the construction of Skyline Drive and hence were built by the Park—more specifically the CCC—from 1933 to 1937.

The Park has not grown greatly in size since establishment—only some dozens of acres—for a number of legal and financial reasons. But the boundaries are subject to change as the Park exchanges property. Southeast of the Park boundaries in the central section, a number of Virginia Wildlife Areas have been established.

Since 1965 the number of hikers and of backcountry hikers have been increasing exponentially, or so it seems. Overuse of the shelter areas became so detrimental that the Park Service discontinued their use for camping except in extremely inclement weather.

Since 1967, when the National Park Service first suggested that wilderness areas be established in the Shenandoah National Park, park officials, citizen conservation groups, and the U. S. Congress have been considering wilderness proposals ranging from 79,000 to 112,000 acres out of the 194,000 total acres in the Park. One such proposal for 80,000 acres—the proposal supported by the National Park Service—passed the U.S. Senate in 1973 but was not acted on by the House.

For further history on the Park, see *Park Guide,* Shenandoah National Park, price, 50¢, on sale in the Park. Also *Skyland, The Heart of the Shenandoah National Park,* by George Freeman Pollock, also on sale there. Three books by Darwin Lambert may be bought through the Shenandoah Natural History Association, Shenandoah National Park, Luray, Va. 22835 and are available in the PATC library: *Illustrated Guide to Shenandoah National Park and Skyline Drive, The Earth-Man Story,* and *Herbert Hoover's Hide-away.* Another book available in the PATC library is *The Shenandoah National Park Travelogue,* 1937, H.K. Hinde, ed.

Natural History of the Park

The area presently composing the Park was once farmed and heavily lumbered. From the middle 1700's to the late 1800's the area was fairly prosperous. In the mid-1800's there was a flurry of interest in mining. But late in the 19th century economic decline began to set in; the demand for handicraft products of the hills dropped off and blight killed most of the chestnut trees. Families began to move elsewhere and population dwindled.

With the decline of farming and lumbering, the forest began to take over. This process was further accelerated with the establishment of the Park. Today nearly all of the land is wooded.

Geology of the Shenandoah Park

Once upon a time (pre-Cambrian time), perhaps 800 million years ago, the area that is now the Shenandoah Park was a relatively level land with hills no higher than a thousand feet above the valleys. The underlying rock was granite or other igneous rock, with only a shallow soil on the hilltops and slopes, but with a deeper accumulation of eroded material in the low areas. Then came the only known major period of volcanic activity for this area. Lava welled up through cracks in the earth's crust and spread out rather evenly over the land, first filling the valleys but finally drowning the hilltops. There was not just a single flow but a series of at least seven for a total thickness of 1500 ft. (Eroded material which accumulated between the flows help mark the divisions.) Finally, the volcanic action ceased and normal erosion again caused soil and gravel to accumulate.

Geologists today believe that mountain building has almost always been caused by collisions of continents. There is evidence that the Atlantic Ocean has opened and closed, perhaps several times, since the creation of the earth. One important era of mountain building occurred about 420 million years ago during a collision between North America and Europe. Although the mountains formed by this collision have been eroded away, traces of their existence still remain. The super-continent of Euro-America existed for a long time. During the period from about 325 to 300 million years ago there is evidence that the sea-level was high and that much of Euro-America was covered by shallow seas with some land along the present eastern coast of North America above sea level while the present Appalachian region was part of an inland sea. Rains eroded these eastern highlands and the streams and rivers which originated in them dumped tremendous amounts of sand, then clay, then more sand into the shallow inland sea covering deeply the older volcanic soil and the lava beds and igneous rock below. As the seas widened and deepened, sea animals (invertebrates only) flourished and their skeletons accumulated on the sea bottom as limey muds atop the earlier sands and clays. Pressure of the top layers caused the lower layers of sediment to harden, the sand into sandstone, the clay into shale and the limey muds into limestone. Apparently, at some point during this geologic period, the land of the Blue Ridge rose above sea level whereas that farther west remained below sea level for many more years, receiving thick deposits of sand, clay and lime.

Then, about 250 million years ago there was a tremendous continental collision as Africa moved in and rammed the continent of Euro-America. The destruction of ocean between Africa and Euro-America and the disappearing ocean floor created volcanic mountains on the Africa side. On the Euro-American side the edge of the continent was rumpled and uplifted, forming mountains. In some places the African plate was shoved over the North American plate. The tremendous pressure, coming from the southeast in our area, caused the earth's crust to fold, like a rug, into long parallel ridges. The mountain chain so formed extended from Poland and Germany (Harz Mtns.) west through Belgium, France and southern England, then on to Newfoundland and thence southwest to Birmingham, Ala. As the pressure continued the folds became higher and steeper and rocks which had been laid down in horizontal beds were tilted vertically in places.

In some places the deeply buried basaltic (lava) and granitic rocks were shoved westward over upturned layers of sandstone, shale and even limestone. The Blue Ridge Thrust Fault can be traced from Alabama to Roanoke and probably as far north as Pennsylvania. The present Blue Ridge mountains were then the lower western edge of a huge anticlinorium which formed a mountain range possibly 5 miles high, although erosion may have kept pace with the lifting of the land in which case this early mountain range was never so high. Besides the folding of the earth's crust here, the same tremendous pressures caused much of the rock, both igneous and sedimentary, to be altered—the basalt into greenstone, the sandstone into quartzite, and the shales, at some localities, into slate.

The supercontinent, made up of Euro-America and Africa and called by geologists *Pangaea,* broke up around 190 million years ago when the Atlantic reopened between North America and Africa (leaving remnants of the African continent along a southeastern strip of N. A.) Separation of North America from Europe was not completed for another 100 million years.

By the beginning of Cretaceous time, 130 million years ago, the period of mountain building was over and erosion had leveled much of the land, leaving low hills here and there. River drainage was now to the east, into the Atlantic Ocean. Sometime in Early Cretaceous time the land was gently tilted, with the Appalachian region lifted as the coastal areas were lowered. This gave the formerly lazily flowing rivers renewed vigor, so they were able to cut through the hard rocks of the Blue Ridge. However as time went on, the headwaters of many of the rivers and streams west of the present Blue Ridge were captured by the biggest rivers, the Potomac, the James and the Roanoke. The gaps the beheaded rivers had cut ceased to deepen and rose as the land rose. They make today's wind gaps. Thornton Gap may have originally been cut by the Thornton River. Manassas Gap, just north of the Park, is one of the deepest of the wind gaps.

Looking at our mountains in the Shenandoah Park of today we can see reminders of their history. Most of the Blue Ridge crest in the Shenandoah National Park is capped by the hard, erosion-resistant greenstone. Although altered from the original basalt this rock still retains many of its original characteristics. One can find amygdules, filled gas bubbles, in almost every greenstone outcrop. In many places columnar jointing, characteristic of basalt, is still quite evident. It can be seen very strikingly at the southeastern viewpoint on Compton Mtn. (One must get down below the rocks to see this display.) It can also be seen on cliffs above the *AT* about 0.15m. north of Hawksbill Gap and again about 200 ft. south of Little Stony Man Parking Area. Evidence of the multiple layers of lava originally laid down can be seen along the *AT* below Franklin Cliffs and Crescent Rocks. In both places the *AT* follows a shelf "between layers" as shown by the vertical cliffs above and below the Trail. One of the ancient granite hills that were drowned by the lava flows can be seen along the walls of White Oak Canyon. The stepwise series of falls in this canyon also indicate the multiple lava flows.

In some places along the Blue Ridge crest in the Shenandoah National Park the greenstone has been completely eroded away and it is the "base rock" that outcrops. One such place is at **Marys Rock** where the outcrop is the igneous rock, granodiorite. Radiogenic age measurements indicated that this rock is 1,100,000,000 years old! Some of the peaks on the eastern side of the main ridge consist primarily of granite. Old Rag Mtn. is one of these. Numerous greenstone dikes are present on Old Rag. Here the greenstone is eroding faster than the surrounding granite, leaving narrow passage ways, with vertical sides and surprisingly regular "steps" made by erosion of the columnar-structured dike material.

To the west of the main crest are the remnants of two lower paralleling ridges, both of sandstone—quartzite. These ridges took shape as the limestones west of them, the shale between them, and the conglomerate between the sandstone and greenstone of the main crest eroded much faster than they did. The remnants of these sandstone ridges show today as peaks on the side ridges that run from the Blue Ridge crest westward. On these side ridges the peak farthest from the main crest is composed of a type of sandstone—quartzite known as the Antietam formation. This sandstone is easily recognized as it is characterized by fine straight parallel tubes that cross the bedding at right angles; these tubes are the fossil burrows of sea worms—skolithos—filled with sand. (Because of its appearance this rock has been called pipe-rock.) Estimated age of the wormhole fossils is 500,000,000 years. Peaks underlain by the old Antietam sandstone include Rockytop (the highest and farthest out peak (2556') of the Rockytop ridge), Lewis Peak, Austin Mtn., Turk Mtn. and Brown Mtn. in the southern section of the park. Those in the central and northern sections are not as obvious to the hiker. In some places the greenstone and base rock were shoved west covering completely the sandstone and shale deposits and even some of the limestone. This is true at the very north end of the park and explains the location of Skyline Caverns, a limestone cave, located under the western slopes of the Blue Ridge.

Park Fauna

The favorite mammal of the Park is the white-tailed deer. This creature of the woods seems to sense that it is protected in the Park so shows little fear of humans. Since 1935 when this area was restocked with 15 deer, they have so multiplied that today there is a stable population of over 1000 deer in the Park. They are most often seen in the early morning and at dusk.

The black bear has returned to the Park in fair numbers, though it is not as plentiful here as in the Great Smokies. Even so, unwary campers may wake to find their food stolen. Black bears weigh up to 700 pounds. Treat them with great caution. Once bears find food at a campground or at a trail shelter they will return again and again, and each time with less fear. So keep a clean camp. At established campgrounds store food and food refuse in the trunk of your hardtopped car (convertibles are not bear-proof). In the back-country suspend your food between two trees well away from your tent or sleeping bag. Do not cook in your tent or take midnight snacks into your sleeping bag. So that bears may continue to be enjoyed as free wild creatures in the SNP do all you can to discourage their developing a dependence on man and his garbage.

Other mammals of the Park include the gray fox, raccoon, opossum, bobcat and, it is claimed by many, the puma or mountain lion. Striped skunks, weasels, gray, flying, and fox squirrels, chipmunks, woodchucks and a number of small rodents all make the Park their home.

The larger streams of the Park are stocked with trout. Fishing is permitted in season and for trout only but a license is required; (a 5-day license may be purchased for use in the Park). Check park regulations. The Staunton River and the Rapidan River are "fish-for-fun" streams with year round season. Here all fish caught (only artificial lures with one barbless hook may be used) must be returned to the water.

Among the birds breeding in the Park uplands are the pileated woodpecker, the woodthrush, veery, chestnut warbler, Blackburnian warbler, Canada warbler, scarlet tanager, rosebreasted grosbeak, slate-colored junco, wood peewee, white-breasted nuthatch, robin, towhee and red-eyed vireo. Turkey buzzards, black vultures, ruffed grouse, wild turkey and the common raven are frequently seen from the Skyline Drive and the *AT*. Redtailed hawks are found here throughout the year; broadtailed hawks in summer only.

A Christmas bird count is conducted annually in the SNP. The count is sponsored by the Park Service in conjunction with the National Audubon Society and local bird-watching clubs.

Snakes are occasionally seen, black racers probably being the most common. There are two poisonous snakes in the Park, the copperhead and the timber rattler. These pit vipers are generally much shorter than the black snakes but thicker. The rattlers vary considerably in color and banding but can be recognized by their triangularly-shaped heads and (usually) tell-tale rattles.

Of all the insects, the pesky gnat is the most annoying to hikers and campers. Mosquitoes are generally troublesome only in the evening. An insect beauty often seen in the Park is the luna moth. In autumn one may discover a mountaintop covered with tiny red ladybugs, getting ready to hibernate. The Allegheny Mound ant lives in large colonies within huge, often two foot high, ant hills. The tent caterpillar and fall webworms often cover whole trees with their heavy webs, the black cherry being a particular favorite to the tent caterpillar.

Two arachnids are a nuisance to the hiker. One is the common tick, often a carrier of Rocky Mountain Spotted Fever; it is most often a problem in spring and early summer. Hikers should always check their bodies and clothes for ticks at a hike's end before these varmints have had a chance to bury their heads under the skin. Once they have taken hold, do not yank them out but use alcohol to encourage them to loosen their hold. A very tiny mite, the chigger or "red bug" of the deep south, can be an annoyance here. These tiny pests may form small red welts on legs or arms but their favorite place for locating on the human body seems to be along waistlines. The bite of a pinhead chigger can be as bad as that from a mosquito a hundred times its size.

Flora of the Park

If one looks at a botanical map of the United States, one will notice a long finger of the hemlock-hardwood forests typical of the Great Lakes Region and the northeastern USA extending down the Appalachian mountains as far as Georgia. The boreal forests of Canada also extend southward, not as a long finger, but as isolated islands along the very highest peaks and ridges of the southern Appalachians. One of these "islands" is located in the Skyland-Big Meadows area of the Shenandoah National Park.

At low elevations in the Park we find flowers and trees typical of the South's Piedmont area. Above 2500 ft. we begin to find many plants more common to the northeast U.S. Finally, at elevations above 3500 ft. we may find Canadian Zone plants. How did such northern plants find their way to these scattered spots? Probably they are relics of the ice age when the country was colder than it is now. Balsam fir, red spruce, speckled alder, gray dogwood, round-leaved dogwood, quaking aspen, fly honeysuckle, and gray birch are native only in the Skyland to Big Meadows stretch of the Park. About six small stands of native white (or paper) birch exist in the Park. Other typically northern trees that are natives here include the American mountain-ash, black ash, and the mountain and striped maples. Small flowers of the Canadian Zone found in the Park include the "common" wood sorrel (oxalis), which is not common here at all but can be found in the Limberlost area, and the three-toothed cinquefoil (potentilla) which may be found along a few very high rock outcrops such as the Hawksbill summit and Betty's Rock. Bunchberry or dwarf cornel (cornus) is known from the southern section of the Park—the only place in Virginia where it is found.

At the other extreme we find a few plants that are near the northern-most limit of their range. Trees in this category include the short-leaf pine, umbrella magnolia and the Carolina willow. The Catawba rhododendron is found only in the southern third of the Park and only in a few spots even there. Though beautiful it does not make the mass displays in the Park that it does just a short distance farther south.

The predominant trees of the Park are the oaks and hickories. The American chestnut was once the queen of the area but this important tree was destroyed by the chestnut blight before the establishment of the Park. The forests of the Park are by no means virgin, except in a few ravines. Man long ago axed or set fire to the trees for use as lumber or tanbark, or to clear the land for homesteads and farms. Virgin timber, chiefly hemlock, can be found in the deep gorges, especially in the Limberlost, Whiteoak Canyon and Cedar Run Canyon. In areas only recently going back to woods from farmlands one will find black locust, hawthorn, sumac, Virginia pine and white pine, trees typical of a "pioneer" forest.

Over 1200 species of flowering plants have been recorded as growing in the Park. It is not unusual to find the Park's first flower of spring blooming in low, wet areas as early as late February. This is the skunk cabbage (*symplocarpus*). Hepatica, coltsfoot (*tussilago*) and spice-bush (*lindera*) soon join it, often blooming in early March after a week of warm weather. By early April the shadbush or service berry (*amelanchier*) will be in bloom and bloodroot (*sanguinaria*), rue-anemone (*anemonella*), cut-leaved toothwort (*centaria*), and violets of many varieties line the trails at low elevations. Look for Dutchman's britches (*dicentra*) and dogtooth violets (*erythronium*) in low areas, golden ragwort (*senecio*) along stream banks and trails, and bright yellow marsh marigold (*caltha*) and the lovely foliage of the false hellebore (*veratrum*) in swampy areas. As April progresses the same sequence of blooms will be found at higher and higher elevations.

In late April redbud (*cercis*) and flowering dogwood (*cornus*) decorate the woods at lower to mid elevations. Star chickweed (*stellaria*), may apple (*podophyllum*), wood betony (*pedicularis*), golden corydalis and a host of other flowers adorn the Park. Early May is blossoming time for the two species of pink azalea or pink honeysuckle, the pinxter-flower at lower to mid altitudes and the roseshell azalea at the mid to higher altitudes, *i.e.*, along the *A T* and Skyline Drive. These showy plants are particularly plentiful in the Central Section of the Park. White (or pink) trillium is plentiful in the Central Section of the Park. Wild geranium and sweet cicily (*osmorhiza*) with its lacy white flowers and aniselike odor are common along the *AT*; observant hikers may see Jack-in-the-pulpit (*ariasaema),* pink and yellow lady's slippers *(cypripedium)* and showy orchises as well. In late May the Catawba rhododendron displays its showy purple-pink flowers along the Riprap Trail and near the Skyline Drive at Turk Gap.

June is the month for mountain laurel (*kalmia*) to show off its beauty. Two interesting members of the lily family—fly-poison (*amianthium*) and turkeybeard (*xerophyllum*)—bloom at this time. The former is very common along the *AT* whereas the latter, which prefers sandy soil, is found growing along the sandstone ridges west of the main Blue Ridge crest in the Southern Section of the Park. On the roadbanks feathery wands of goatsbeard (*aruncus*) and tall plumes of black cohosh (*cimicifuga*) are much in evidence. In July the turkscap lily (*lilium*) is quite common along the Drive. Many umbelliferae, including the huge cow-parsnip (*heracleum*) will be found in bloom. By August, members of the compositae predominate— black-eyed Susans, sunflowers, coreopsis, Joe-Pye-weed, knapweed and goldenrods. Asters continue to bloom until late in the fall.

Ripening berries help color the September woods; beautiful clusters of vivid mountain-ash berries peek out between the rocks along the rocky crest of the Blue Ridge. The cardinal-flower (*lobelia*) and great lobelia brighten stream banks. Brightest fall foliage often appears in early October when the dogwoods, sour gum, sumac and woodbine put on their leaf display. The peak of autumn brilliance is usually mid-October. By late in the month the entire Park turns to gold as the oaks and hickories blend their yellows, deep reds and browns. Last flower of the year, the witchhazel, will be found in bloom from late September to early December.

Winters in the Park are unpredictable. There may be periods of balmy springlike weather, followed by a week of severe cold, with Park temperatures hovering around zero. Some years there is much snow, other years almost none. One big ice storm can turn the ridges into fairyland; but such a storm can also do indescribable damage to the trees of the Park, especially those growing in exposed locations.

Among the plants of the Park one should mention a few that are immigrants from Europe and Asia that have made themselves very much at home here. Japanese honeysuckle (*lonicera*) is so thick in some of the low elevation areas of the Park that it has made an almost impenetrable jungle. Dyers woad (*isatis*) has a special liking for the Skyline Drive and grows profusely along the roadbanks. Viper bugloss *(echium)*, the common ox-eye daisy, chicory, mulleins, Queen Anne's lace, and bull thistle are thick along the roadsides during the summer months. Deep in the woods one may walk into thick patches of the shiny-leaved periwinkle (vinca), often a sign of an old family cemetery site. Plants of daylilies (*hemerocallis*) also persist near former homesites and the plants have continued to flourish though they seldom bloom in the deep shade. The princess tree (*paulownia*), often mistaken for a catalpa, and the fast growing tree of heaven (*ailanthus*) are also immigrants. Wineberry, a type of raspberry, is found at certain spots in the Southern Section.

Two very common plant pests should be mentioned. One of these is poison ivy, which is common in brushy areas and among exposed rocks. It is similar in appearance to woodbine (Virginia creeper) except that each leaf contains three leaflets rather than five. Another very annoying plant is the wood nettle (*laportea*) which is densely covered with stinging hairs. Nettles are particularly troublesome on side trails of the Park which often get only one time a year maintenance. Best protection from nettles, ivy, greenbriers and berry bushes are long pants. The juice from the fleshy stems of jewelweed (*impatiens*) may help to relieve the stinging sensation of nettle and the itching of poison ivy. It is often found growing near these pests.

HEIGHTS OF WATERFALLS IN
SHENANDOAH NATIONAL PARK

(This chart is reproduced, with permission, from the Shenandoah National Park's PARK GUIDE, copyrighted in 1968.)

Waterfall	Height (feet)	District	Stream
Big Falls	93	North	Overall Run
Whiteoak #1	86	Central	Whiteoak Run
South River Falls	83	Central	South River
Lewis Falls	81	Central	Hawksbill Creek
Dark Hollow Falls	70	Central	Hogcamp Branch
Rose River Falls, Upper	67	Central	Rose River
Big Falls, Doyle R.	63	South	Doyle River
Whiteoak #2	62	Central	Whiteoak Run
Whiteoak #6	60	Central	Whiteoak Run
Whiteoak #5	49	Central	Whiteoak Run
Jones Run Falls	42	South	Jones Run
Whiteoak #4	41	Central	Whiteoak Run
Whiteoak #3	35	Central	Whiteoak Run
Twin Falls	29	North	Overall Run
Little Falls, Doyle R.	28	South	Doyle River
Rose River Falls, Lower	22	Central	Rose River

(*NOTE:* The waterfalls on Whiteoak Run are numbered from top to bottom.)

Measurements were made by Robert Momich and Gary Miller (Volunteers in the Parks) using a Wallace and Tiernan Altimeter accurate within 2 ft. One might consider an unrestricted drop of water a waterfall and the steeply slanting, downhill rush of water a cascade. Shenandoah Park falls of water are usually a combination; in particular, the tops and bottoms of the Park waterfalls are often indefinite and so the establishment of recording stations for the above measurements was necessarily arbitrary.

APPALACHIAN TRAIL DATA

SECTION VI NORTHERN SHENANDOAH PARK
U.S. 522 TO THORNTON GAP
NORTH TO SOUTH

27.5 miles (44.3 Kilometers)   (Map No. 9: E-1)

Section VI of the Appalachian Trail in Virginia begins at U.S. 522 at a point 3.2m. southeast of its junction with U.S. 55 in Front Royal. Except for the first three and a half miles the *A T* lies entirely within the Shenandoah Park. There are no longer open areas in the northern section of the park, so that good viewpoints are limited to occasional rock outcroppings. Trail description has been divided into two subsections, U.S. 522 to Gravel Springs Gap, and Gravel Springs Gap to Thornton Gap.

Maps:

PATC map #9, USGS map of Shenandoah National Park, northern section, 1969, scale 1:62500. Also USGS 7½′ quads: Front Royal, Bentonville, Chester Gap, Luray, Thornton Gap, and Washington, Va.

SUBSECTION:
U.S. 522 TO GRAVEL SPRINGS GAP

12.9 miles (20.8 kilometers)   (Map No. 9: E-1)

General description:

From U.S. 522 just below Lake Front Royal, elevation 940 ft., the *A T* leads south along the edge of National Zoological Park Conservation Center property. The Trail crosses Va. Sec. 602 in about 1½ miles and comes into Va. Sec. 601 1¼ miles farther, elevation about 1475 ft. From here the *A T* climbs steadily via graded trail, crossing into the SNP a short distance before reaching the crest of the Blue Ridge where it comes into the old road from Chester Gap to Compton Gap, former route of the *A T*. It follows the Compton Gap Rd. south to the Skyline Drive at Compton Gap; el. 2415′. From here it climbs over Compton Mtn. and over both North and South Marshall Mtns.

before reaching Gravel Springs Gap. The *AT* either crosses the Skyline Drive, or comes quite close to it, in several places, so that all parts of it are easily accessible. Spring water is available in several locations near the Trail.

Side trails:

The Dickey Ridge (or Dickey Hill) Trail, the Bluff Trail, the Lands Run Fire Road, the Mt. Marshall Fire Road, and the old Browntown Road offer good walking. In addition, there are two short but interesting trails, Big Devils Stairs Trail and The Peak Trail. The old Compton Gap Rd. north of its junction with the *AT*, together with Va. Sec. 610 from the Park boundary down to Chester Gap, and a blue-blazed trail along the mountain north of the gap to Mosby Shelter (the former route of the *AT*) (see PATC map No. 8) can be used with the *AT* for a circuit hike. For details on side trails see Chap. 5: "Side Trails, Northern Section." Also refer to the PATC publications: *Circuit Hikes in the Shenandoah National Park* and *Walkers' Chart No. 1.*

Accommodations:

There are many motels and restaurants in Front Royal and a number of private campgrounds in the Front Royal area. Near the *AT* there are two open-faced shelters but they can only be used for camping in very inclement weather. They are: Indian Run Shelter, 5.2m. along the *AT* (then follow side trail 0.4m. from *AT* to the shelter) and Gravel Springs Shelter, 12.9m. along the *AT* (then at Gravel Springs Gap follow the Harris Hollow Rd. left from the Skyline Drive 0.3m. to the shelter.)

Matthews Arm Campground is a few miles south of Gravel Springs Gap at SDMP 22.2. It is generally open mid-April thrugh October.

Located on the *AT*, 3.1m. (between Va. Sec. 601 and the Park boundary), there is the Tom Floyd Wayside, a primitive camping area with a few tent sites and a rain shelter. This Wayside is for the use of the through hiker.

Detailed Trail data:

0.0 *AT* crosses U.S. 522 just below Lake Front Royal, el. 940 ft., at a point 3.2m. SE of its junction with Va. Rt. 55 in Front Royal. The *AT* leads south, across a stile into a field, the property of the National Zoological Park Conservation and Research Center. The Trail follows bridges over stream and a swampy area, Sloan Creek Swamp, then climbs along edge of fields. From high on the hill one may see, with the help of field glasses, various zoo animals.

0.4 Enter woods. In early May there are showy orchises along the trail here.

0.9 Climb stile and immediately beyond reach summit of hill.

1.4 Cross Va. Sec. 602, a dirt road. (Trail leaves National Zoological Park property here and enters property of the Northern Virginia 4H Educational Center.) Just beyond road cross Moore Run.

1.6 Beyond a wet weather stream come into a field. Midway across the field there are good views of the fruit orchards in Harmony Hollow.

2.1 Cross a wet weather creek.

2.2 Cross through a narrow fence opening. (Trail leaves 4 H Educational Center land here and follows easements on private property. STAY ON TRAIL.)

2.4 Here a side trail leads right 0.2m. through PATC property to a parking area on Va. Sec. 601. A tenth of a mile farther come into a farm road and follow it right. Pass white house on left of *AT*.

2.6 Come into Va. Sec. 601 at a sharp turn of the road. (From here it is 0.4m. down Rt. 601 to the PATC parking lot and 0.7m. to the main road through Harmony Hollow, Va. Sec. 604.) The *AT* follows up Rt. 601 just a few feet, then turns left onto a footpath, passing through a gap in a rock wall, then crossing a small creek. Trail now climbs by switchbacks toward the crest of the Blue Ridge.

3.1 Enter the Tom Floyd Wayside, a primitive camping area with tent sites and a rain shelter for the use of through hikers only. No open fires permitted. Ginger Spring is 800 ft. to the right of the *AT* here.

3.6 Enter the Shenandoah National Park.

3.8 Come into old Compton Gap Rd. and follow it to the right. (To the left the road leads 0.5m. down to Va. Sec. 610 at the Park boundary. Via 610 it is 1.8m. farther to U.S. 522 at Chester Gap. This, until 1974, was the route of the *AT*.)

4.9 Old road leads right 0.7m. to intersect the Dickey Ridge Trail at a point on that trail 0.6m. north of its junction with the *AT*.

5.2 Reach trail junction marked by cement post. (To the right the Dickey Ridge Trail leads 9.2m. north to Front Royal town limits and entrance to the Skyline Drive, SDMP 0.0. Interesting Fort Windham Rocks are 0.2m. from the *AT* on this trail. To left of *AT*, a Park service road leads 0.4m. to Indian Run Shelter, northernmost shelter in the SNP. A spring is 250 ft. from the service road, on the left, about 0.1m. before reaching the shelter. Shelter may be used for camping only in inclement weather. See Chap. 6: "Shelters and Cabins.")

5.4 A cement post marks a trail leading left 0.5m. to Indian Run Shelter.

5.5 Cross to the right of (south of) the Skyline Drive, SDMP 10.4, in Compton Gap, el. 2415'. Ascend Compton Mtn. by switchbacks. There is a patch of white clintonia (speckled wood lily) along the Trail here and a small clump of yellow lady's-slippers. (The latter bloom in mid-May, the former in early June.)

6.3 Signpost marks short blue-blazed trails leading right and left to viewpoints. Both are ungraded and offer only rough footing but are worthwhile. (Trail on left leads down 0.2m. to an interesting outcrop of columnar basalt. To see the columnar structure it is necessary to climb down below the rocks. Top of the outcrop affords good view east. Trail to right of *AT* leads over the top of Compton Mtn., el. 2909', and down 0.2m. to a rocky ledge offering excellent views to west and north.)

6.7 Pass Compton Springs. One is 50 ft. uphill on left; another is to right of *AT*, about 15 ft. away and downhill. *AT* descends fairly steeply for about a half-mile, then levels off.

There is much mountain laurel (blooming in early June) and pink azalea (mid-May) between here and Jenkins Gap.

7.3 *AT* bears right as an old road goes straight ahead through the laurel.

7.5 Cross gravel road in Jenkins Gap, el. 2398'. (Road leads right 100 ft. to former dump. Below dump area are two old roads, one now a fire foot trail, that descend the mountain to Va. Sec. 634 at a point 2.2m. from Browntown. To left of *AT* road leads 150 ft. to Skyline Drive, SDMP 12.3. Some parking is available at Jenkins Gap, more at the Jenkins Gap Overlook, SDMP 12.4. Mt. Marshall Fire Rd. can be reached by walking south along the Skyline Drive about 0.2m.)

9.0 Trail passes along the foundations of an old homestead.

9.2 Cross to left of Skyline Drive at Hogwallow Gap, SDMP 14.2, el. 2739'. Trail now ascends gently through the Hogwallow Flats area.

9.8 Pass Hogwallow Spring 30 ft. on left of Trail.

10.7 Reach summit of North Marshall, el. 3368'. (The name of this mountain grows out of the fact that these lands were formerly a part of the Blue Ridge holdings of John Marshall, the noted Chief Justice of the United States from 1801 to 1835. See "The Manor of Leeds" by Jean Stephenson in the April, 1934 PATC Bulletin.) Along the crest of the mountain, cliffs to the right of the Trail offer many good views to the west. As the Trail descends, just where it jogs sharply to the left, there is one outstanding viewpoint. At the next switchback some high cliffs on the left of the *AT* are worth scrambling up on. (These cliffs are quite visible from the Skyline Drive south of Mount Marshall.)

11.3 Cross to the right of the Skyline Drive, SDMP 15.9, el. 3087'.

11.9 Reach summit of South Marshall, el. 3212'. Trail now descends gradually with ledges on right affording splendid views.

12.9 Reach Gravel Springs Gap at intersection of old Browntown-Harris Hollow Rd. with the Skyline Drive, SDMP 17.7, el. 2666'. (To right of the *AT* the old Browntown Rd. leads northwest down the mountain 3.4m. to Va. Sec. 631 at a point about 1m. south of Browntown.)

SUBSECTION:
GRAVEL SPRINGS GAP TO THORNTON GAP

14.6 miles (23.4 kilometers)   (PATC map no. 9:G-10)

General description:

From Gravel Springs Gap, el. 2666' the *AT* climbs, reaching its highest elevation in the northern section of the Shenandoah Park on the Second Peak of Hogback, el. 3475'. It then descends over a thousand feet before reaching Elkwallow Gap, from which it climbs over several lesser high points including the summit of Pass Mtn. before descending to Thornton Gap, el. 2307'. Near the Range View Cabin and also south of Pass Mountain the Trail passes through areas that were once quite open. Large old oak trees with wide-spreading low branches show that they grew to maturity in open fields. They are still to be seen, but now they must compete for light with the young but tall forest trees that surround them.

The *AT* is never very far from the Skyline Drive and crosses it several times. Many good one-day hikes can be made by utilizing short stretches of the *AT* plus connecting side trails. Water is available at the shelters and at other points along the Trail in this section.

Side trails:

At 3.8m. (PATC map No. 9:E-12) the Big Blue-Tuscarora Trail connects with the *AT*. This trail, when completed will offer a 220 mile route west of the *AT*, rejoining it northeast of Carlisle, PA. From the juction in the SNP the Big Blue utilizes the Overall Run Trail for 4.5 miles, then forks to the right, eventually crossing U.S. 340 just south of Bentonville. From there it crosses the Massanutten range and continues generally west to the VA.-W. VA. state line where it then heads northeast, more or less paralleling the *AT*. By 1974 approximately 55m. of the southern portion had been completed, starting at its southern terminus here. In 1976, another 25m. remained to be done to reach the Potomac River. The Tuscarora section, that part of the Big Blue-Tuscarora Tr. north of the Potomac, has been finished.

The Gravel Springs-Thornton Gap area is rich with side trails, too many to enumerate here. See Chap. 5: "Side Trails, Northern Section;" also the PATC publications: *Circuit Hikes in the Shenandoah Park* and *Walkers' Charts.*

Accommodations:

Four open-faced shelters along this section are available for use by campers in inclement weather: Gravel Springs, 0.2m. along the *AT* (then follow the Bluff Trail for 0.2m.), Elkwallow, 6.4m., Byrd's Nest #4, 10.6m., and Pass Mtn. 13.3m. (then follow spur trail 0.2m.) In addition to these there is one locked cabin, Range View, 5.1m. Reservations for the use of this cabin must be obtained in advance from PATC Headquarters. See Chap. 6: "Shelters and Cabins."

Matthews Arm Campground, SDMP 22.2, offers extensive camping facilities. Meals are available at Panorama Restaurant at Thornton Gap and lunches can be purchased at the Elkwallow Wayside, SDMP 24.0. None of these facilities are available during the cold months.

Detailed Trail Data:

0.0 Intersection of old Browntown-Harris Hollow Rd. with the Skyline Drive, SDMP 17.7, el. 2666 ft. *AT* crosses to left (east) side of the Drive and parallels the old Harris Hollow Rd. for several hundred feet. (Harris Hollow Rd., on the left of the *AT*, is utilized as an access road to the Gravel Spring Shelter, 0.3m. Below the spring the old road continues, as a fire foot trail, to Va. Sec. 622 intersecting it at a point about 5m. from Washington, Va.)

0.2 *AT* turns sharply to the right at concrete post where Bluff Trail comes in on left. (Bluff Tr. starts here, descends by switchbacks to Gravel Springs, 0.2m., where it crosses the old Browntown-Harris Hollow Rd. It continues on, slabbing the east sides of South and North Marshall Mtns. ending at the Mt. Marshall Fire Rd. (4.7m.) Gravel Springs Shelter is 50 ft. south of the spring.) The *AT* now passes through an extended level area.

1.3 Cross to right side of Skyline Drive, SDMP 18.9.

1.5 Spur trail to left leads 100 ft. to Skyline Drive, SDMP 19.4, at junction of the Jinney Gray Fire Rd. on east side of Drive. (Jinney Gray Fire Rd. leads south along the east slopes of the Blue Ridge, passing the point known as "Four-Way" in 1.0m. See Chap. 5: "Side Trails;" also the PATC booklet, *Circuit Hikes in the Shenandoah Park*.)

1.8 *AT* reaches top of Little Hogback where there is a fine outlook from ledge 30 ft. to right of the Trail.

1.9 Spur trail, at signpost, leads straight ahead 50 ft. to Little Hogback Parking Overlook on the Skyline Drive, SDMP 19.7, as the *AT* veers right and descends, passing below the overlook. Trail then ascends steeply, by switchbacks, up the east face of First Peak of Hogback.

2.5 Reach crest; continue along ridge.

2.6 Pass a few feet to the left of the First Peak of Hogback, el. 3420'.

2.7 Graded trail leads to left, downhill, 0.2m. to a walled-in spring which is within sight of the Skyline Drive. *AT* now ascends.

2.9 Pass antenna towers on summit of the Second Peak of Hogback, el. 3474 ft. Trail follows tower road across its turn-around area, then goes to right of road and descends. Trail crosses to left of road in 0.1m.

3.1 *AT* comes into tower road just before it reaches the Drive. (Here a trail leads left 300 ft. to Drive.) Cross to left of Skyline Drive, SDMP 20.8. Ascend toward Third Peak of Hogback, 3440', Near the top a side trail leads right 15 ft. to a spot offering a splendid view north over Browntown Valley and Dickey Ridge. Skyline drive is directly below; there are enormous rocks here.

3.4 Cross to right of Skyline Drive, SDMP 21.1. Continue along crest of Hogback Mtn.

3.7 Side trail leads left 30 ft. to summit of Fourth Peak, el. 3440', with fine view south. From Fourth Peak, *AT* descends.

3.8 Junction with Big Blue-Overall Run Trail. (This is the southern terminus of the Big Blue-Tuscarora Trail which will, when completed, provide a 220m. route connected to the *AT* at each end. 5.6m. of the Big Blue Trail lies within the SNP. From the junction with the *AT* the Big Blue-Overall Run Trail, right, descends, passing at 0.7m. a trail leading left to Matthews Arm Campground. It passes near Overall Falls at 2.7m. The Big Blue Tr. parts from the Overall Run Tr. at 4.5m. and reaches U.S. 340 at 6.6m. at a point 2.6m. south of Bentonville.)

4.1 Spur trail on right leads 50 ft. to summit of Sugarloaf. *AT* continues to descend.

4.4 Cross to left of Skyline Drive, SDMP 21.9. (0.2m. to right along the Drive is entrance road to Matthews Arm Campground. Fifty yds. left of the *AT*, on the Drive, is Rattlesnake Point Overlook, 3105', with views east over Piney Branch.) On *AT* pass Rattlesnake Point to right of the Trail.

4.7 Junction with Piney Branch Trail which leads left from *AT*. (See Chap. 5: "Side Trails") Immediately beyond, *AT* comes into Range View cabin service road and follows it left a few feet before turning left away from it. (This road comes in on right from Skyline Drive, SDMP 22.1, passing the Piney River Ranger Station. See large scale map of Elkwallow-Range View Cabin area on back of PATC map #9.)

5.0 Pass under power line. A trail, left, follows power line 0.1m. to Range View Cabin.

5.1 A second side trail, left, leads 0.1m to Range View Cabin. Spring is below cabin. (Cabin is a locked structure. Reservations are required for its use. See Chap. 6: Shelters and Cabins.) Two hundred feet beyond, *AT* crosses access road to cabin. (A few feet down this road the Piney Ridge Trail takes off from the right of the road, just as the road bends left toward the cabin. See Chap. 5: "Side Trails;" also PATC publication, *Circuit Hikes in the Shenandoah Park*). *AT* now descends gently toward Elkwallow Gap.

5.9 Cross to right of Skyline Drive, SDMP 23.9, el. 2480'. (200 yds. south on Drive is the Elkwallow Wayside where lunches may be obtained from mid-May through October; Elkwallow Picnic area is beyond the Wayside. There are no overnight accommodations.) *AT* now swings right, then circles the wayside and picnic area. 250 ft. beyond the Drive, cross Elkwallow Trail. (Left, trail leads 0.1m. to the wayside; right, trail leads 1.9m. to Matthews Arm Campground.)

6.2 A trail to the left leads 200 ft. to Elkwallow Picnic Grounds. *AT* turns sharply right here and descends.

6.3 Spur trail, right, leads 150 ft. to Elkwallow Shelter, el. 2280'. (See Chap. 6: "Shelters and Cabins.")

6.4 Cross service road to shelter. To the right, road leads 150 ft. to shelter. To the left, road is about 0.5m. to the Skyline Drive. Also to the left of the *AT* here is a short trail to spring.

6.5 Junction with Jeremys Run Trail which is straight ahead here. (Jeremys Run Tr. leads 6.5m. to Va. Sec. 611 at a point 3.5m. from Big Spring on U.S. 340. See Chap. 5: "Side Trails" for details of this trail and circuit hikes possible in this area; also see PATC booklet, *Circuit Hikes in the Shenandoah Park*). *AT* turns sharply left at this junction, crossing creek in 100 ft. and ascends.

6.7 Spring 5 yds. to right.

7.5 Reach crest of narrow ridge and follow along it.

9.8 Cross Jeremys Hollow FFT. (This trail leads left 300 ft. to Skyline Drive. To right it leads downhill 1.2m. to Jeremys Run Trail.) A short distance farther a graded trail leads left 0.1m to unofficial parking area on Skyline Drive, SDMP 26.8.

10.1 Near top of rise reach intersections (two forks of trail, 50 ft. apart) with the Neighbor Trail. (Neighbor Trail leads right 4.6m. to Jeremys Run, first following an almost level spur ridge to the peak of "The Neighbor", then descending sharply.) *AT* now tops the rise, descends to a sag, then climbs again.

10.5 Reach a knob, the highest point of Neighbor Mtn. Short trails, one left, one right, lead to observation points, the one to the left badly overgrown with scrub oak.

10.6 Reach Byrd's Nest #4. Piped water available May through October. From the shelter *AT* descends, crossing access road several times in the next 0.3m.

11.1 Trail on right leads 100 ft. to a spring. A step or two farther, *AT* intersects the Kemp Hollow A FFT. (This trail leads right 0.4m. to Park boundary but is closed outside the Park.)

11.3 Spur trail on left leads 0.1m. to Beahms Gap Parking Overlook on Skyline Drive, SDMP 28.5.

11.5 Cross to left of Skyline Drive, SDMP 28.6. *AT* ascends gently from here.

12.2 Rocky area affords wintertime views to the right— views of Kemp Hollow, the Neighbor and Knob Mtn.

12.6 Reach summit of Pass Mtn., el. 3052'.

13.4 Graded trail, left, leads downhill 0.2m. to Pass Mtn. Shelter. (See Chap. 6: "Shelters and Cabins.")

14.2 *AT* comes into service road and follows it to right for 150 ft., then turns off the road to right.

14.5 Trail descends bank to service road within sight of the Drive. Follow road to the Drive and cross to the right side of the Drive.

14.6 Cross U.S. 211 at a point 0.15m. west of Skyline Drive in Thornton Gap, SDMP 31.5, el. 2307'.

SUMMARY OF DISTANCES ALONG THE *AT*
Section VI Northern

	Miles	Kilometers
U.S. Rt. 522	0.0	0.0
Indian Run Shelter	5.2 + 0.4	8.4 + 0.6
Compton Gap	5.5	8.9
Jenkins Gap	7.5	12.1
North Marshall Summit	10.7	17.2
Gravel Springs Gap	12.9	20.8
Gravel Springs Shelter	13.0 + 0.2	20.9 + 0.3
2nd Peak of Hogback (tower)	15.8	25.4
Junction with Big Blue	16.7	26.9
Piney Branch Tr. junction	17.6	28.3
Range View Cabin	17.9 + 0.1	28.8 + 0.2
Piney Ridge Tr.	18.0	29.0
Skyline Drive, Elkwallow Gap	18.8	30.3
Elkwallow Shelter	19.2	30.9
Jeremys Run Tr. junction	19.3	31.1
Neighbor Tr. junction	23.0	37.0
Byrd Shelter #4	23.5	37.8
Skyline Drive, Beahms Gap	24.4	39.3
Pass Mtn.	25.5	41.1
Pass Mtn. Shelter	26.3 + 0.2	42.3 + 0.3
U.S. Rt. 211 (Thornton Gap)	27.5	44.3

SUMMARY OF DISTANCES BY SKYLINE DRIVE TO POINTS ON *AT*
Section VI Northern

SDMP		From Thornton Gap S to N
0.0	Park Entrance, Rt. 340 at edge of Front Royal	31.5
10.4	Compton Gap, *AT* crossing	21.1
12.3	Jenkins Gap, *AT* is 0.1 m. to the west	19.2
14.2	*AT* crossing, Hogwallow Gap	17.3
15.9	*AT* crossing just south of North Marshall Mtn.	15.6
17.7	*AT* crossing, Gravel Springs Gap	13.8
18.9	*AT* crossing, 1.3 m. via Trail south of Gravel Springs Gap	12.6
19.4	Jinney Gray Fire Rd. *AT* is 100 ft. north via spur trail	12.1
19.7	Little Hogback Parking Overlook, *AT* 50 ft. to north via spur trail	11.8
20.8	*AT* crossing, sag between Second and Third Peaks of Hogback	10.7
21.1	*AT* crossing, between Third and Fourth Peaks of Hogback	10.4
21.9	*AT* crossing at Rattlesnake Point. Range View Cabin is 0.7 m. south from here via the *AT*. Entrance to Matthews Arm Campground is 0.3 m. farther south along the Drive.	9.6
23.9	*AT* crossing, Elkwallow Gap. Wayside is 200 yds. south.	7.6
24.2	Elkwallow Picnic Grounds. Trail to the *AT* leads off from the second parking area for 200 ft.	7.3
26.8	Parking area for Neighbor Tr. Spur Tr. leads 0.1 m. west to *AT*.	4.7
28.5	Beahms Gap Overlook. *AT* is west of Drive, 0.1 m. via spur trail.	3.0
28.6	*AT* crossing, Beahms Gap	2.9
31.5	Thornton Gap. *AT* crosses U.S. 211 0.15 m.	0.0

SECTION VII CENTRAL SHENANDOAH PARK
THORNTON GAP TO SWIFT RUN GAP
NORTH TO SOUTH

34.3 miles (55.2 kilometers)   (PATC map No. 10; G-2)

General Description:

U.S. 211 crosses the Blue Ridge and intersects the Skyline Drive in Thornton Gap, SDMP 31.5, at a point 9 miles east of Luray, 7 miles west of Sperryville. and 83 miles from Washington, D.C. The southern end of this section is at Swift Run Gap, SDMP 65.7, where U.S. 33 crosses the mountain. From Swift Run Gap it is 7 miles west to Elkton, 8 miles east to Stanardsville, and 110 miles to Washington, D.C.

The Blue Ridge crest is higher in this section of the Park than in the northern and southern sections. The highest peak in the Park, Hawksbill, just south of Skyland, has an elevation of 4050 ft. The *AT* reaches its highest point in the Park, 3812 ft., on Hazeltop Mtn. which is 4.0m. south of Big Meadows Campground. The Skyline Drive itself reaches its highest altitude, 3680 ft., right at the northern entrance to Skyland.

The central part of the Shenandoah Park is the section most widely used by the motoring public, by campers, and by hikers. The *AT* is heavily used, as are the chief side trails. Favorite short hikes include the Stony Man and Swamp Nature Trails, the Stony Man Trail and *AT* loop trip, the Dark Hollow Falls Trail and the Limberlost Trail. Longer favorites are the White Oak Canyon Trail, the trails up Old Rag Mtn., the trails up Hawksbill, and the stretch of the *AT* from Thornton Gap (Panorama) to Marys Rock. There are also special trails for horseback riding, with stables at Skyland and Big Meadows.

There are two large campgrounds located in the area, one at Big Meadows (open all year) and another at Lewis Mountain. Skyland, Big Meadows, and Lewis Mountains have lodging facilities available for tourists—both lodge and cabins; only at Big Meadows are these open during the winter months. For complete information on tourist facilities and for reservations write to the ARA Virginia Sky-Line Co., Inc., Box 727, Luray, Va. 22835.

The Skyland resort antedates the Park, having been developed by George F. Pollock, with its beginnings in the 1880's. The Hoover Camp, developed when Herbert Hoover was President, is on the eastern slopes of the Blue Ridge near Big Meadows. It is now managed by the Park Service, but is still reserved for use by presidential guests. For more information about the history of this area read "Skyland Before 1900" by Jean Stephenson in the July, 1935 PATC Bulletin and the book, *Skyland,* by George Freeman Pollock.

For convenience Section VII is divided into 3 subsections: Thornton Gap to Skyland, Skyland for Fishers Gap, and Fishers Gap to Swift Run Gap.

Maps:

PATC Trail Map No. 10. Also available are the USGS map of the Shenandoah Park, Central Section, scale 1:62.500 and the USCG 7½´ quads (scale 1:24,000) of Thornton Gap, Old Rag, Big Meadows, Fletcher, Elkton East, and Swift Run Gap. (The following quads cover areas of the central section of the Park not traversed by the *AT*: Washington, Va., Luray, Stanley, Madison, and Stanardsville.)

SUBSECTION
THORNTON GAP TO SKYLAND
NORTH TO SOUTH

9.4 miles (15.1 kilometers)   (PATC map No. 10: G-2)

General description:

From U.S. 211, about 0.1m. west of the Skyline Drive at Thornton Gap (SDMP 31.5, el. 2307 ft.) the *AT* swings through the woods, passing to the west of Panorama Restaurant. A spur trail leads to the upper parking area there. The Trail climbs steadily, reaching the ridge crest just beyond the peak of Marys Rock, 3514 ft. A side trail, to the right, leads to the northern tip of Marys Rock which affords one of the most outstanding panoramic views in the entire Park. The *AT* then follows the ridge crest, climbs over The Pinnacle, 3730 ft., passes below the Jewel Hollow Overlook, and then goes through the Pinnacles Picnic Grounds. From here on, the **AT** generally stays a little below the ridge crest on the western side. As the western slopes are generally quite steep in this area there are many good views westward. The *AT* passes below the main cliffs of Little Stony Man along a very scenic shelf of rock. It enters the Skyland area through a lovely grove of white pine, crosses one of the Skyland paved roads and passes just below the long Dining Hall building. Here the section ends.

There are no dependable sources of water on the *AT* along this stretch of trail except the piped water, available "in season" at Byrd Shelter No. 3, at the Pinnacles Picnic Grounds, and at Stony Man Mountain Parking Overlook. The springs at Meadow Springs and Shavers Hollow Shelter are each 0.3m. downhill from the *AT*.

Side trails:

The Park is wide on the east side of the Drive in this area and there are many trails. One group of trails is centered around "Hazel Country", that section near the Hazel River and Hazel Mountain. These interconnect with trails centered around Nicholson (Free State) Hollow and Corbin Cabin. The Skyland area includes a wide variety of trails. See Chap. 5: "Side Trails", Central Section, for detailed descriptions of these trails.

Accommodations:

In season, Panorama, at the northern end of the section, offers meals and gasoline but no lodging facilities. Skyland has an excellent restaurant, a lodge, and cottages. A stable is maintained here and there is a network of horse trails as well as hiking trails in this area. The nearest public campground is at Big Meadows, SDMP 51.2, about 9 miles south of Skyland. One section of the campground is kept open during the winter. The lodge, wayside and Byrd Visitor Center at Big Meadows are also kept open.

There are two open-faced shelters, which can be used for camping only in very inclement weather, Byrd's Nest No. 3 (3.0m.) and Shavers Hollow Shelter (6.5m.). A locked structure, Corbin Cabin, reached via the Corbin Cabin Cut-Off Trail, is 1.4m. east of the Skyline Drive, SDMP 37.9. For its use reservations must be obtained in advance from PATC Headquarters. See Chap. 6: "Shelters and Cabins."

Detailed Trail data:

0.0 This section of the *AT* begins at the Trail's intersection with U.S. 211, about 0.1m. west of the Skyline Drive, SDMP 31.5, el. 2307 ft. Proceed through the woods passing west of the Panorama Restaurant. (A spur trail here leads left to the parking area at Panorama.) The *AT* ascends along the northern and then eastern slopes of the mountain.

0.8 At a bend in the Trail, the non-maintained Tunnel Tr. leads left 0.2m. downhill, to the Skyline Drive. (The Tunnel Tr. forks about halfway down, the left fork leading to the north portal of the tunnel, the right fork leading to the south portal, SDMP 32.2.) As the *AT* nears the crest of the ridge it ascends by switchbacks through laurel and scrub oak.

1.7 Spur trail leads right 0.1m. to the northern tip of Marys Rock. The view from this point is unsurpassed anywhere in the Park. (Highest point, 3514 ft., is reached by climbing to the top of the huge rock outcrop, dangerous in wet or windy weather. The rock is granodiorite and geologists have determined its age to be over a billion years!) Beyond the junction, the *AT* follows the ridge crest south, with occasional views westward, and descends gradually.

2.4 In a sag the Buck Hollow Trail intersects the *AT*. (Buck Hollow Trail leads left, downhill, passing Meadow Springs on its left in 0.3m. It continues downhill crossing the Skyline Drive, SDMP 33.5, in 0.7m. and contining down to reach U.S. 211 in 3.7m. at a point on Rt. 211 3.4m. west of Sperryville.) The *AT* continues along the ridge crest which is narrow here. There is an excellent view to the west from an rock outcrop 0.1m. farther along the Trail.

2.7 Reach another good viewpoint. Here Trail switches back to the left, then descends toward sag at base of The Pinnacle.

3.0 *AT* comes into service road and follows it right 180 ft. to Byrd's Nest Shelter #3. (To left, service road leads 0.3m. to Skyline Drive, SDMP 33.9. Piped water available at the shelter during the warmer months. See Chap. 6: "Shelters and Cabins.) Beyond shelter *AT* ascends gradually.

3.5 An obscure trail, left, leads down to Skyline Drive near

Pinnacle Overlook. (This trail is useful for connecting the *AT* with the Hannah Run Trail for circuit hikes.) Beyond side trail, *AT* climbs by switchbacks.

3.7 Obscure spur trail, right, leads 100 ft. to fine view north.

3.8 Fifty feet to right of *AT* are jagged rocks forming the North Peak of The Pinnacle. Beyond, the *AT* leads for a short distance along the level ridge crest, affording splendid views of the sheer western slopes of this ridge.

4.0 Pass to left of highest point of The Pinnacle, el. 3730 ft. Descend through heavy growth of mountain laurel (blossoming in early June) with occasional views of Stony Man Mtn. ahead.

4.7 Cross yellow blazed but obscure trail, the Leading Ridge Fire Foot Trail. (To left, trail leads 0.1m. to the Drive. To right it climbs over Leading Ridge, then descends steeply toward the Shenandoah Valley, and comes into VA. Sec. 669 outside the Park boundary, at a point about 2 m. from U.S. 211 using the shortest route. (See PATC Map No. 10.)) *AT* now passes through some tall white pine, descending gently.

4.8 Side trail, left, leads 100 ft. to scenic Jewell Hollow Parking Overlook, SDMP 36.4, el. 3335'. *AT* passes below the Overlook.

5.0 A second trail, left, leads back 75 ft., to the Jewell Hollow Overlook. *AT* ascends gradually along the crest of a narrow ridge. There are fine views westward across Jewell Hollow.

5.1 *AT* comes up to, then parallels to the right, the entrance road to Pinnacles Picnic Grounds, SDMP 36.7. At fork in the path the *AT* follows the unpaved right fork which leads around the picnic grounds. Follow white blazes! Trail route is through tall laurel.

5.3 Trail passes toilets and drinking fountain. There are large Appalachian Trail signs at adjacent parking area; bear right here and also 200 ft. beyond, where paved picnic area path bends to the left. Enter woods, ascend slightly, then descend.

5.7 An impressive old white pine grows to left of the *AT* here. A tenth of a mile farther the *AT* passes under power line. Trail then ascends over knob at head of Nicholson Hollow.

6.1 Where the *AT* switchbacks sharply to the right, descending, there is an excellent viewpoint. The *AT* here is close to, but above the Skyline Drive and presents an unobstructed view of Nicholson (Free State) Hollow and Old Rag Mountain beyond. (The mountaineers who once lived in Nicholson Hollow were reputed to be so mean they were a "law unto themselves" and the local sheriffs were afraid to enter the hollow, hence the name "Free State." See George F. Pollock's book, *Skyland*.)

6.2 Intersection with trail to Shaver Hollow Shelter. (The shelter is 0.3m. downhill to right of the *AT*. It is situated on a ridge crest between two valleys in an unusually attractive setting. A spring is 300 ft. southwest of the shelter. Left of the *AT*, the trail leads 150 ft. to Skyline Drive at the Shaver Hollow Parking Area, SDMP 37.9. Across the Drive here the Corbin Cabin Cut-Off Trail leads 1.5m. to Corbin Cabin and the Nicholson Hollow Trail. See Chap. 6: "Shelters and Cabins.") From the trail intersection the *AT* continues with several gentle dips and climbs.

6.8 Cross Crusher Ridge FFT which here follows an old woods road known as Sours Lane. (To the right, the fire foot trail leads along Crusher Ridge, then down into Shaver Hollow near Va. Sec. 669. To left, the fire foot trail ends on the Nicholson Hollow Trail just a few feet from the Skyline Drive.)

7.0 Junction with the blue-blazed Nicholson Hollow Trail. (The Nicholson Hollow Trail leads 0.1m. to the Drive, SDMP 38.4, and diagonally across it. It then drops down into Nicholson Hollow and follows the Hughes River for another 5.8m. to reach VA. Sec. 600 west of Nethers.)

7.3 A side trail, left, leads 200 ft. to south end of the Stony Man Mtn. Overlook in Hughes River Gap, SDMP 38.6, el. 3097'. Drinking water and toilets here. Continuing around the head of Nicholson Hollow, the *AT* parallels the Drive. Trail emerges from woods with fine view west of Page Valley, the Massanutten Range, New Market Gap and Luray, and a near view south of Little Stony Man cliffs and the Stony Man Mtn. "profile." The *AT* ascends, paralleling the Skyline Drive.

7.7 Spur trail, left, leads 150 ft. to Little Stony Man Parking Area on the Skyline Drive, SDMP 39.1. Ascend Stony Man

Mtn. gradually, by long switchbacks, first left, then right.

8.0 At trail junction marked by a concrete signpost, take right fork. (Left fork is the Stony Man Trail which affords an alternate route over Stony Man Mtn., el. 4011 ft., rejoining the Appalachian Trail at Skyland (see map of Skyland area on back of PATC map No. 10.) The Stony Man Trail involves more climbing and is 0.2m. longer. Combined with the *AT* it makes an excellent short circuit hike. Via the Stony Man Tr. it is uphill 0.2m. to Little Stony Man where cliffs offer fine views west, 0.8m. to Stony Man Nature Tr., 1.1 to Stony Man cliffs and 1.5m. to Dining Hall area of Skyland. *AT* crosses Skyland just below the Dining Hall.)

8.1 Follow ledge below Little Stony Man cliffs. Excellent views here. (Stony Man Tr. is directly above the *AT* here, atop the cliffs.) The route of the *AT* around Little Stony Man and Stony Man Mtn. is a slight relocation of George Freeman Pollock's original Passamaquoddy Trail in 1932. (Passamaquoddy is a Main Indian word signifying "abounding in pollock".) This bit of *AT* is exceptionally beautiful as it follows the base of rocky cliffs and passes by huge hemlock trees.

9.0 Pass Skyland power line and housed Furnace Spring 25 ft. to left of Trail. Enter fine hemlock grove. Then in 200 ft. turn left on the old Skyland-Luray Road. (To right road leads 3m. to the "foot of the mountain". Road is gated at Park boundary, where it becomes VA. Sec. 672 at a point about 8m. from Luray.)

9.1 Turn left off road at signpost. Ascend through woods, largely white pine.

9.2 Cross paved Skyland road and continue through woods. (Road leads left to northern entrance of Skyland and the Nature Trail parking area. To right it leads down to the cabin area of Skyland.)

9.3 Come into paved path and follow it left, uphill, toward the Skyland Dining Hall. At a sharp bend to the right, a side trail leads straight ahead. (This trail leads to service road, in the vendor's dormitory area of Skyland. Road can be followed uphill toward north entrance of Drive, to where the Stony Man Trail begins.)

9.4 This section of the *AT* ends just below the Dining Hall where the *AT* forks to the right leaving the paved path. There is a wooden sign board here.

Skyland is located between SDMP 41.7 and 42.5 about 23m. north of U.S. 33 at Swift Run Gap and 10m. south of U.S. 211 at Thornton Gap via the Drive.

SUBSECTION:
SKYLAND TO FISHERS GAP
NORTH TO SOUTH

6.3 miles (10.1 kilometers)   (PATC map No. 10: G-7)

This stretch of the Appalachian Trail starts at Skyland, just below the Skyland Dining Hall. The Blue Ridge in this area was at one time covered by a series of lava flows. (See Chap. 3: "The Shenandoah Park", Geology of the Park.) Today this lava, in its present form of greenstone, is the rock seen in the many rock outcrops along the Skyline Drive and Appalachian Trail in this section. On the west side of the ridge, where the slope is very steep, the old layers of lava show as a series of vertical cliffs, one above another, thus affording a very rugged and photogenic section of Trail.

The summit of Hawksbill Mtn, el. 4050', is the highest point in the Park. The *AT* slabs along the northwestern slopes of this mountain but side trails lead to the summit.

Two typically northern evergreens, red spruce and balsam fir, are found in this area. The spruce is native to Hawksbill, the balsam to Crescent Rock, and both are found in the Limberlost area east of Skyland and on Stony Man Mtn. just north of Skyland. Going north on the *AT* these trees are not found again until one reaches Vermont. They are found farther south but at much higher elevations such as on Mt. Rogers, el. 5729 ft. (and

White Top near by) in southwestern Virginia. Another northern plant, the tiny three-toothed cinquefoil, can be found atop Hawksbill, Crescent Rock, and Bettys Rock nearby.

Side trails:

As in the preceding subsection the Park is wide here, especially to the east of the Skyline Drive. The lovely Whiteoak Canyon-Cedar Run Circuit Hike is in this area. The scenic rock-sculptured top of Old Rag Mountain beckons the hiker here. Several routes lead to the top of Hawksbill Mountain. For details of these and other side trails see Chap. 5: "Side Trails", Central Section.

Accommodations:

Public accommodations are available at Skyland from mid-April to early November. The lodge and cottages can accommodate 350 persons. A stable is maintained here and there is a network of horseback trails in the area. The Big Meadows Developed Area just south of Fishers Gap offers the Byrd Visitor Center, a picnic grounds, a lodge and cabins with lodging and meals for 200 persons, a wayside, stables, and a tremendous camping area with standard facilities for campers—both tent and trailer—store, laundry, showers, etc. Big Meadows is the only campground in the Park open year-round; the visitor's center and service station also remain open during the winter. For information and lodging reservations write to the ARA Virginia Sky-Line Co., Inc., Box 727, Luray, Va. 22835.

There are two open-faced shelters available for *AT* hikers, but they may be used for camping only in very inclement weather. They are: Hawksbill Gap Shelter, 3.1m. (across the Drive and 0.3m. from the *AT*) and Byrd's Nest N2, 3.1 and 4.1m. (this shelter is atop Hawksbill Mtn. about 1m. from the *AT* from either Trail junction.) Considerably east of the Drive are two additional shelters, Byrd's Nest #1 on the western ridge of Old Rag Mtn., and the Old Rag Shelter, 0.4m. up the Saddle

Trail from the junction of three Park fire roads, the Old Rag
Fire Rd., the Weakley Hollow Fire Rd. and the Berry Hollow
Fire Rd.. See PATC map No. 10.

One locked cabin, Rock Spring, 4.4m. (spur trail to cabin
0.2m.) is also available. Reservations for its use must be
obtained in advance from PATC Headquarters. (See Chap. 6:
"Shelters and Cabins.")

Detailed Trail data:

0.0 Signpost on path 75 ft. below the Skyland Dining Hall
marks start of this section. The *AT* follows an unpaved path
south through woods. (To reach the *AT* at start of the section
follow paved path leading downhill (west) from the Skyland
Dining Hall for 75 ft. Turn left onto the *AT* at signpost.)

0.2 *AT* bears left, then crosses paved road; there is a small
trail marker visible in the distance. (The Millers Head Trail
starts from the road about 200 ft. to the right of the *AT* crossing.
This trail leads 0.8m. over Bushytop to Millers Head with
beautiful views.) The *AT* continues along a power line, then
through the woods.

0.5 Cross paved road leading to stables a short distance to
the right of the *AT*. At trail intersection just beyond, a horse
trail leads left to Whiteoak Canyon and on to Big Meadows,
while *AT* bends right. Follow *AT* blazes and Park signs. The
Trail proceeds along a fence. It then descends slightly toward
the west edge of an escarpment.

0.8 Trail leads along cliffs on west edge of ridge under
Pollock Knob, el. 3560 ft. (named for George Freeman Pollock,
founder of Skyland). There are occasional views to the right
from the Trail.

1.3 Here, where the *AT* begins descent by switchbacks, there
is a spectacular view of Hawksbill Mtn. and Ida Valley. Beyond,
the *AT* parallels the Drive, passing through a thicket of laurel.

1.8 Spur trial, left, leads uphill 300 ft. to Timber Hollow
Parking Overlook on the Skyline Drive, SDMP 43.3.

1.9 Pass a piped spring 4 ft. left of the *AT*. Trail climbs over a
small ridge, then descends gently, slabbing the steep western

slopes of the Blue Ridge. Here the Trail passes some pictures-que contorted trees. A big oak on the right extends a "sitting limb".

2.5 Cement post marks spur trail leading uphill for 0.1m. to a junction a few feet north of the parking area, with short (0.3m.) trail leading north from the Crescent Rock Parking Overlook, SDMP 44.4, to Bettys Rock. (The views from Bettys Rock are lovely. The "rare in Virgina" three-toothed cinquefoil is found here; it blooms from late May on into the summer.) The *AT* next passes under the cliffs of Crescent Rock. Excellent views of Nakedtop and Hawksbill Mtn. from the Trail along here.

3.1 Reach Hawksbill Gap. (Buracker Hollow FFT leads right, down the mountain, passing a spring in 450 ft. To left, a trail leads uphill 300 ft. to Hawksbill Gap Parking Area on the Drive, SDMP 45.6, el. 3361 ft. On the east side of the Drive here is the start of the Cedar Run Trail. To reach Hawksbill Gap Shelter, follow this trail for 0.2m., then take spur trail on right for 250 ft.) (From the Hawksbill Gap Parking Area, the Hawsbill Tr. leads steeply up for 0.8m. to Byrd's Nest #2 and the summit just beyond. From the summit, el. 4050 ft., the Hawksbill Trail descends southward to the Upper Hawksbill Parking Area on the Drive, SDMP 46.7. The Nakedtop Trail also starts at the shelter and descends the west ridge of Hawksbill, intersecting the *AT* in 0.9m. and continuing on to Nakedtop. See Chap. 6: "Shelters and Cabins".) From Hawksbill Gap the *AT* ascends, then slabs along the steep northern face of Hawksbill Mtn., passing under cliffs in a wild, rugged setting. There are splendid views, looking backward, of Crescent Rocks, Stony Man and Old Rag Mountain; also northward views of Ida Valley and Luray. Note the balsam fir along the Trail here.

4.1 Intersection with the Nakedtop Trail in a sag between Hawksbill and Nakedtop. (The Nakedtop Trail leads right 0.4m. to the peak, Nakedtop; two viewpoints have been cleared on the peak.) A few feet farther along the *AT*, at a signpost, the Nakedtop Tr. leads left 0.9m. to the summit of Hawksbill. (Hawskbill Mtn., 4050', is the first summit near the *AT* to reach this much elevation south of Killington, Vt. Its exposed top affords a magnificent panoramic view. Among the hardwoods on its upper slopes are a scattering of conifers—balsam fir and red spruce—both rare in Virginia. North of the Stony Man to Hawksbill area they are not found again growing as natives along the *AT* until Vermont; Farther south they are found again along the Trail in the Mt. Rogers area of SW Virginia and down into North Carolina and Tennessee at elevations above 5000 ft.)

4.4 Here the *AT* comes out of deep woods into an old field now rapidly being overgrown with locust and pines. A road enters the Trail from the left. It comes 0.2m. from the Skyline Drive, SDMP 47.8, and serves as a Park service road to Rock Spring Cabin. Twenty ft. farther along the *AT* a signpost marks the graded spur trail leading right 0.2m. down to Rock Spring Cabin, a locked structure. (For its use reservations must be obtained in advance from PATC Headquarters. See Chap. 6: "Shelters and Cabins.") A spring is 50 yds. north of the cabin.

5.0 Spur trail, left, marked by post, leads 150 ft. uphill to the Skyline Drive at Spitler Knoll Parking Overlook, SDMP 48.1, nearest parking spot for Rock Spring Cabin. Beyond the Overlook the *AT* continues, again slabbing along the western slopes of the main Blue Ridge.

5.8 Pass a wet weather spring 15 ft. to the right of the *AT*. One hundred feet farther, at cement post, an obscure trail leads left, uphill, 0.3m. to the north end of Franklin Cliffs Overlook.

6.1 Pass a second trail, marked by post, leading left 0.1m. to the south end of Franklin Cliffs Overlook, SDMP 49.0, el. 3135'.

6.3 Intersect the Red Gate Fire Road in Fishers Gap. (To the right, the road, gated at the Drive and again at the Park boundary, leads down the mountain 4.8m. to VA. Sec. 611 about 4m. east of Stanley. Although hikers can use this road it is not recommended, as Park personnel and concessioners use this road for hauling supplies and for commuting to Big Meadows. To the left the road leads 350 ft. to the northern end of the Fishers Gap Parking Overlook, SDMP 49.3, el. 3061'. East of the Drive here is the northern end of the Copper Mine-Dark Hollow Falls Loop Trail. Also from here the Dark

Hollow Falls Fire Road, gated at the Drive, leads down 1.0m. to the creek in Dark Hollow, crossing it a few hundred feet below the main falls. See Chap. 5: "Side Trails", Central Section. Also PATC map No. 10 and PATC publication: *Circuit Hikes in the Shenandoah National Park.*)

FISHERS GAP TO SWIFT RUN GAP
NORTH TO SOUTH

18.6 miles (30.0 kilometers)   (PATC map No. 10: I-26)

General Description:
    From Fishers Gap, el. 3061', the *AT* skirts the Big Meadows Developed Area, then continues on to Milam Gap where it crosses the Skyline Drive. It climbs to the summit of Hazeltop where the *AT* reaches its highest elevation in the Shenandoah Park, 3816', then descends to Bootens Gap. The Trail now climbs two low mountains, Bush and Bearfence; the latter is very scenic. The *AT* skirts the Lewis Mtn. Developed Area, climbs over Baldface Mtn., drops down to skirt around the South River Picnic Grounds, then follows an old road over a spur of Saddleback Mountain and finally descends steeply to Swift Run Gap, el. 2367'.

Side trails:
    In the Big Meadows Area there are many trails and a number of circuit hikes that are popular; the Dark Hollow Falls-Copper Mine Loop circuit is probably the favorite one. The Rapidan Fire Rd. and several trails lead eastward from the Skyline Drive and *AT* to Hoover Camp, located within the Park on the Rapidan River. On Laurel Prong near Hoover Camp one can find growing the rosebay rhododendron, (R. maximum).
    Farther south is the short, but very scenic, South River Falls Trail. An excellent circuit hike can be made from Pocosin Cabin by using the Pocosin Fire Rd., the Pocosin (Horse) Tr., the South River Fire Rd., the South River Falls Trail and the *AT*. (See Chap. 5: "Side Trails", Central Section, and the South River inset on the back of map #10.)

Many fire foot trails, fire roads, and other old roads beckon the hiker. Some are well marked and easy to follow, but others may be poorly marked or badly overgrown and should be attempted only by the experienced woodsman.

Accommodations:
Both picnic and camping (tent and trailer) facilities are available at Big Meadows (open year-round) and Lewis Mtn. Cabins are also available at both places. For use of the latter, reservations can be made with the ARA Virginia Sky-Line Co., Inc, Box 727, Luray, Va. 22835. Big Meadows also has a lodge, a wayside and the Byrd Visitor Center. Lewis Mtn. has a camp store.

There are two open-faced shelters for use by *AT* hikers but camping in them is permissable only during very inclement weather. These are the Bearfence Mtn. Shelter, 9.5m., and the South River Shelter, 16.1m. (then follow old road from the *AT* for 0.3m.)

One locked structure, Pocosin Cabin, 12.3m, is near the Trail here. A second cabin, the Jones Mtn. Cabin, is located too far to the east for easy accessibility from the *AT*. Best approach to this cabin is from the Piedmont. See Chap. VI: "Shelters and Cabins".

Detailed Trail Data:
0.0 Intersection with the Red Gate Fire Road 350 ft. west of the Skyline Drive, just north of the Fishers Gap Overlook, SDMP 49.3, el. 3061'. (To right of the *AT*, fire road leads 4.8m. down the mountain to VA. Sec. 611 at a point about 4m. from Stanley. This road is not ideal for hiking as it is used by Park personnel and concessioners for commuting to Big Meadows and for hauling supplies. Across the Drive here is the northern end of the Copper Mine-Dark Hollow Falls Loop Trail. Also from here the Dark Hollow Falls Fire Road leads down 1.0m. to the creek in Dark Hollow, crossing it a few hundred feet below the main falls. See Chap. 5: "Side Trails", Central Section, also PATC map No. 10 and PATC publication: *Circuit Hikes in the Shenandoah National Park.*)

0.1 Pass post marking spur trail, left, which leads 100 ft. to Fishers Gap Parking Overlook.

0.2 Pass to right of split rock. Ascend gradually. Pass through beautiful hemlock grove. Continue to ascend.

1.0 Swamp Nature Trail enters from the left and follows (in reverse direction) the *AT*.. David Spring is 50 ft. to right of the *AT* here. (To the left, the Swamp Nature Trail leads 0.8m. to its junction with the Dark Hollow Trail, then continues on to its end near the amphitheatre in Big Meadows. See Big Meadows inset on back of PATC map No. 10.) The *AT* skirts the north edge of the Big Meadows Campground, several small unmarked trails leading left to the campground. Openings along the *AT* give fine views to the north and west—of Hawksbill Mtn. in the foreground, Stony Man Mtn. farther away, and, in the distance, Knob Mtn. and The Neighbor. Across the Page Valley Signal Knob can be seen at the north end of the Massanutten range.

1.3 Cross over a small rocky knob, the Monkey Head. There are views here also. Beyond, the *AT* skirts the western edge of the ridge.

1.5 Here the Swamp Trail "in reverse" leaves the *AT* and goes left uphill about 0.1m. to its starting point at the Amphitheatre (and Picnic Grounds) Parking Area of Big Meadows. *AT* now passes below the open-air amphitheatre.

1.6 Cement posts mark trail intersection. Trail straight ahead is route of the *AT*. (Trail to left leads 0.2m. to the end of the Swamp Trail and along the Swamp Trail "in reverse" about 0.8m. farther to the beginning of the Dark Hollow Falls Tr. The trail to right of the *AT* leads 1.2m. to Lewis Falls. The Lewis Falls Tr. and *AT* together offer a 3.1m. circuit hike. See back of map, PATC No. 10.)

1.9 Pass under sheer cliffs of Black Rock.

2.1 Trail to left of *AT* leads 0.1m., to Black Rock viewpoint and another 0.2m. to Big Meadows Lodge. The *AT* continues along the west slope of the ridge, descending, with occasional views to the west from rocks to the right of the Trail.

2.5 Cross service road. (To left this road leads about 0.3m. to the Skyline Drive, SDMP 51.4, at a point 0.1m. south of the Big Meadows Wayside. Lunches are available at the wayside year-round. Here too is located the Harry F. Byrd Sr. Visitor Center. To right of the *A T* the service road leads down to a sewage disposal area. To reach Lewis Falls follow the road downhill for about 150 ft. (Note small pumphouse to right of road here.) Turn left off the road onto a footpath that leads 0.5m. downhill to Lewis Falls and on to Big Meadows.) Beyond the service road intersection the *A T* passes the outlet of housed-in Lewis Spring. The Trail continues through woods, descending gradually.

2.8 Cross horse trail. Continue straight ahead and cross the horse trail again in about 0.1m. Cross open field with cemetery to the right. Here are splendid views; ahead is Hazeltop Mtn.

3.1 Cross Tanners Ridge Fire Road. (Road, gated at the Drive and at the Park boundary, leads right for 1.4m. to the Park boundary where it becomes VA. Sec. 682. To left it leads 0.1m. to the Drive, SDMP 51.6.)

3.3 Pass spring 50 ft. to left of the *A T*. Beyond, pass through fields still fairly open.

4.2 Cross Skyline Drive, SDMP 52.8, just south of Milam Gap, el. 3257'. *A T* bears east through a field. Cement post marks the Mill Prong Trail which leads left from the *A T*. (This trail, of which the first 0.1m. is blue-blazed, leads 1.8m. to Hoover Camp. The latter 0.8m. of the trail is coincident with the Mill Prong Horse Trail.) Beyond the junction of the *A T* ascends along the north ridge of Hazeltop.

4.6 Bear right along ridge crest. From rock to left of Trail is wintertime view of Doubletop and Fork Mtns. (Former Pres. Herbert Hoover's Camp is in the Rapidan Valley between these peaks.) The *A T* ascends very gradually along the ridge crest. Here may be found a fine stand of stiff gentians among the white and purple asters in the autumn.

5.7 Reach the north end of Hazeltop.

6.1 Cross the wooded summit of Hazeltop, 3812', highest point on the *A T* in the SNP.

6.6 Junction with graded Laurel Prong Trail. (Laurel Prong Tr. leads left from the *A T* down 2.8m. to Hoover Camp. This is one of the few trails in the Park that pass through areas with rosebay rhododendron (or great laurel) which blooms in late

June or early July. Other wild flowers found here include the false lily-of-the-valley, trillium, and wild iris.)

7.0 In Bootens Gap, el. 3243', cross the Conway River Fire Road, gated. Skyline Drive, SDMP 55.1, is 150 ft. to right, with parking space for two cars. To left, the road leads down the Conway River, one fork of the road becoming Va. Sec. 615 and continuing to Graves Mill: the other fork, which continues down the Conway River, becomes VA. Sec. 667 and comes into VA. Rt. 230 about 3m. north of Stanardsville.) The *AT* descends gradually for 0.2m., then continues with little change in elevation, paralleling the Skyline Drive.

7.7 Ascend gradually, following along the western slope of Bush Mtn.

7.9 *AT* approaches within 150 ft. of the Drive. Ascent continues for about 0.2m., then Trail is level for about 0.3m. before again ascending along the ridge of Bearfence Mtn.

8.4 Trail intersection. (To right, trail leads 0.1m. to the Skyline Drive at the Bearfence Mtn. Parking Area, SDMP 56.4. Naturalist led hikes start here in the summer. To left, an unimproved trail (blazed) leads to spectacular jagged rocks of Bearfence Mtn. Views from the rocks are excellent. This is a rough trail requiring the use of hands in some places. In 0.3m. it connects with the graded loop trail over Bearfence Mtn., the two trails, with the *AT*, making a rough figure eight.)

8.6 Bearfence Mtn. Loop Trail (graded) leaves *AT* on left. (Views along this trail are rewarding. The loop trail is only 150 ft. longer than the stretch of *AT* between the junctions.)

8.8 The Bearfence Loop Trail comes in from the left. The *AT* now descends steeply with a series of zigzags, with a splendid view to the east from a rock ledge near the top.

9.4 In gap, cross the Bearfence Mtn. Shelter access road. (Road leads down 0.3m. to the shelter. Below the shelter, as the Slaughter Fire Foot Trail it continues down to the Conway River where it joins a branch of the Conway River Fire Road. To right of the *AT* the road leads a few feet to the Skyline Drive, SDMP 56.8. On west side of the Drive, the road continues as the Meadows School Fire Road and descends to VA. Sec. 759.)

9.5 Spur trail, left, leads downhill 0.2m. to Bearfence Mtn. Shelter. Spring is 50 ft. south of the shelter. (See Chap. 6: "Shelters and Cabins.") The *AT* now ascends gradually the north slope of Lewis Mtn. As Trail levels off at about 3400 ft., several paths lead right, first to the Lewis Mtn. Picnic Grounds (water available "in season") and then to the Lewis Mtn. Campground. There is a camp store on the campground road, open June thru October.

10.4 Here a post marks a trail, right, leading 300 ft. to the campground. (Water fountain "in season" directly across camp road.)

10,5 Pass trail intersection. (To right a trail leads to the campground. To left the Lewis Mtn. FFT leads along the ridge crest of Lewis Mtn. but soon gives out. Across the Skyline Drive from the entrance to the Lewis Mtn. Campground the Allen Hollow FFT leads 3m. down to VA. Sec. 625 at a point about 8m. from Elkton.) The *AT* now descends steadily.

11.1 Left of the *AT* an old road descends toward Pocosin Hollow. To the right of the Trail, Skyline Drive is only a few feet away. *AT* soon bears away from the Drive.

12.0 Pass spring to the right of the Trail.

12.2 Cross Pocosin Fire Rd. (To right, fire road leads 0.1m to Skyline Drive, SDMP 59.5. Across the Drive a few feet north of here, the Hensley Church FFT, badly overgrown at present, leads down to Va. Sec. 625 at a point about 7m. from Elkton. To left of the *AT*, the Pocosin Fire Rd. leads downhill passing Pocosin Cabin in 0.1m. About 0.8m. farther along the fire road, the Pocosin Horse Trail leads right from the road for 1.3m. to join the South River Fire Rd., making an excellent loop trail possible (or a complete circuit by returning to Pocosin Fire Rd. via the *AT*.) See Chap. 5: "Side Trails", Central Section, and PATC map no. 10.) Beyond the fire road intersection the *AT* ascends gradually.

12.3 Graded spur trail leads left, downhill, 250 ft. to Pocosin Cabin and to the spring just south of the cabin. (Pocosin Cabin is a locked structure; reservations for its use must be obtained in advance from PATC Headquarters. See Chap. 6: 'Shelters and Cabins." From the cabin there is a fine view east over the

Conway River Valley. Three mountains can be seen across the valley. The local mountaineers called these, from right to left: Panther, Bear Stand, and Sawney Macks; these names are not recognized on current maps. "Pocosin" is said to be of Indian derivation, meaning a "dismal" or swamp.)

12.5 AT ascends steeply by switchbacks for 0.1m. It next passes through a relatively flat area known as Kites Deadening, now completely wooded. (A deadening was an area where the early settlers, instead of felling the trees to clear the land for a field, saved time and effort by just ringing the trees— removing the lower bark—to kill the trees without the task of cutting them down. They would then plant their crops amid the "deadened" trees.)

12.7 Blue blaze marks short spur trail, right, leading 0.1m. to Skyline Drive, SDMP 60.2. AT now ascends.

13.5 Reach crest of Baldface Mtn., el. 3600 ft.

13.8 Rocks to right of the Trail offer views to the west.

14.2 Cross old road which leads left past an old quarry. (To the right road leads 0.1m. past the site of a former CCC camp to the Skyline Drive, SDMP 61.8.)

15.1 Cross South River Fire Road. (To left road leads down toward South River Falls. In 0.8m. from the AT a road leads right from the fire road down to the South River at a point 0.1m. below the Falls. The South River Falls Tr. utilizes the lower portion of this road. Follow a footpath for 0.1m. up the river to the base of the South River Falls. The South River Fire Rd. continues eastward. In another 1.2m. the Pocosin Horse Trail leads left from it for 1.3m. to its junction with the Pocosin Fire Rd. Beyond this junction the South River Fire Rd. descends, becoming Va. Sec. 642 outside the Park. To the right of the AT , the fire road leads 0.3m. to the Skyline Drive, SDMP 62.7, el. 2960'. Across the Drive here the Dry Run Falls Fire Rd. leads 2.6m. down the west slope of Dean Mtn. to VA. Sec. 625.) From the fire road intersection, the AT ascends, then skirts the east slope of the knob on which the South River Picnic Area is located.

15.6 Cross graded trail, the South River Falls Trail. (To left this trail leads 1.5m. downhill to the South River Falls. To the right it leads 0.1m. to the eastern edge of the South River Picnic Grounds. Water is available here "in season".)

15.9 In pine thicket old road comes in on right from the Drive, SDMP 63.1. *AT* turns left onto this road and follows it.

16.1 *AT* takes right fork of road. (Left fork leads across overgrown fields and young woods 0.3m. to South River Shelter. Spring is 200 ft. west of the shelter.)

16.5 At bend in Trail an old road comes in from the left. The *AT* ascends.

16.7 Still following the old road, reach top of rise, just west of the westernmost peak, el. 3296', of Saddleback Mtn. There is much trillium along the trail here in early May.

17.2 Junction with the Saddleback Mtn. FFT which comes in from the left and follows the *AT*. (Fire foot trail leads back to South River Shelter. It is labeled South River FFT on PATC map #10 but marked Saddleback Mtn. FFT on metal post. This trail is fairly open but not well blazed so should be used with caution.)

17.3 Saddleback Mtn. FFT leaves the *AT* on the left. (Here the fire foot trail leads south, coming into Big Bend Fire Road near U. S. 33. The trail is badly overgrown but easy to follow; there are almost no blazes.)

17.9 *AT* turns left off of the old road it has been following.

18.3 Trail passes under power line.

18.5 Pass a side trail, on right, at a sign which reads: "Danger Power Cable".

18.6 Reach Skyline Drive, just where the entrance road from U. S. 33 comes into the Drive in Swift Run Gap, SDMP 65.5, el. 2367'. (Swift Run Gap is 7 miles east of Elkton and 8 miles west of Stanardsville via U.S. 33.)

SUMMARY OF SKYLINE DRIVE DISTANCES
TO REACH POINTS ON *AT*
Section VII Central

SDMP		Mileage from Thornton Gap
31.5	U.S. 211 at Thornton Gap	0.0
33.5	Buck Hollow Trail crossing, 0.7 m. to *AT*	2.0
33.9	Service Road to Byrds Nest #3, 0.3 m. to *AT*	2.4
36.4	Jewell Hollow Overlook	4.9
36.7	Pinnacles Picnic Grounds	5.2
37.9	Shaver Hollow Parking Area	6.4
38.4	Nicholson Hollow Trail Crossing, 0.1 m. to *AT*.	6.9
38.6	Stony Man Mtn. Overlook	7.1
39.1	Little Stony Man Parking Area	7.6
41.7	Skyland, North Entrance, 0.3 m. to *AT*	10.2
42.5	Skyland, South Entrance, 0.1 m. to *AT*	11.0
43.3	Timber Hollow Overlook	11.8
44.4	Crescent Rock Overlook	12.9
45.6	Hawksbill Gap	14.1
48.1	Spitler Knoll Parking Overlook (parking for Rock Spring Cabin)	16.6
49.0	Franklin Cliffs Overlook	17.5
49.3	Fishers Gap	17.8
51.2	Big Meadows Developed Area, 1.0 m. to *AT* via Campground Rd.	19.7
51.6	Tanners Ridge Fire Rd., 0.1 m. to *AT*	20.1
52.8	Milam Gap, *AT* crossing	21.3
55.1	Bootens Gap	23.6
56.4	Bearfence Mtn. Parking Area, 0.1 m. to *AT*	24.9
56.8	Bearfence Mtn. Shelter Access Road	25.3
57.5	Lewis Mtn. Campground, 0.1 m. to *AT*	26.0
59.5	Pocosin Fire Rd., 0.1 m. to *AT*	28.0
62.7	South River Fire Rd., 0.2 m. to *AT*	31.2
62.8	South River Picnic Grounds, 0.3 m. to *AT*	31.3
63.1	Service Road to South River Shelter, 0.1 m. to *AT*	31.6
65.5	Swift Run Gap	34.0

SUMMARY OF DISTANCE ALONG THE *AT*
Section VII Central

	Miles	Kilometers
Thornton Gap and U.S. 211	0.0	0.0
Marys Rock Summit	1.7 + 0.1	2.7 + 0.2
Buck Hollow Trail	2.4	3.9
Byrds Nest #3	3.0	4.8
Pinnacles Picnic Grounds	5.3	8.5
Shavers Hollow Shelter	6.2 + 0.3	10.0 + 0.5
Nicholson Hollow Trail	7.0	11.3
Stony Man Parking Overlook	7.3	11.8
Little Stony Man Parking Area	7.7	12.4
Skyland (Dining Hall)	9.4	15.1
Whiteoak Canyon Trail	9.9 + 0.1	15.9 + 0.2
Hawksbill Gap	12.5	20.1
Hawksbill Gap Shelter	12.5 + 0.2	20.1 + 0.3
Byrds Nest #2 and summit of Hawksbill	12.5 + 0.8	20.1 + 1.3
Rock Spring Cabin	13.8 + 0.2	22.2 + 0.3
Fishers Gap	15.7	25.2
Big Meadows—Amphitheatre area	17.3	27.8
Lewis Spring Service Rd.	18.2	29.2
Skyline Drive crossing, Milam Gap	19.9	31.9
Hazeltop Mtn. summit	21.8	35.0
Bearfence Mtn. Loop Trail	24.3	39.0
Bearfence Mtn. Shelter	25.2 + 0.2	40.5 + 0.3
Lewis Mtn. Campground	26.2	42.2
Pocosin Cabin	27.9 + 0.1	44.9 + 0.2
South River Falls Trail	31.3	50.3
South River Shelter	31.8 + 0.3	51.1 + 0.5
Swift Run Gap and U.S. 33	34.3	55.2

SECTION VIII SOUTHERN SHENANDOAH PARK
SWIFT RUN GAP TO ROCKFISH GAP
NORTH TO SOUTH

Distance 44.3 miles (71.2 kilometers)   (PATC Map No. 11: J-2)

This section of the Appalachian Trail commences where U.S.
Rt. 33 (Spotswood Trail) crosses the Blue Ridge at Swift Run
Gap, SDMP 65.5, el. 2367 ft. Swift Run Gap is 7 miles east of
Elkton and 8 miles west of Stanardsville, (110 miles from
Washington, D. C.) Rockfish Gap is 4 miles east of
Waynesboro via U.S. 250 and 22 miles west of Charlottesville,
(about 140 miles from Washington, D. C.)

The southern section of the Shenandoah Park is the wildest
and least developed section. Much of it lies in an area proposed
for wilderness status. The *AT* itself follows the main crest of the
Blue Ridge, so is rarely far from the Skyline Drive and crosses it
frequently. There are many interesting side trails and fire roads
in the section that can be used in conjunction with the *AT* for
interesting hiking trips. The *AT* leaves the Shenandoah Park at
Jarman Gap and is on private land from there to Rockfish Gap
at the south end of the section. Here the Trail crosses U. S.
Interstate 64 and U. S. 250. Plans are being made to relocate the
7.6m. stretch of *AT* between Jarman and Rockfish Gaps.
*Hikers should be on the alert for a trail route different from that
described in this Guide.*

One large campground, the Loft Mountain Campground, is
in this section of the Park. In addition to a picnic area and
campsites, there are shower and laundry facilities, and a camp
store. The Campground is closed during the winter. Dundo
Campground is open from April through October for Group
use only; the remainder of the year Dundo is open as a picnic area,
facilities are limited.

There is one locked cabin, the Doyle River Cabin, in this
section that may be rented by hikers. Reservations for its use
must be made through PATC Headquarters. See Chap. 6:
Shelters and Cabins.

Section VIII is divided for convenience into four subsections: Swift Run Gap to Simmons Gap, Simmons to Browns Gap, Browns to Jarman Gap, and Jarman to Rockfish Gap.

Maps: PATC Hiker's map, #11. Also available are the USGS map of Shenandoah National Park, Southern Section, 1969, scale 1:62,500, and the USGS 7½' quads: Swift Run Gap, McGaheysville, Browns Cove, Crimora and Waynesboro East. (Other 7½' quads covering areas of the southern section not traversed by the *AT* include Grottoes, Elkton East, and Crozet.)

SUBSECTION:
SWIFT RUN GAP TO SIMMONS GAP
NORTH TO SOUTH

9.6 miles (15.4 kilometers)   (PATC map No. 11:J-2)

General description:

From Swift Run Gap, el. 2367 ft. the *AT* climbs over 1200 ft. to near the summit of Hightop Mtn., el. 3587 ft. This is the highest elevation of the *AT* in the southern section of the Park. The Trail then loses even more elevation than it had gained as it descends to Powell Gap. Still following the main crest of the Blue Ridge it climbs over a shoulder of Flattop Mtn. before reaching Simmons Gap.

Side trails:

Because the SNP is very narrow through most of this subsection there are few side trails and those that do exist lead out of the Park.

Accommodations:

There is one open-faced shelter, Hightop Shelter, 3.4m. (follow spur trail 0.1m.) along this section. See Chap. 6: "Shelters and Cabins."

There are no public accommodations along this section. Closest public lodgings, open only during the warmer months, are at Lewis Mtn., SDMP 57.5, in the Central Section of the Park. There is neither gasoline nor food available at Swift Run Gap.

Detailed Trail data:

0.0 The cement post on east side of Skyline Drive, directly opposite the place where the entrance road from U.S. 33 reaches the Drive, is the starting point for this section. *AT* follows pedestrian footway along edge of bridge. Beyond the bridge, cross to right side of the Skyline Drive and climb bank. Trail shortly comes into old road which it follows for a few feet.

0.1 Trail turns sharply left from the old road and climbs. It soon levels off and follows an old farm road through what remains of an apple orchard. Then descends gently.

1.3 Trail crosses to left of Skyline Drive in grassy sag, SDMP 66.7, el. 2637 ft. From sag Trail ascends steeply, by switchbacks, up the north slope of Hightop Mtn.

2.7 As *AT* nears summit there are two excellent viewpoints from ledges right of the Trail, one about 100 ft. farther along the Trail than the other. In another 100 ft. a spur trail, left, leads 350 ft. to site of former Park Service Lookout Tower at the summit of Hightop Mtn., el. 3587 ft. No view from the summit. *AT* now descends.

2.9 There is a protected spring at the foot of a large boulder just to the left of the *AT*. Trail continues to descend.

3.4 Spur trail leads right 0.1m. to Hightop Shelter. (Spring is 400 ft. downhill from shelter on graded trail. Hightop Shelter FFT leads from shelter 0.5m down to Skyline Drive, SDMP 67.2.)

3.5 Cross dirt road. (Service road leads right, to Hightop Shelter. To left it leads to the Smith Roach Gap Fire Rd. at a point about 0.8m. from the Drive.) *AT* descends steadily.

4.6 Trail crosses Smith Roach Gap Fire Road, then turns right and parallels it to the Skyline Drive.

4.7 Cross to right of Skyline Drive in open Smith Roach Gap, SDMP 68.6, el. 2622'. Trail continues with little change in elevation around the east and south sides of Roundtop Mtn., affording wintertime views of Powell Gap and Flattop Mtn. Continue along ridge crest.

5.8 Summit of Little Roundtop Mtn. is 50 yds. to the right here. View of Powell Gap is to be had, just as Trail starts to descend steeply the west slope of the mountain.

6.3 Reach Powell Gap, SDMP 69.9, el. 2294', and cross to left of Drive. A trail, formerly the Powell Gap Road, crosses the mountain here. To the northwest it descends down Eaton Hollow to VA. Sec. 628. To the southeast it leads down to VA. Sec. 627.) The *AT* now ascends a shoulder of Flattop Mtn.

6.6 Turn sharply left here, where old road, which *AT* has been following, continues straight ahead. Continue to ascend.

6.8 Excellent views of the Roach River Valley (Powell Gap and Bacon Hollows) from rock ledges just to the left of the Trail. Continue to ascend very gently.

8.0 Reach summit of the shoulder of Flattop Mtn. and start gradual descent.

8.1 The *AT* comes close to the edge of the SNP here. There is an open field about 50 ft. to left of the Trail. From the field, but not from the *AT*, there are views, especially of Flattop Mtn., el. 3325'. Trail continues to descend.

8.7 Trail bends right to parallel an old road on its left and descends steeply.

9.1 Come into the old road and follow it right for about 0.2m. (The road leads down to the Simmons Gap Ranger Station, formerly the Simmons Gap Episcopal Mission.)

9.3 Turn slightly right, away from the road. Come into Simmons Gap Rd. and follow it 40 ft. to the Drive.

9.6 Reach Simmons Gap, SDMP 73.2, el. 2253 ft., at the intersection of the Simmons Gap Fire Rd. and Skyline Drive. (The Simmons Gap Rd. is barred on both sides of the Drive and at the Park boundaries. Outside the Park, on both east and west sides of the Drive, the road becomes VA. Sec. 628. A short distance south on the road is the ranger's residence and beyond it are the Park Service maintenance facilities. Water available here.) *AT* crosses to right (west) of Skyline Drive.

SUBSECTION:
SIMMONS GAP TO BROWNS GAP
NORTH TO SOUTH

12.2 miles (19.6 kilometers)   (PATC map No. 11:I-7)

General description:

This portion of the Trail starts at Simmons Gap, SDMP 73.2, el. 2253 ft. There are two 600 ft. climbs and one 800 ft. one, from Ivy Creek to the summit of Loft Mtn., but little other climbing. Between the peak of Loft Mtn. and Big Flat Mtn., site of the Loft Mtn. Campground, the *AT* passes through considerable open area, a pleasant change from wooded territory. On Big Flat Mtn. the *AT* skirts the east, south, and then western edges of the Loft Mtn. Campground, then descends very gently toward Browns Gap, SDMP 82.9, el. 2599 ft.

The Shenandoah Park is much wider in this subsection than in the preceding one. A roughly triangular area between the ridges of Rockytop, Browns Mtn. and Loft Mtn. and drained by tributaries of Big Run comprises the largest watershed in the Park, 11 square miles.

Side trails:

The greater width of Park here gives space for a wide variety of trails. The Big Trail and the Falls Trail are both Park Service loop trails, connected at each of their ends with either the *AT* or Skyline Drive. There are, in addition, several blue-blazed trails and a number of fire foot trails. Finally there are several gated Park roads—Simmons Gap Rd., Big Run Fire Rd., Browns Gap Fire Rd., Madison Run Fire Rd. and Paines Run Fire Rd. For details of these see Chap. 5: "Side Trails," Southern Section.

Accommodations:

The Loft Mtn. Developed Area includes a wayside, camp store, campground with shower and laundry facilities, picnic grounds and two nature trails. Campground and other facilities are generally open April through October . (Store opens in mid May through October).

There are two open-faced shelters for use of hikers in inclement weather, Pinefield Shelter, 2.1m., and Ivy Creek

Shelter, 5.8m. A third shelter, Big Run Shelter, can be reached by hiking down 2m. along the Big Run Trail from either of its ends. (*A T* mileages at termini of Big Run Trail, 10.0 and 11.6m.)

One locked cabin is available, the Doyle River Cabin, one quarter mile from the *A T* (10.0m.) down the Falls Trail. Reservations for the use of this cabin must be obtained in advance from PATC Headquarters. See Chap. 6: *Shelters and Cabins.*

Detailed Trail data:

0.0 West side of the Skyline Drive, at junction with the Simmons Gap Fire Rd., SDMP 73.2, el. 2253 ft. (A short distance to the south on the fire road is the ranger's residence and beyond it are the Park Service maintenance facilities. Water available here. The Simmons Gap Rd. is barred on both sides of the Drive and at the Park boundaries. Outside the Park, on both east and west sides of the Drive, the road becomes VA. Sec. 628.) Trail ascends the northwestern face of Weaver Mtn.

1.1 Reach top of Weaver Mtn., then descend gently through sparse, scraggly woods, primarily black locust.

1.9 Cross to left of Skyline Drive at Pinefield Gap, SDMP 75.2. Continue through level area.

2.1 Cross access road to Pinefield Shelter. Spring is located along this road, 20 yds. left of the *A T*. Shelter is 150 yds. farther down the road. (A second spring is 250 ft. behind the shelter. See Chap. 6: "Shelters and Cabins.") Trail now ascends.

2.3 Here *A T* comes withing 100 ft. of the Skyline Drive.

2.7 At a spot where the *A T* turns sharply left, an unmarked trail leads right approximately 200 ft. to Skyline Drive. (From here one can follow the Drive north a few feet to reach the start of the Two-Mile Ridge FFT. The Two-Mile Run Parking Overlook is 0.1m. farther north, SDMP 76.2, and the start of the Rocky Mount Trail another 0.2m.) *A T* continues to ascend.

3.1 Reach unnamed summit, 3050 ft., then descend gently.

3.7 Reach north end of the Ivy Creek Overlook, SDMP 77.5. *A T* passes along the overlook, parallels the Drive a few feet farther, then crosses to the right (west) of the Skyline Drive.

3.9 Cross to the left of the Skyline Drive, SDMP 77.7, and ascend unnamed peak, el. 3080', then descend.

4.4 Trail reaches excellent viewpoint, with Skyline Drive immediately below the Trail. (View covers an area from Trayfoot Mtn. on the left to Rockytop on the right.) *AT* continues to descend.

5.1 Cross Ivy Creek in a very lovely miniature canyon at an elevation of about 2550 ft. Trail now starts the ascent of Loft Mtn., the longest climb in this portion of the *AT*, climbing along the east bank of Ivy Creek for 0.2m., then bearing left away from it.

5.8 A spur trail leads right 0.1m. to Ivy Creek Shelter and spring. (See Chap. 6: *Shelters and Cabins.*)

6.1 *AT* passes to right of the peak of Loft Mtn., about 3320 ft., and follows crest of the ridge. For the next mile or so, as far as Big Flat Mtn., the *AT* passes through Patterson Field, an area that was once a large, 240 acre pasture. Now grass is gradually being replaced by blackberry vines and other shrubby growth, but at least a half mile of *AT* is still out in the open with good views (in 1975 as this edition is being written). In places, especially near the pasture edges, black locust now covers the land. But in the midst of the young woods stand several old oak trees with very large low-spreading branches, showing that these oaks gained their maturity while the land was still open pasture.

6.7 Panoramic (270°) view from the Trail. A short distance farther the Deadening Nature Trail (See Loft Mtn. inset, back of map. #11), a Park Service trail, enters from the right and follows along the *AT*. (This nature trail starts from the Skyline Drive at the entrance to the Loft Mtn. Campground, SDMP 79.5, climbs to the *AT*, follows it south about 0.1m., then descends to its starting point.)

6.8 Deadening Nature Trail leaves *AT* here. *AT* begins descent toward sag between Loft and Big Flat Mtns.

7.4 *AT* crosses old road in sag. (To right, road leads to the paved Loft Mtn. Campground road. To left, road soon deadends.)

7.9 A spur trail leads right, uphill, to the Loft Mtn. Camp Store which is open "in season", generally mid May through October. (Store carries a complete line of groceries. Adjoining laundromat is equipped with coin-operated washers and dryers.) Trail climbs gently toward Big Flat Mtn., el. 3387 ft.

8.1 Loft Mtn. Nature Trail enters *AT* from right and follows it south for about one mile as the *AT* circles clockwise around the Loft Mtn. Campground. Excellent views can be had, first to the east, then south and finally to the west, as the *AT* swings around the camping area located on summit of Big Flat Mtn. The Trail is almost level here. Several unmarked trails lead right to the campground.

9.2 Cement post marks junction where the Loft Mtn. Nature Trail leaves the *AT* to return to the campground. *AT* now descends Big Flat Mtn.

9.7 Here there is an excellent panoramic view: from left to right: Rockytop, Brown Mtn., Rocky Mtn., Rocky Mount, and, to right (east) of the Drive, Loft Mtn. *AT* continues to descend.

10.0 *AT* intersects the Falls Trail. (Skyline Drive, SDMP 81.1, is 200 ft. to right. To reach northern end of Big Run Trail at the Big Run Parking Overlook, go south on Drive for 250 ft. Big Run Tr. leads west 2.2m. to Big Run Shelter.) (Falls Trail leads down on the left of the *AT*, passing below the Doyle River Cabin in 0.3m. Reservations for the use of this cabin must be obtained in advance from PATC Headquarters. See Chap. 6: *Shelters and Cabins* and Chap. 5: *Side Trails*.) From the Falls Tr. intersection the *AT* closely parallels the Skyline Drive and is relatively level.

10.9 Trail passes through the Doyle River Parking Overlook, SDMP 81.9 A tenth of a mile farther, to the left of the *AT*, can be seen the remains of earthworks and trenches erected in 1864 by Jubal Early's men after their retreat from Winchester.

11.1 Trail follows along ledges affording wintertime views south.

11.3 *AT* crosses to the right of the Skyline Drive, SDMP 82.2, with fine view of Cedar Mtn. and Trayfoot Mtn. from the Drive.

11.6 Junction with Big Run Trail. (Big Run Trail, 4.2m. long, runs from here to Big Run Parking Overlook, SDMP

81.1, near the Falls Trail. Big Run Shelter is 2.0m. down this trail from *AT* junction.) Beyond junction, *AT* gradually descends.

12.2 Junction with the Madison Run Fire Road at a point 100 ft. to the right of the Skyline Drive, SDMP 82.9, el. 2599 ft. in Browns Gap. Junction is marked with cement post. (Madison Run Rd. leads west down Dundo Hollow to the Park boundary, 5.7m. and joins VA. Sec. 663 and 629 at a point 1.8m. from Grottoes on U.S. 340, East of the Drive the Browns Gap Fire Rd. leads beyond the Park boundary and becomes VA. Sec. 629.) Browns Gap was used several times by Gen. Stonewall Jackson during the Civil War's Valley Campaign.

SUBSECTION:
BROWNS GAP TO JARMAN GAP
NORTH TO SOUTH

15.1 miles (24.3 kilometers)   (PATC map No. 11: G-14)

General description:
   After crossing the Skyline Drive in Browns Gap, SDMP 82.9, el. 2599', the *AT* passes along the east side of the Dundo Area (used as a group campground April through October and as a picnic grounds November through March). It then recrosses the Drive and climbs to Blackrock, a mammoth rock pile and one of the most interesting spots in the entire Shenandoah Park. The Trail then descends to Blackrock Gap, losing 750 ft. of elevation. From the gap it follows the crest of the Blue Ridge with a succession of short climbs and shorter dips, gradually reaching an altitude of over 3000 ft. The final five miles of this section is primarily downhill all the way to Jarman Gap, el. 2173'. Jarman Gap marks the southern end of the Shenandoah Park. The Skyline Drive itself continues on to Rockfish Gap, SDMP 105.4.
   This most southern area of the Park, like the preceding section, Simmons Gap to Browns Gap, is quite wild and much of it may be designated a Wilderness Area. Rhododendron, which is quite scarce in the Park, is found along the Riprap Trail and along the *AT* in the same general area. Mountain Laurel

(kalmia) is very plentiful in this area, especially along the Moormans River Fire Rd. east of the Drive from Blackrock Gap.

Side trails:

There are a number of very worthwhile side trails. Some lead to places of special scenic interest such as Riprap Ravine, Calvary Rocks, Trayfoot Mtn. and the falls on both Jones Run and Doyle River. The old Moormans River Fire Road, which was at one time the route of the *A T*, leads down the north fork of the Moormans River from Blackrock Gap and up the south fork to Jarman Gap. For more information refer to Chap. 5: "Side Trails", Southern Section; also the separate PATC publications, *Circuit Hikes in the Shenandoah National Park* and *Walkers' Chart No. 3.*

Accommodations:

The Dundo Group Campground, SDMP 83.7, is reserved for organized groups from April through October. Reservations should be made with Park Headquarters in advance. Fee $3.00. There is no store here and no shower or laundry facilities. The remainder of the year the Dundo area is operated as picnic grounds.

Two open-faced shelters, Blackrock Shelter, 3.0m. (follow spur trail 0.2m.) and Sawmill Run Shelter, 13.0m. (follow spur trail 0.3m.) are available for use, but for camping only in inclement weather. In addition to these, the Riprap Shelter about 3m. from the *A T* via the Riprap Trail from either of its junctions (6.2m. and 9.3m.) is available for camping in inclement weather.

Detailed Trail data:

0.0 Cement post marks junction of the *A T* and the Madison Run Fire Road at a point 100 ft. to the west of the Skyline Drive, SDMP 82.9, el. 2599'. (Madison Run Rd. leads west down Dundo Hollow to Park boundary where it joins VA. Sec. 663 and 629 at a point 1.8m. from U. S. 340 at Grottoes. East of the Drive the Browns Gap Fire Rd. leads down into Browns Cove, crossing the Falls Trail in 1.7m. Both roads are gated at the Drive and Park boundaries.) The *A T* crosses diagonally to the left side of the Skyline Drive, then ascends gently.

0.4 The Trail skirts the east side of the Dundo Area, SDMP 83.7, for the next 0.2m. Several unmarked paths lead up to Dundo. Water is obtainable there from April through October.

0.6 *AT* turns sharply left. A trail to right leads to Dundo.

1.2 Intersection with the Falls Trail. (To right, the Falls Tr. leads uphill 100 ft. to the Falls Trail Parking Area, SDMP 84.1; to the left, the Falls Tr. descends Jones Run, then ascends Doyle River, intersecting the Browns Gap Road about halfway up, passing below the Doyle River Cabin, and recrossing the *AT* to reach the Skyline Drive, SDMP 81.1. Hiking distance along the Falls Trail, 4.6m.) The *AT* now passes through remnants of an old apple orchard.

1.4 Cross to right side of Skyline Drive, SDMP 84.3, and ascend very gently.

2.1 Here the *AT* and Trayfoot Mtn. Fire Rd. come within a few feet of each other, then parallel but do not cross. (Trayfoot Mtn. Fire Rd. leads back 250 yds. to the Skyline Drive, SDMP 84.7. This road is the shortest approach to Blackrock from the Drive.) After about 0.1m. the *AT* bears right, away from the road, and circles the north, west, and south sides of Blackrock, el. 3092'. Blackrock is a tremendous mass of lichen-covered blocks of rock, piled haphazardly one upon another. The area is reminiscent of New Hampshire's White Mountain terrain above tree-line. The view from the rocks is excellent.

2.4 A graded trail leads right from the *AT* at its highest elevation at Blackrock and follows the ridge leading to Trayfoot Mtn. (It comes into the Trayfoot Mtn. Rd. where that road reaches the ridge, about 0.2m. from the *AT*.)

2.5 *AT* crosses the Trayfoot Mtn. Rd. From here Trail descends steadily toward Blackrock Gap, following along the east side of a narrow ridge. (An old road parallels the trail on the west side of the ridge, just out of sight of the trail.)

3.0 Spur trail, left, leads steeply down 0.2m. to Blackrock Shelter. (Shelter is located in a deep ravine. Spring is 10 yds. in front of shelter.) One hundred feet beyond spur trail, the *AT* crosses to west of the old road, parallels it for 0.2m., then comes into it and follows it on down to its intersection with the Skyline Drive.

3.5 Cross to the left of the Skyline Drive, SDMP 87.2, and continue along the east side of the Drive for a quarter mile.

3.7 Cross the Moormans River Fire Rd. in Blackrock Gap, SDMP 87.4, el. 2321 ft. (Moormans River Fire Rd. follows the north fork of the river down to the Charlottesville Reservoir where it meets VA. Sec. 614. From there the fire road climbs along the south fork of the river, reaching the Skyline Drive at Jarman Gap, hiking distance 9.4m. This fire road was at one time the route of the *A T*.) (On the west side of Blackrock Gap, the Paine Run Fire Rd. descends 3.7m. to the Park boundary at a point approximately 2m. from Rt. 340.) From the road intersection the *A T* climbs over a small knob, descends to a sag at 4.8m, with the Skyline Drive 50 ft. to the right. Trail now climbs over a second small knob.

5.: Trail crosses to right of Skyline Drive, SDMP 88.9, in a sag, then climbs.

6.2 At summit of a knob, el. 2988 ft., reach junction with Riprap Trail. (Riprap Tr. leads west to Calvary Rocks, 1.0m. and on by the Riprap Shelter and up Wildcat Ridge to its southern junction with the *A T*. Hiking distance via the Riprap Trail, 6.2m.) From junction, *A T* descends rather steeply.

6.6 A graded trail, left, leads 300 ft. down to Calvary Rocks Parking Area on the Skyline Drive, SDMP 90.0. Trail continues to descend steeply for another 0.1m., then more gradually. For the next two miles Trail alternately climbs and dips gently. There is occasional rhododendron (Catawba) here. It is found in only a few other places in the SNP.

9.3 Intersection with Riprap Trail. (To left Riprap Trail leads 0.1m. to Skyline Drive at the Wildcat Ridge Parking Area, SDMP 92.1. To right, it follows the Wildcat Ridge west, then drops down into Riprap Hollow and passes Riprap Shelter, then climbs passing Calvary Rocks before again reaching the *A T*.) From junction with Riprap Trail, *A T* ascends gently.

9.6 *A T* crosses to left of Skyline Drive, SDMP 92.4, and continues to ascend, reaching a summit, el. 3080 ft., in 0.5m. Beyond summit there are wintertime views of peaks in the George Washington National Forest, Pedlar District, south of Rockfish Gap. Trail descends to a slight sag, reclimbs to about the same elevation, then descends fairly steeply toward Turk Gap.

11.6 Cross to the right of the Skyline Drive at Turk Gap, SDMP 94.1, el. 2610 ft. (Turk Gap Rd., now trail, leads down the west slope of the Blue Ridge for 1.6m. to the Park boundary near the old Crimora mines.) About 0.1m beyond the Drive, the Turk Mtn.-Sawmill Ridge Fire Foot Trail comes into the *AT* from the left and follows along it. (Skyline Drive is 100 ft. via the fire trail. South on the Drive about 0.2m. from here is start of the Turk Branch Trail which leads down to the South Fork of the Moorman River.)

11.8 The Turk Mtn.-Sawmill Ridge Fire Foot Trail leaves the *AT*, right, and follows along a side ridge which shortly divides into two ridges, one Turk Mtn., the other Sawmill Ridge. The hiker will find the 1.1m. side trip to the top of Turk Mtn. via the Turk Mtn. Fire Foot Trail well worth his time. See Chap. 5,: "Side Trails." 250 ft. beyond the fire trail junction, the *AT* reaches crest and starts long gentle descent.

13.0 A trail to the right leads steeply downhill 0.3m. to openfaced Sawmill Run Shelter. This shelter is the southernmost shelter in the SNP. (Spring is 50 ft. left of shelter; it often fails to flow in dry weather.) *AT* continues to descend.

13.2 Cross to left of Skyline Drive, SDMP 95.3, in a deep sag at the north edge of Sawmill Run Parking Overlook. Trail now climbs. Looking backwards while ascending, there are views of Turk Mtn., Sawmill Ridge and the city of Waynesboro.

13.8 Reach summit of unnamed hill, el. 2453 ft. As Trail starts to descend there are views to the east of Bucks Elbow Mtn.

14.2 Cross grass-covered pipeline diagonally to the right. Continue to descend.

14.6 Reach South Fork of the Moormans River, a small creek here, and follow up the creek along its west bank to its source.

14.9 Cross Moormans River Fire Road. (Road leads right 0.1m. to Skyline Drive at Jarman Gap, SDMP 96.8, el. 2173 ft. To left it follows down the South Fork of the Moormans River to the Charlottesville Reservoir, then ascends the North Fork of the Moormans River.) 200 ft. farther, pass spring on left of *AT*, then climb.

15.1 Reach Bucks Elbow Mtn. Fire Road, 100 yds. east of the Skyline Drive, SDMP 96.8, and end of this section of *AT*. (To right, road leads to Skyline Drive at its intersection with the Moormans River Fire Rd. in Jarman Gap. To left it leads out along the ridge of Bucks Elbow Mtn. to a radio tower. A branch of the road leads down the Lickinghole Hollow and becomes VA. Sec. 611.) (West of the Drive the Jarman Gap Fire Rd. leads down 1.8m to Sawmill Run and VA. Sec. 622 at a point about 3m. east of Dooms on U.S. 340 and 4m. NE of Waynesboro (U. S. 340))

SUBSECTION:
JARMAN GAP TO ROCKFISH GAP
NORTH TO SOUTH

7.4 miles (11.9 kilometers)   (PATC map No. 11:J-24)

General description:

There is a good chance that this section of the *AT* will be relocated in the near future. *Hikers should be on the alert for signs indicating a change of route.* Present (1975) route of the Trail is described here.

The route of the *AT* from Jarman Gap to Rockfish Gap is entirely on private land. From Jarman Gap the *AT* climbs Calf Mtn., descends to Beagle Gap, where it crosses the Skyline Drive, climbs over Bear Den Mtn., drops to McCormick Gap, where it recrosses the Drive, climbs up Scott Mtn., then continues along the ridge as it gradually drops toward Rockfish Gap. Descending steeply to the Skyline Drive just before reaching the Gap, it follows the Skyline Drive bridges over Interstate 64 and U. S. 250, where the section ends, as does the Drive, at milepost 105.4. For continuation of the *AT* south see PATC map 12. Much of the Trail's route is bare of trees, so views are excellent, but caution is needed in following the Trail in rain, snow, or fog. Rock outcrops on the summits in this section consist of a green shale, rather than greenstone, the basaltic rock so predominant along the ridge crest in the SNP.

Side Trails:
None other than old roads.

Accommodations:
Gasoline, restaurant, and lodging facilities are available at Rockfish Gap and in Waynesboro 4 miles northwest via U. S. 250. There are no cabins or shelters along this stretch of Trail.

Detailed Trail data:
Start of this section is on the Bucks Elbow Mtn. Fire Road, about 0.1m. east of the Skyline Drive in Jarman Gap, SDMP 96.8, el. 2175 ft. (Bucks Elbow Mtn. Fire Rd. is the more southerly of the two roads that intersect at the Skyline Drive. The other is the Moormans River Fire Rd. West of the Drive is the Jarman Gap Fire Road.)

0.0 From Bucks Elbow Mtn. Fire Rd., ascend southward through pine woods, soon coming out into open pasture.

0.2 Cross gravel road.

0.5 Pass under power line. In 0.2m. come into the gravel road that was crossed earlier and follow it uphill.

0.8 Where road ends continue straight ahead, still climbing. Pass through an area covered with staghorn sumac.

1.3 Reach top (highest peak) of Calf Mtn., el. 2974 ft. Continue along the ridge, passing to the left of the second peak of Calf Mtn., 2910 ft. *AT* now descends.

2.2 Cross Skyline Drive in Beagle Gap, SDMP 99.5, el. 2532 ft. Trail now ascends open slopes of Bear Den Mtn.

2.8 Reach summit, 2885 ft. (A police radio installation here.) Continue past a second summit, 2810 ft. As the Trail descends from here, Scott Castle is visible on the far side of McCormick Gap.

4.0 Cross Skyline Drive in McCormick Gap, SDMP 102.1, el. 2434 ft. From the Gap, climb stile and follow a dirt road a few feet, then turn right from the road and ascend steeply through brush and locust trees.

4.2 Come out into open field and continue to climb, but more gently.

4.3 Reach top of Scott Mtn. 2762 ft. Follow along grass-covered road, through briers and sumac. Scott Castle is visible to the south.

4.8 Cross gate into woods and follow old road along the ridge. In 0.1m. a road enters from left. (This road comes from Scott Castle and leads up through an orchard.)

5.6 Cross over gate into open area. Continue along ridge with a small knob and an abandoned building to right of the Trail.

6.1 Climb over gate and follow old road along the ridge crest through woods, gradually descending.

6.9 Turn sharply right and descend steeply by switchbacks.

7.2 Reach Skyline Drive, SDMP 105.2. and follow it left, walking along the left side of the Drive.

7.3 Cross Interstate 64 and beyond cross U. S. 250.

7.4 End of section at south end of Skyline Drive bridge over U. S. 250, in Rockfish Gap, SDMP 105.4, el. 1902 ft. (For description of *AT* south of Rockfish Gap see *Guide to the Appalachian Trail in Central and Southwestern Virginia* and PATC map #12.)

SUMMARY OF DISTANCE ALONG THE *AT*
Section VIII Southern

	Miles	Kilometers
Swift Run Gap	0.0	0.0
Hightop Shelter	3.4 + 0.1	5.5 + 0.2
Smith Roach Gap, Skyline Drive crossing	4.7	7.6
Powell Gap, Skyline Drive crossing	6.3	10.1
Simmons Gap, Skyline Drive crossing	9.6	15.4
Pinefield Shelter	11.7 + 0.1	18.7 + 0.2
Ivy Creek Overlook, S. Drive	13.3	21.3

continued -

	Miles	Kilometers
Ivy Creek Shelter	15.4 + 0.1	24.7 + 0.2
Loft Mtn. Camp Store	17.5	28.1
Falls Trail (near north end of Big Run Trail)	19.6	31.5
Doyle River Cabin	19.6 + 0.3	31.5 + 0.4
Big Run Shelter	19.6 + 2.3	31.5 + 3.7
Big Run Trail, south end	21.2	34.0
Browns Gap, Skyline Drive crossing	21.8	35.0
Falls Trail, south end	23.0	36.9
Blackrock	24.2	38.9
Blackrock Shelter	24.8 + 0.2	39.8 + 0.3
Blackrock Gap—Moorman's River Fire Road	25.5	41.0
Riprap Trail, north end	28.0	45.0
Riprap Shelter	28.0 + 3.0	45.0 + 4.9
Riprap Trail, south end	31.1	50.1
Turk Gap, Skyline Drive crossing	33.4	53.7
Sawmill Run Shelter	34.8 + 0.3	55.9 + 0.5
Skyline Drive crossing just north of Sawmill Ridge Overlook	35.0	56.3
Jarman Gap, *AT* 0.1 m. east of Skyline Drive	36.9	59.3
Beagle Gap, Skyline Drive crossing	39.1	62.9
McCormick Gap, Skyline Drive crossing	40.9	65.7
Rockfish Gap, end of Section VIII	44.3	71.2

DISTANCES (MILES) BY SKYLINE DRIVE TO POINTS ON THE *AT*
Section VIII Southern

	SDMP	from Swift Run N to S	from Rockfish Gap S to N
Swift Run Gap	65.5	0.0	39.9
Smith Roach Gap	68.6	3.1	36.8
Powell Gap	69.9	4.4	35.5
Simmons Gap	73.2	7.7	32.2
Pinefield Gap	75.2	9.7	30.2
Ivy Creek Overlook	77.5	12.0	27.9
Loft Mtn. Developed Area (1.3 m. to *AT* thru campground)	79.5	14.0	25.9
Falls Trail and Doyle River Cabin Parking (200 ft. to *AT*)	81.1	15.6	24.3
Doyle River Parking Area	81.9	16.4	23.5
Browns Gap	82.9	17.4	22.5
Falls Trail (south end 100 ft. to *AT*)	84.1	18.6	21.3
Trayfoot Mtn. Rd., closest auto approach, 0.1 m. to *AT*	84.7	19.2	20.7
Blackrock Gap	87.4	21.9	18.0
Calvary Rocks Parking Area 300 ft. to *AT*	90.0	24.5	15.4
Riprap Trail, Wildcat Ridge Parking Area, 0.1 m. to *AT*	92.1	26.6	13.3
Turk Gap	94.1	28.6	11.3
Sawmill Run Parking Overlook	95.3	29.8	10.1
Jarman Gap, 0.1 m. to *AT*	96.8	31.3	8.6
Beagle Gap	99.5	34.0	5.9
McCormick Gap	102.1	36.6	3.3
Rockfish Gap	105.4	39.9	0.0

SECTION VIII SOUTHERN SHENANDOAH PARK
ROCKFISH GAP TO SWIFT RUN GAP
SOUTH TO NORTH

44.3 miles (71.2 kilometers)   (PATC map No. 11:I-30)

Section VIII of the Appalachian Trail begins in Rockfish Gap where U. S. 250 (and Interstate 64) meet the Skyline Drive at its southern end (and the Blue Ridge Parkway at its northern end). Rockfish Gap is four miles east of Waynesboro via U. S. 250 and 22 miles west of Charlottesville (and about 140 miles from Washington, D.C.) The highway junction is 105.4m. from the northern end of the Skyline Drive in Front Royal. Distance covered by the *AT* from Rockfish Gap to U. S. 522 just north of the Park is 106.1 miles (170.7 kilometers.) Section VIII ends at Swift Run Gap where U. S. 33 crosses the Blue Ridge and intersects the Drive, SDMP 65.5. Swift Run Gap is 7m. east of Elkton, 8 miles west of Stanardsville and about 111 miles from Washington, D.C.

The 7.6 mile stretch of Appalachian Trail from Rockfish Gap to Jarman Gap will probably be relocated in the near future, *so hikers are alerted to watch for changes from the route as presently (1975) described in this Guide.* This stretch lies entirely outside the Shenandoah Park. At present it follows the mountain crest through open fields and with the Skyline Drive often visible below it.

The *AT* enters the Shenandoah Park at Jarman Gap. For most of the distance from here to Swift Run Gap it follows the ridge crest, crossing the Skyline Drive frequently. The southern section of the Park is the wildest and the least developed. Much of it lies in an area proposed for wilderness status. There are many interesting side trails and fire roads in this section that can be used either alone or in conjunction with the *AT* for interesting hiking trips.

Loft Mountain Campground facilities include showers, coin laundry and camp store, as well as campsites and a picnic area. It is closed in winter. Dundo, from April through October, is open only for group camping and reservations are needed. In the winter this area is open only for picnicking. Doyle River

Cabin, a locked structure, can be rented by hikers: reservations must be made at PATC Headquarters. See Chap. 6: "Shelters and Cabins."

Section VIII has been divided for convenience into four subsections: Rockfish Gap to Jarman Gap, Jarman to Browns Gap, Browns to Simmons Gap, and Simmons to Swift Run Gap.

Maps: PATC Map #11. Also available is the USGS map of Shenandoah National Park, Southern Section, 1969, scale 1:62500 and the USGS 7½' quads: Waynesboro East, Crimora, Browns Cove, McGaheysville, and Swift Run Gap. (Other 7½' quads, covering areas on the southern section of the Park not traversed by the *AT*, include Crozet, Grottoes and Elkton East.)

SUBSECTION:
ROCKFISH GAP TO JARMAN GAP
SOUTH TO NORTH

7.4 miles (11.9 kilometers)   (PATC map No. 11:I-30)

General description:

There is a good chance that this section of the *AT* will be relocated in the near future. *Hikers should be on the alert for signs indicating a change of route.* Present route of the Trail is described here.

The stretch of the Appalachian Trail from Rockfish Gap is entirely on private land. Much of the route is bare of trees so views are excellent, but caution is needed in following the Trail in rain, snow or fog. Rock outcrops on the summits in this section consist of a green shale, rather than greenstone, the basaltic rock so predominant along the ridge crest in the Shenandoah Park itself.

This section of Trail starts at the south end of the Skyline Drive Overpass over U. S. 250 and follows along the east side of the Drive, passing over Interstate 64 and continuing along the Drive for another tenth mile where it turns right, away from the road, and ascends steeply until reaching the ridge crest. From here the Trail follows the ridge, ascending gently, until reaching the summit of Scott Mtn.; then it descends to McCormick Gap where it crosses the Drive. It climbs over Bear Den Mtn., drops into Beagle Gap where it recrosses the Drive, climbs over Calf Mtn., then drops to Jarman Gap.

Side trails:
   None other than old roads

Accommodations:
   Gasoline, lodging and restaurant facilities are available at Rockfish Gap and in **Waynesboro 4** miles northwest via U. S. 250. There are no shelters or cabins along this stretch of Trail.

Detailed Trail data:
   0.0 Skyline Drive at south end of overpass over US Rt. 250 in Rockfish Gap, SDMP 105.4, el. 1902 ft. Trail follows the footway along the right (east) side of the Drive.
   0.1 Cross over Interstate 64, utilizing the Skyline Drive overpass. Continue along the right side of the Drive.
   0.2 At cement post and *AT* trail marker, turn right away from the Drive. Ascend steeply with switchbacks.
   0.5 Reaching the ridge crest, the Trail turns left along it and follows an old road, gradually ascending.
   1.3 Climb fence gate and enter an open area. Pass small knob and an abandoned building to left of the Trail.
   1.8 Pass through gate and follow road through woods.
   2.5 Take left fork of road. (Right fork leads down through an orchard to Scott Castle.) A tenth of a mile beyond, cross fence and come into open area. Follow grass-covered road through field overgrown with berry bushes and staghorn sumac.
   3.1 Reach open summit of Scott Mtn., 2762 ft. Scott Castle can be seen to the south.
   3.2 Dip into woods and descend steeply.
   3.4 Cross Skyline Drive in McCormick Gap, SDMP 102.1, el. 2434 ft. Ascend through pine thicket, then across open land, along the ridge of Bear Den Mtn. Looking back, Scott Castle can be seen.
   4.6 Reach bare summit of Bear Den Mtn., 2885 ft. (Police radio installation here.) Trail now descends northeastward.

5.2 Cross Skyline Drive in Beagle Gap, SDMP 99.5, el. 2532 ft. Trail ascends Calf Mtn., skirting to the right of the first peak, el. 2910 ft.

6.1 Reach the open summit of Calf Mtn., 2974 ft. Descend through low sumac brush, soon coming into gravel road and continuing down it.

6.7 Turn somewhat right off the road and continue through pasture, passing under power line in 0.2m.

7.2 Cross the gravel road and descend through a pine thicket.

7.4 Reach Bucks Elbow Mtn. Fire Rd. at a point on the road, 0.1m. east of the Skyline Drive at Jarman Gap, SDMP 96.8, el. 2175 ft.

SUBSECTION:
JARMAN GAP TO BROWNS GAP
SOUTH TO NORTH

15.1 miles (24.3 kilometers)   (PATC map No. 11: J-24)

General description:

This section starts at the intersection of the *AT* with the Bucks Elbow Mtn. Fire Road at a point about 100 yds. east of the Skyline Drive in Jarman Gap, SDMP 96.7. The Trail first descends along the South Fork of the Moormans River from its source for a short way, then climbs to the crest of the main ridge of the Blue Ridge, which it continues to follow for the most part throughout this section. It crosses the Skyline Drive at a number of points. Much of this section of the Park is in a proposed wilderness area. There are a number of side trails, some of which, like the Riprap Trail, can be used along with the *AT* for interesting circuit hikes. Blackrock, a tumbled mass of large lichen-covered blocks of stone, is interesting in itself and also affords splendid views. The *AT* skirts the east side of Dundo shortly before reaching Browns Gap.

Accommodations:

There is one developed area, Dundo, SDMP 83.7, used from April through October as a group campground for which reservations should be made at SNP Headquarters; fee is $3.00.

The remainder of the year Dundo is open only for picnicking. There are no shower or laundry facilities here and no store. Water is available from April through October.

There are two open-faced shelters along the *AT* for camping only during inclement weather, Sawmill Run Shelter, 2.1m. (plus 0.3m. along spur trail) and Blackrock Shelter, 12.1m. (plus 0.2m. along spur trail). In addition to these the Riprap Shelter can be used. It is on the Riprap Trail about 3 miles from the *AT* from either junction of this trail with the *AT* (5.8m. and 8.9m.) See Chap. 6: "Shelters and Cabins".

Side trails:

This is one of the wildest areas of the Park. There are a number of very worthwhile side trails. Some lead to places of special scenic interest such as Riprap Ravine, Calvary Rocks, Trayfoot Mtn., and the falls on both Jones Run and Doyle River. The old Moormans River Road, which was at one time the route of the *AT*, leads from Jarman Gap down the south fork of the Moormans River and up the north fork to Blackrock Gap. Refer to Chap. 5: "Side Trails," Southern Section; also the separate PATC publication, *Circuit Hikes in the Shenandoah National Park.*

Detailed Trail data:

To reach the *AT* at Jarman Gap, follow the Bucks Elbow Mtn. Fire Road east from the Skyline Drive, SDMP 96.9, el. 2173', for 0.1m. (Bucks Elbow Mtn. Fire Rd. and the Moormans River Fire Road intersect right at the east side of the Drive, the Bucks Elbow Mtn. Fire Rd. being the more southerly one. West of the Drive the Jarman Gap Fire Road leads from the gap down to Sawmill Run and VA. Sec. 622, at a point about 3m. east of Dooms and 4m. NE of Waynesboro.)

0.0 Junction of *AT* with Bucks Elbow Mtn. Fire Rd. Trail descends.

0.2 Pass spring on right of the *AT*. 100 yds. farther, cross the Moormans River Fire Rd. Continue descent along the west bank of the South Fork of the Moormans River at its upper end.

0.5 Here the *AT* leaves the creek and ascends unnamed hill. Partway up it crosses diagonally to the right a grasscovered pipeline area.

1.3 Reach summit of the hill, el. 2453'. Looking backwards, toward the east, is a view of Bucks Elbow Mtn. Then, as Trail begins to descend, there are forward views of Turk Mtn., Sawmill Ridge and the city of Waynesboro.

1.9 *AT* crosses to the left of the Skyline Drive, SDMP 95.3, in a sag at the north edge of Sawmill Run Parking Overlook.

2.1 From the *AT* a trail to the left leads steeply downhill 0.3m. to Sawmill Run Shelter. (This shelter is the southernmost of the ones in the Shenandoah National Park. Spring is 50 ft. to left of shelter but is unreliable.) From this junction the *AT* ascends gently.

3.3 Trail reaches summit of knob, 2650 ft.; 250 ft. farther along the *AT* the Turk Mtn.-Sawmill Ridge Fire Foot Trail comes in from the left along a side ridge. The fire trail utilizes the *AT* north for 0.2m., then goes off on the right, reaching the Skyline Drive in 100 ft, SDMP 94.2.

3.5 *AT* crosses over to the right of the Skyline Drive at Turk Gap, 2625 ft, SDMP 94.1. Trail ascends 400 ft., dips gently, then ascends to a second summit with about the same elevation as the first. There are backward views in winter of peaks in the George Washington Nat. Forest, Pedlar District, south of Rockfish Gap. Trail now descends.

5.5 *AT* crosses to the west side of the Skyline Drive, SDMP 92.4.

5.8 Junction of *AT* and Riprap Trail. (Riprap Tr. leads east 0.1m. to Skyline Drive, SDMP 92.1, and west 3.2m. to Riprap Shelter and on via Calvary Rocks to its more northern junction with the *AT*. Total distance via Riprap Trial, 6.2m.) *AT* continues along west side of ridge crest, passing through one of the few areas in the SNP having any rhododendron.

8.3 Here Trail ascends steeply for half a mile around slope of Riprap Hollow.

8.5 A graded trail to right leads 300 ft. down to Calvary Rocks Parking Area on the Skyline Drive, SDMP 90.0.

8.9 Reach summit of knob, 2988 ft. Riprap Trail comes in from the left. *AT* now descends.

9.6 In a sag, cross to right of Skyline Drive, SDMP 88.9. *AT* now climbs over a small knob.

10.3 Trail comes into a sag with Skyline Drive 150 ft. to left. *AT* now climbs a second knob, then descends steadily.

11.4 Cross the Moormans River Fire Rd. in Blackrock Gap, SDMP 87.4, el. 2329 ft. From here Trail continues along east side of Drive for a quarter mile.

11.6 *AT* crosses to left (west) of Drive, SDMP 87.2. It now ascends along an old road for 0.2m., then angles off slightly to the left of the road and parallels it.

12.1 Trail crosses to the east of the old road. One hundred feet beyond, a graded trail leads right, steeply down, for 0.2m. to the Blackrock Shelter. (Shelter is located in a very deep ravine. Springs is 10 yds in front of the shelter.) *AT* continues to ascend along east side of ridge. (The old road parallels it on Trail's left, just out of sight along the ridge crest.)

12.6 *AT* crosses Trayfoot Mtn. Rd. 300 ft. farther, Trail starts circling around Blackrock, 3092 ft., a curious mass of dark lichen-covered blocks heaped upon each other. It is reminiscent of terrain above tree-line on Mt. Washington. Views are excellent here.

12.7 A graded trail leads left from the *AT* along the ridge leading to Trayfoot Mtn. (It joins the Trayfoot Mtn. Rd. where that road reaches the ridge, about 0.2m. from the *AT*.)

12.9 Here the *AT* and the Trayfoot Mtn. Rd. come within a few feet of each other but do not cross. They are parallel for about 0.1m. Then the *AT* bears off to the left. (The road leads out 750 ft. to the Skyline Drive, SDMP 84.7. This is the shortest approach to Blackrock from the Drive. There is parking space for several cars a few hundred feet up this road from the Drive.)

13.7 Cross to right side of Skyline Drive, SDMP 84.3. From here Trail passes through remnants of an old apple orchard.

13.9 Junction with the Falls Trail. (To left of *AT*, uphill, trail leads to the Falls Trail Parking Area, SDMP 84.1; to the right the Falls Tr. descends Jones Run, then ascends Doyle River, passing below the Doyle River Cabin and recrossing the *AT* to reach the Skyline Drive, SDMP 81.1. Hiking distance along Falls Trail, 4.7m.) From junction *AT* continues with little change in elevation.

14.4 *AT* turns sharply to the right, while a trail straight ahead leads to Dundo Developed Area (summer a group campground, winter a picnic grounds) SDMP 83.7. *AT* skirts the east side of the developed area. Several unmarked trails lead left to this area. (Water available at Dundo April through October.) Beyond Dundo, Trail descends gently.

15.1 Trail reaches Browns Gap, where the Skyline Drive intersects the old Browns Gap Rd. Here *AT* crosses Drive, SDMP 82.9, el. 2599 ft. (The Falls Trail is 1.4m. east, downhill, via the old Browns Gap Rd.; this road continues outside the Park eventually becoming Va. Sec. 629 about a mile before reaching Va. Sec. 810 at Browns Cove. From Browns Cove it is 11m. to Crozet and 12.5m. to U. S. 250 via Va. Sec. 810 and 18m. north to Stanardsville and U. S. 33, also via Va. Sec. 810. The Madison Run Rd., west of the Drive, leads down Dundo Hollow to the Park Boundary at junction of Va. Sec. 663 and 629 1.8m. from Grottoes. Both the Browns Gap Rd. and the Madison Run Rd. are gated at the Skyline Drive and at the Park boundaries.)

SUBSECTION:
BROWNS GAP TO SIMMONS GAP
SOUTH TO NORTH

12.2 miles (19.6 kilometers)   (PATC map No. 11:G-14)

General description:

This part of the Trail starts at its junction with Madison Run Road about 100 ft. west of the Skyline Drive, SDMP 82.9, in Browns Gap. (On the east side of the Drive this road is called the Browns Gap Road.) The *AT* at Browns Gap is 22.7m. by trail from Rockfish Gap and 21.6m. from Swift Run Gap.

The elevation of the *AT* at Browns Gap is 2599 ft. The trail reaches elevations of 3300 ft. and above in the area of Big Flat Mtn. (Where the Loft Mtn. Campground is located) and Loft. Mtn., drops to 2550 ft. where it crosses Ivy Creek, gains 500 ft., then loses it again to reach Pinefield Gap, climbs over Weaver Mtn., then descends to Simmons Gap at 2253 ft. For a mile south of the peak of Loft Mtn. the Trail passes through considerable open area; otherwise it is heavily wooded. The *AT* crosses the Drive several times and comes within a few hundred feet of it in a few other places.

A roughly triangular area between the ridges of Rockytop, Brown Mtn. and Loft Mtn. and drained by tributaries of Big Run comprises the largest watershed in the Park, about eleven square miles.

Accommodations:

The Loft Mtn. Developed Area includes a wayside, camp store, picnic grounds, and campground with shower and laundry facilities; also two nature trails. Campground and other facilities are generally open April through October. (Exception: store open mid May-October)

There are two shelters along the *AT* for use of hikers during inclement weather, Ivy Creek Shelter (6.4m.) and Pinefield Shelter (10.1m.) A third, Big Run Shelter, can be reached by hiking about 2 miles along the Big Run Trail from either of its junctions with the *AT* (at 0.6m. and 2.2m.)

One locked cabin is available, the Doyle River Cabin, 0.4 mile from the *AT*, (2.2m.) Reservations for the use of this cabin must be obtained in advance from PATC Headquarters. See Chap 6: "Shelters and Cabins."

Side trails:

This region has several side trails which provide an opportunity for making interesting circuit hikes, the Falls Trail and the Big Run Trail being the chief ones. See Chap. 5: "Side Trails:" Southern Section.

Detailed Trail data:

0.0 Browns Gap. (Gen. Stonewall Jackson used this gap several times during the Valley Campaign of the Civil War.) Start of this section of *AT* is at junction with the Madison Run Rd. (the western portion of the old Browns Gap Rd.) about 100 ft. to the left (west) of the Skyline Drive in Browns Gap and is marked by a cement post. (SDMP 82.9, el. 2599 ft.) Trail ascends gaining 250 ft. altitude, then levels off.

0.6 From the *AT* graded Big Run Trail leads off to left. (From this intersection Big Run Shelter is 2.0m.)

0.9 *AT* crosses to the right of the Skyline Drive, SDMP 82.2, with fine view of Cedar Mtn. and Trayfoot Mtn.

1.1 Trail follows along ledges affording wintertime views south.

1.2 To the right of *AT* can be seen the remains of earthworks and trenches erected in 1864 by Jubal Early's men after their retreat from Winchester.

1.3 Trail passes through Doyle River Parking Overlook, SDMP 81.9.

2.2 *AT* intersects the Falls Trail. (Skyline Drive is 200 ft. to left, SDMP 81.1. Follow Drive south for 250 ft. to reach northern end of Big Run Tr. at the Big Run Parking Overlook. Big Run Tr. passes Big Run Shelter in 2.2m.) (Falls Trail leads down on the right of the *AT*, passing below the Doyle River Cabin in 0.3m. See Chap. 6: "Shelters and Cabins") *AT* now ascends Big Flat Mtn., el. 3389 ft.

2.5 There is an excellent panoramic view here of, from left to right: Rockytop, Brown Mtn., Rocky Mountain, Rocky Mount, and, to the right (east) of the Drive, Loft Mtn.

3.0 Cement post marks junction where the Loft Mtn. Nature Trail comes in from left. (Nature trail then follows *AT* north a full mile before leaving *AT* to return to the Loft Mtn. Campground.) *AT* now skirts the southern and eastern edges of the campground for about a mile. There are a number of good views along this stretch; at first views are to the west, then south, and finally due east. Several unmarked trails lead left to the campground.

4.1 Nature trail leaves *AT* on the left, looping back to the campground.

4.3 From the *AT* a trail leads left, uphill, to the Loft Mtn. Camp Store which is open mid-May through October. (Store carries a complete line of groceries. Laundromat, with coin-operated washers and dryers, adjoins store.) For the next mile or so, as far as the summit of Loft Mtn., the Trail passes through Patterson Field, an area that was once a large, 240 acre pasture. Now grass is gradually being replaced by blackberry vines and other shrubby growth but at least a half mile of Trail is still out in the open with good views (true in 1975). In places, especially near the pasture edges, black locust now covers the land. But in the midst of the young woods stand several old oak trees with very large lowspreading branches indicating that these oaks gained their maturity while the land was still pasture.

4.8 Trail crosses old road. (To left, road leads to paved road to Loft Mtn. Campground. To right, road soon dead-ends.)

5.4 Reach crest of Loft Mtn. ridge, Here a trail enters the *AT* from the left. (The Deadening Nature Tr., which starts from the Skyline Drive at the entrance to the Loft Mtn. Campgrounds, SDMP 79.5, enters the *AT* at this point, follows it north about 0.1m., then descends to its starting point. See inset, back of PATC map No. 11.) Along the *AT*, about 150 ft. beyond the junction, is an excellent 270° panoramic view.

6.1 Trail passes slightly to left of the peak of Loft Mtn., el. about 3320 ft., then starts descending toward Ivy Creek.

6.4 From the *AT* a trail leads left 200 yds. to Ivy Creek Shelter and spring. The *AT* continues to descend, following the right bank of Ivy Creek.

7.1 Trail crosses Ivy Creek, very picturesque here, at an elevation of about 2550 ft. It then ascends.

7.8 Trail reaches an excellent viewpoint showing an area from Trayfoot Mtn. on the left to Rockytop on the right. Skyline Drive is immediately below the Trail here. *AT* continues to ascend for 0.2m., then descends.

8.3 *AT* crosses to the left of the Drive, SDMP 77.7, then in 0.1m. recrosses it.

8.5 Trail reaches the south end of the Ivy Creek Overlook, SDMP 77.5. It passes along the Overlook, then ascends gently for a half mile.

9.1 *AT* reaches summit of hill, 3080 ft., then descends through patches of white pine, interspersed with areas of locust and young oak.

9.5 At a spot where the *AT* turns sharply to the right, an unmarked trail leads left approximately 200 ft. to the Skyline Drive. (From here one can follow the Drive north a few feet to reach the Two-Mile Ridge Fire Foot Trail, or continue 0.1m. farther to reach the Two-Mile Run Parking Overlook, and another 0.2m. to reach the start of the Rocky Mount Trail, SDMP 76.1.)

9.9 *AT*, still descending, again comes within a hundred feet of the Drive.

10.1 *AT* crosses access road to Pinefield Shelter. Twenty yards to the right of the *AT* along this road is a spring. (Shelter is 0.1m. on down the road. There is another spring about 250 ft. behind the shelter.)

10.3 *AT* crosses to left of Skyline Drive at Pinefield Gap, SDMP 75.2. Trail now ascends, winding through sparse, scraggly woods, primarily black locust.

11.1 Reach top of Weaver Mtn. Trail descends along the northwestern side of the ridge.

12.2 *AT* reaches Simmons Gap at the junction of the Simmons Gap Fire Rd. and Skyline Drive, SDMP 73.2, el. 2253 ft. (A short distance to the south on the fire road is the Ranger's residence and beyond it are the Park Service maintenance facilities. Water available here. The Simmons Gap Rd. is barred on both sides of the Drive and at the Park boundaries. Outside the Park, on both east and west sides of the Drive, the road becomes Va. Sec. 628.)

SUBSECTION:
SIMMONS GAP TO SWIFT RUN GAP
SOUTH TO NORTH

9.6 miles (15.4 kilometers)   (PATC map No. 11:I-7)

General description:

This part of the *AT* starts at Simmons Gap at the junction of Simmons Gap Fire Road and the Skyline Drive (SDMP 73.2.) The Simmons Gap Road becomes VA. Sec. Rt. 628 outside the Park on both east and west sides. The road is barred on both sides of the Drive and at the Park boundaries. (To the west Rt. 628 leads 10m. past Beldor on to U. S. 33. To the east Rt. 628 leads 5.8m. to VA. Sec. 810.)

From Simmons Gap the *AT* climbs a ridge on the east side of the Skyline Drive, then descends to Powell Gap where it crosses the Drive. It then climbs, skirting the south and east sides of Roundtop Mtn. and crosses again to the east of the Drive in Smith Roach Gap. From here it ascends steadily to the top of Hightop Mtn. Open ledges to the west of the summit afford excellent views south and west. The Trail now descends the north slope of Hightop by switchbacks. It crosses the Drive in a sag and continues on through scraggly woods to Swift Run Gap where U. S. Rt. 33 (Spotswood Trail) crosses the Blue Ridge.

Swift Run Gap, SDMP 65.5, el. 2367', is 39.8m. from Rockfish Gap and 34.0m. from Thornton Gap via the Skyline Drive; it is 6 miles from Elkton and about 110 miles from Washington, D. C.

Accommodations:

There are no public accommodations along this section. The nearest public lodgings are at Lewis Mtn., SDMP 57.5, but these are closed during the winter. There is no gas or food available at Swift Run Gap.

There is one open-faced shelter, Hightop Shelter, 6.1m., along this section that is available, but for camping only in inclement weather. See Chap. 6: "Shelters and Cabins."

Side trails:

Because the Shenandoah Park is very narrow in this area, there are few side trails, and these lead out of the Park.

Detailed Trail data:

0.0 Intersection of Simmons Gap Fire Road and Skyline Drive, SDMP 73.2, el. 2253'. *AT* follows Simmons Gap Rd. east of the Drive for about 40 ft., then turns left onto path.

0.3 *AT* turns slightly left to follow old road. (To the right the road leads down to the Simmons Gap Ranger Station, formerly the Simmons Gap Episcopal Mission.) Two-tenths of a mile farther, the Trail turns slightly left off the old road but parallels it.

0.9 *A T* turns sharply left while the old road continues straight ahead. Trail continues to ascend.

1.5 Near top of rise there is open field about 50 ft. to right of the Trail and beyond a wire fence. There are views, especially of Flattop Mtn., 3325', from the field but not from the *A T*.

1.6 Reach summit of a shoulder of Flattop Mtn. Trail continues along northern ridge crest.

2.8 Excellent views of the Roach River Valley (Bacon and Powell Gap Hollows) from rock ledges just to the side of the Trail. *A T* descends gradually.

3.0 Turn sharply right onto well-worn trail, a former road, leaving the old road bed, now overgrown, in 0.1m. Continue descent.

3.3 Reach Powell Gap, SDMP 69.9, el. 2294', and cross to left of Drive. Trail crosses grass and angles along edge of woods. Avoid old Powell Gap Road, now just a trail, to the left of the *A T*. (On the left side of the Drive the old road leads down Eaton Hollow to VA. Sec. 628. On the right side of the Drive it continues, also as a trail, down to Va. Sec. 627.) The *A T* ascends the west slope of Little Roundtop Mtn.

3.8 Summit of Little Roundtop Mtn. is 50 yds. to left of the *A T* here. Trail continues along the ridge crest, then swings around the south and east sides of Roundtop Mtn., affording wintertime views of Powell Gap and Flattop Mtn. Trail now continues with little change in elevation.

4.9 Cross to right of Skyline Drive in open Smith Roach Gap, SDMP 68.6, el. 2622'. From the Drive the *A T* parallels the Smith Roach Gap Fire Road, a few feet to the right of this road, for about 300 ft. Then the *A T* crosses the road and ascends steadily through woods.

6.1 Cross the Hightop Shelter service road. (On left of the *A T*, the service road leads to Hightop Shelter; to the right it leads to the Smith Roach Gap Fire Rd. at a point 0.8m. from the Skyline Drive.)

6.2 From the *A T* a trail leads left 0.1m. to Hightop Shelter. (Spring is 400 ft. downhill from shelter on graded trail. The Hightop Shelter FFT leads 0.5m. from the shelter down to the Skyline Drive across from the "north" end of the Swift Run Parking Overlook, SDMP 67.2.)

6.7 There is a piped, covered spring at the foot of a large boulder just to the right of the *AT*. Trail continues to ascend.

6.8 From the *AT* a trail leads to the right 350 ft. to site of former Park Service Lookout Tower at the summit of Hightop Mtn., el. 3587'. There is no view from the summit now. One hundred feet farther along the *AT* there is an excellent view from ledges to the left of the Trail. Shortly farther along the Trail there is a second good viewpoint. Beyond, the Trail descends steeply, veering first to the east, then switchbacking down the north slope of the mountain.

8.3 Trail crosses to left (west) of Skyline Drive in grassy sag, SDMP 66.7, el. 2637'. *AT* continues along former farm road, ascending slightly, passing through the remains of an old apple orchard, then descending.

9.5 Trail turns sharply right on an old road which comes in from the left. It follows this road for a few feet only, then climbs to its right. Just beyond, the Trail drops steeply down to the highway bridge which carries the Skyline Drive over U. S. Rt. 33. *AT* follows pedestrian footway along edge of bridge.

9.6 Reach cement sign post marking the *AT*. It is located on the east side of the Drive, about 300 ft. north of the bridge and directly opposite the place where the entrance road from U. S. 33 reaches the Skyline Drive in Swift Run Gap, SDMP 65.5, el. 2367'.

SUMMARY OF DISTANCES ALONG THE *AT*
Section VIII Southern

	Miles	Kilometers
Rockfish Gap	0.0	0.0
McCormick Gap, Skyline Drive crossing	3.4	5.5
Beagle Gap, Skyline Drive crossing	5.2	8.4
Jarman Gap	7.4	11.9
Sawmill Ridge Overlook,		

continued-

	Miles	Kilometers
Skyline Drive crossing	9.3	15.0
Sawmill Run Shelter	9.5 + 0.3	15.3 + 0.5
Turk Gap, Skyline Drive Crossing	10.9	17.5
Riprap Trail junction (southern)	13.2	21.3
Riprap Shelter	13.2 + 3.2	21.3 + 5.2
Riprap Trail junction (northern)	16.3	26.2
Blackrock Gap, Moormans River Fire Rd.	18.8	30.3
Blackrock Shelter	19.5 + 0.2	31.4 + 0.3
Blackrock	20.1	32.4
Falls Trail, south end	21.3	34.3
Browns Gap, Skyline Drive crossing	22.5	36.2
Big Run Trail, south end	23.1	37.2
Big Run Shelter	23.1 + 2.0	37.2 + 3.2
Falls Trail, north end (near north end, Big Run Tr.)	24.7	39.8
Doyle River Cabin	24.7 + 0.3	39.8 + 0.4
Loft Mtn. Camp Store	26.8	43.1
Ivy Creek Shelter	28.9 + 0.1	46.5 + 0.2
Ivy Creek Overlook, Skyline Drive	31.0	49.9
Pinefield Shelter	32.6 + 0.1	52.5 + 0.2
Simmons Gap, Skyline Drive crossing	34.7	55.9
Powell Gap, Skyline Drive crossing	38.0	61.1
Smith Roach Gap, Skyline Drive crossing	39.6	63.7
Hightop Shelter	40.9 + 0.1	65.7 + 0.2
Swift Run Gap, end of Section VIII	44.3	71.2

For summary of distances by Skyline Drive to points on the *AT* see end of Section VIII, North to South.

SECTION VII. CENTRAL SHENANDOAH PARK
SWIFT RUN GAP TO THORNTON GAP
SOUTH TO NORTH

34.3 miles (55.2 kilometers)   (PATC map No. 10: J-26)

General description:

The section starts at Swift Run Gap. SDMP 65.6, where U.S. 33 crosses the mountain. Swift Run Gap is 7m. east of Elkton **and 8m. west of Stanardsville** (and 108m. from Washington, D. C.) The northern end of Section VII is at Thornton Gap, SDMP 31.5, where U. S. 211 crosses the Blue Ridge. Thornton Gap (Panorama) is 9m. east of Luray and 7m. west of Sperryville (and 83m. from Washington, D. C.)

The Blue Ridge crest is higher in this section of the Park than in either the southern or northern section. The *AT* reaches its highest point in the Park on Hazeltop, el. 3816', about 4m. south of Big Meadows Campground. The Skyline Drive itself reaches its maximum elevation, 3680', right at the northern entrance to Skyland. The highest peak in the Park, Hawksbill, has an elevation of 4050'.

The central part of the Shenandoah Park is the part most widely used by the motoring public, by campers, and by hikers. The *AT* is heavily used, as are the chief side trails. Favorite short hikes include the Stony Man and Swamp Nature Trails, the Stony Man Trail—*AT* loop, the Dark Hollow Falls Trail and the Limberlost Trail. Longer favorites are the Whiteoak Canyon Trail, the trails up Old Rag Mtn., the trails over Hawksbill, and the stretch of *AT* from Thornton Gap to Marys Rock. There are also special trails for horseback riding, with stables at Skyland and at Big Meadows.

Two large campgrounds, Lewis Mountain and Big Meadows (the latter open all year), are located in the area. Skyland, Big Meadows, and Lewis Mountain also offer lodging for 350, 200 and 25 persons, respectively. For complete information on tourist facilities at these places and for reservations write to the ARA Virginia Sky-Line Co., Inc., Box 727, Luray, VA. 22835.

The Skyland resort antedates the Shenandoah Park, having been developed by George Freeman Pollock, with its beginning in the 1880's. The Hoover Camp, developed when Herbert Hoover was President of the USA (1929-33), is on the eastern slopes of the Blue Ridge near Big Meadows. It is now managed by the Park Service but is still reserved for use by presidential guests. For more information about the history of this area read "Skyland Before 1900" by Jean Stephenson in the July, 1935 PATC Bulletin and the books, *Skyland*, by George Freeman Pollock (Washington, Judd and Detwiler, 1960) and *Herbert Hoover's Hideaway* by Darwin Lambert (Shenandoah Natural History Assoc. Inc., Luray, Va. 1971.)

For convenience Section VII is divided into 3 subsections: Swift Run Gap to Fishers Gap, Fishers Gap to Skyland, and Skyland to Thornton Gap.

Maps:

PATC Trail Map #10; also available is the USGS map of the Shenandoah National Park, Central Section, 1969, scale 1:62,500, and USGS 7½' quads, scale 1:24,000 for: Thornton Gap, Old Rag, Big Meadows, Fletcher, Elkton East, and Swift Run Gap. (USGS quads that cover parts of the central section not traversed by the *AT* include those of Luray, Washington, Va., Stanley, Madison, and Stanardsville.)

SUBSECTION:

SWIFT RUN GAP TO FISHERS GAP
SOUTH TO NORTH

18.6 miles (30.0 kilometers)   (PATC map No. 10: J-26)

General description:

From the intersection of the Skyline Drive and the entrance road from U. S. 33 in Swift Run Gap, el. 2367', the *AT* climbs, soon coming into an old road which it follows over a spur of Saddleback Mountain. The Trail skirts the South River Picnic Grounds, then starts a long gradual ascent over Baldface Mountain, el. 3600'. It loses 500 ft. of altitude to reach the gap beyond Pocosin Cabin. The *AT* skirts the east side of the Lewis Mountain Campground, passes a very scenic area on Bearfence Mountain, then, beyond Bush Mountain, descends to Bootens

Gap. North of Bootens Gap the *A T* reaches its highest elevation in the Park, 3816', on Hazeltop. At Milam Gap the *A T* crosses to the west of the Drive. It then skirts the west and north edges of the Big Meadows Campground before reaching Fishers Gap, el. 3061'.

Side trails:

The South River Falls Trail is short, but steep and very scenic. An excellent circuit hike can be made using this trail, the South River Fire Road, Pocosin (Horse) Trail, Pocosin Fire Road, and return via the *A T.*

In the Big Meadows Area there are many trails and a number of popular circuit hikes, the Dark Hollow Falls-Copper Mine Loop-*A T* circuit is probably the favorite one. Trails and a fire road lead down from the Drive and the *A T* to Hoover Camp, located in the Park on the Rapidan River. The Hoover Camp area is one of the few places in the SNP where one can find rhododendron growing.

Many fire foot trails, fire roads, and other old roads beckon the hiker. Some are well marked and easy to follow, but others may be poorly marked or badly overgrown and should be attempted only by the experienced woodsman.

Accommodations:

The Lewis Mountain Developed Area has picnic grounds, camp store and a campground; a few cabins are available. The Area is closed from November until mid-April. The Big Meadows Areas includes a large campground, picnic grounds, both lodge and cabins, stables, a wayside, and the Byrd Visitor Center. The wayside (including the service station), visitor center, lodge, and one section of the campground are open all year round. Reservations for lodging can be made with the ARA Virginia Sky-Line Co., Inc., Box 727, Luray, Va. 22835.

There are two open-faced shelters to be used by *A T* hikers for camping only during inclement weather. These are the South River Shelter, 2.9m. (follow old road right 0.3m. from the *A T*) and Bearfence Mtn. Shelter, 9.3m.

In addition, one locked structure, Pocosin Cabin, 6.6m., is found on this stretch of Trail. A second cabin, the Jones Mountain Cabin (map #10: M-15, 16) is located on the eastern slopes of the Blue Ridge, about 4m. "as the crow flies" from the *AT* on Bush Mtn. For the use of these cabins, reservations must be obtained in advance from PATC Headquarters. (See Chap. 6: "Shelters and Cabins.")

Detailed Trail data:

0.0 A signpost on the eastern side of the Skyline Drive in Swift Run Gap, SDMP 65.5, el. 2367', at a point where the entrance road from U. S. 33 joins the Drive, marks the start of this section of the *AT*. From here Trail ascends through the woods.

0.1 Pass a side trail, right, at a sign which reads "Danger Power Cable."

0.3 *AT* passes under power line.

0.7 Trail turns right onto old road which it follows over Saddleback Mountain, passing west of the summit, for a distance of about 2 miles.

1.3 Saddleback Mtn. FFT comes into the *AT* from the right. (The fire foot trail leads back south, joining the Big Bend Fire Road near U. S. 33. It is easy to follow, though overgrown and with no blazing.)

1.4 Saddleback Mtn. FFT leaves *AT* and proceeds right toward South River Shelter. (This section of the fire foot trail is blazed but care must be used where other old trails intersect.)

1.9 Still following the old road, the *AT* reaches the top of the rise just west of the westernmost peak of Saddleback Mtn., el. 3296'. One will find trilliums blooming here in profusion in early May. Trail now descends.

2.1 At sharp left bend in the *AT* an old road comes in from the right.

2.5 At junction of old roads, the *AT* follows the left fork. (To the right, a road leads across overgrown fields and young woods for 0.3m. to the South River Shelter. A spring is 200 ft. west of the shelter.)

2.7 *AT* turns right off the old road and passes through a pine woods. (Road bears left and leads 0.1m. to Skyline Drive, SDMP 63.1.) *AT* now skirts the east side of the South River Picnic Grounds.

3.0 Cross the graded South River Falls Trail. (To left trail leads 0.1m. to picnic grounds. Water available here "in season". To right of the *AT* the trail leads steeply downhill for 1.5m. to lovely South River Falls.)

3.5 Cross South River Fire Road. (To right road leads down toward South River Falls. About a mile from the *AT* a road leads right from the fire road down to the South River at a point 0.1m. below the falls. The South River Falls Trail utilizes the lower part of this road. A foot trail leads up to the falls. The South River Fire Rd. itself swings northeast at the road intersection and in another mile the Pocosin (Horse) Trail enters it from the left. From here the road descends, becoming VA. Sec. 642 outside the Park. To left of the *AT* the fire road leads 0.2m. to the Skyline Drive, SDMP 62.7, el. 2960 ft. Across the Drive here the Dry Run Falls Fire Rd. leads 2.6m. down the west slope of Deans Mountain to VA. Sec. 625.) From the South River Fire Rd. intersection the *AT* begins a long gentle ascent of Baldface Mountain.

4.4 Cross old road which leads, right, past an old quarry. (To left road leads past the site of a former CCC camp 0.1m. to the Drive, SDMP 61.8.)

4.8 Rocks to left of the Trail offer views to the west.

5.1 Reach summit of Baldface Mtn., el. 3600 ft., and descend gently.

5.9 Blue blaze marks short spur trail, left, leading 0.1m. to Skyline Drive, SDMP 60.2. *AT* here passes through a relatively flat area known as Kites Deadening, now completely wooded. (A deadening was an area where the early settlers, instead of felling the trees for a field, saved time and effort by just ringing the trees, removing the lower bark, to kill the trees without the task of removing them. They would then plant their crops amid the "deadened" trees.)

6.0 Trail descends steeply, by switchbacks, for 0.1m.

6.3 Spur trail leads right, downhill, 250 ft. to Pocosin Cabin and to spring south of the cabin. (Pocosin Cabin, el. 3120 ft., is a locked structure. Reservations for its use must be obtained in advance from PATC Headquarters. See Chap. 6: "Shelters and Cabins." From the cabin there is a fine view east over the Conway River Valley. Three mountains can be seen across the valley. The local mountaineers called these, from right to left: Panther, Bear Stand and Sawney Macks; these names are not shown on today's maps. The word "Pocosin" is said to be of Indian derivation meaning a "dismal" or swamp.) Beyond spur trail *AT* descends gently.

6.4 Cross Pocosin Fire Road. (To left fire road leads 0.1m. to Skyline Drive, SDMP 59.5. Across the Drive and a few feet north the Hensley Church FFT leads down to VA. Sec. 625 at a point about 7m. from Elkton. To right, the fire road leads downhill passing Pocosin Cabin in 0.1m. About 0.8m. farther along the fire road, the Pocosin (Horse) Trail leads right from the road approximately 1.3m. south to intersect the South River Fire Rd., making an excellent loop trail possible. See Chap. 5: "Side Trails;" also PATC map No. 10.)

6.6 Pass spring to the left of the *AT*.

7.5 Where *AT* is close (30 ft.) to the Drive, an old road leads right from the *AT* descending toward Pocosin Hollow. *AT* soon ascends.

8.1 Pass trail intersection. (To left a trail leads to Lewis Mountain Campground. To the right the Lewis Mtn. FFT leads along the ridge crest of Lewis Mtn., then disappears.

8.2 A post marks a trail, left, leading 300 ft. to Lewis Mtn. Campground. (Water fountain "in season" directly across camp road here. A Camp store is located on road. Across the Skyline Drive from the entrance to the Lewis Mtn. Campground, SDMP 57.5, the Allen Hollow FFT leads 3m. down to VA. Sec. 625 at a point about 8m. from Elkton.) *AT* now descends gently. Several paths, unmarked, lead left to camping area and then the picnic area of Lewis Mtn. Water available "in season".

9.1 Spur trail, right, leads downhill 0.2m. to Bearfence Mtn. Shelter. Spring 50 ft. to right of shelter. (See Chap. 6: Shelters and Cabins.)

9.2 In gap, cross access road to Bearfence Mtn. Shelter. (Road leads right 0.3m. to shelter. Below shelter, as the Slaughter FFT, it continues down to the Conway River and joins the Conway River Fire Road. Left of the *AT*, road leads to the Drive, SDMP 56.8. On west side of Drive, the old road continues as the Meadows School Fire Road and descends to VA. Sec. 759.) *AT* now ascends steeply, by switchbacks, the southwest slope of Bearfence Mtn.

9.8 Junction with Bearfence Loop Trail which leads right. (Views on this short trail are very rewarding. Loop Tr. is only 150 ft. longer than the stretch of *AT* between the junctions.)

10.0 Loop Trail reenters *AT* from the right.

10.2 Cross blazed trail. (To left, trail leads 0.1m. to the Bearfence Mtn. Parking Area on the Skyline Drive, SDMP 56.4. Here hikes lead by a SNP Naturalist start during the summer. To the right of the *AT* an unimproved trail leads to spectacular jagged rocks of Bearfence Mtn; they offer excellent views. This rough trail requires the use of hands in some places. It connects with the loop trail over Bearfence Mtn., the two trails marking a rough figure eight with the *AT*.) Beyond the intersection the *AT* remains rather level for 0.3m., then descends gradually along the western slope of Bush Mtn.

10.7 *AT* approaches within 150 ft. of the Drive. Trail continues to descend for another 0.2m., then levels off and finally climbs again gently for 0.2m.

11.6 In Bootens Gap, el. 3243 ft., cross old road, the Conway River Fire Road (Skyline Drive, SDMP 55.1, is 150 ft. to left, with parking space for two cars. To right, the fire road leads down the Conway River, becoming VA. Sec. 667 outside the Park. Rt. 667 comes into VA. Rt. 230 3m. north of Stanardsville), *AT* now starts ascent of Hazeltop Mtn.

12.0 Pass graded Laurel Prong Trail on right. (Laurel Prong Tr. leads down 2.8m. to Hoover Camp. It passes through one of the few areas in the Park where rhododendrons grow. About 1m. from the *AT* it passes through Laurel Gap. Here an overgrown trail leads over Cat Knob to "The Sag".) *AT* continues to ascend.

12.5 Cross wooded summit of Hazeltop, el. 3812', highest point on the *AT* in the SNP. *AT* now descends gently.

13.0 Along a level area of the *AT* there is a fine stand of stiff gentians, mixed with purple and white asters, each autumn. Beyond this area the *AT* again descends.

14.0 Trail bears left, due west. From a rock to right of the *A T* at this turn is a good wintertime view of Doubletop and Fork Mtns. (Former President Hoover's Camp is in the Rapidan Valley between these peaks.)

14.4 Come into overgrown field. A cement post marks the Mill Prong Trail leading right from the *A T*. (This trail, of which the first 1.0m. is blue-blazed, leads 1.8m. to Hoover Camp. The latter 0.8m. of the trail is coincident with the Mill Prong Horse Trail.) A few feet farther, just south of Milam Gap, the *A T* crosses the Skyline Drive, SDMP 52.8. (This is the only crossing of the Drive in the central section of the Park.) Cross a field and enter woods.

15.3 Pass a spring 50 ft. to right of the *A T*.

15.5 Cross Tanners Ridge Fire Road. (To right, the fire road leads 0.1m. to the Drive, SDMP 51.6. To left, it leads down the mountain becoming VA. Sec. 682 outside the Park.) Cross open field with cemetery to the left. Here are fine views, back, of Hazeltop.

15.7 Cross Tanners Ridge Horse Trail. Cross the horse trail again in about 0.1m. Ascend gradually.

16.1 Pass outlet of housed-in Lewis Spring. Immediately beyond, cross Park service road. (To left of the *A T* the road leads down to a sewage disposal area. To reach Lewis Falls follow the road down for about 150 ft. to a small pumphouse on right of road. Turn left off the road here, onto a footpath that continues downhill 0.5m. to the falls.) To the right of the *A T* the road leads about 0.3m. to the Skyline Drive, SDMP 51.4, 0.1m. south of the Big Meadows Wayside. Lunches are available at the wayside. Here too is located the Harry F. Byrd Sr. Visitor Center.) *A T* ascends steadily along west slope of ridge with occasional views from rocks to the left of the Trail.

16.5 Trail to right of *A T* leads 0.1m. to Black Rock Viewpoint and 0.2m. farther to Big Meadows Lodge. 0.2m. farther along the *A T*, pass under the sheer cliffs of Black Rock.

17.0 Trail intersection marked by two cement posts, *A T* is straight ahead. (Trail to left leads back 1.2m. to Lewis Falls. The Lewis Falls Tr. and *A T* together offer a 3.1m. circuit hike. To right of *A T*, trail leads between the Big Meadows Lodge and Picnic Grounds. Along this trail it is 0.2m. to the "end" of the

Swamp Nature Tr. and, following this nature trail "in reverse", about 0.8m. farther to the beginning of the Dark Hollow Falls Trail.) *A T* now passes below the Big Meadows Amphitheatre.

17.1 Junction with the Swamp Trail which enters from the right (0.1m. from its start at Amphitheatre Parking Area) and follows the *A T* for a half mile. *A T* now skirts the northwestern and northern edge of the ridge.

17.3 Cross over small rocky knob, the Monkey Head, where there are views. Beyond, *A T* skirts the north edge of the Big Meadows Campground. Several small unmarked trails lead right to the camping area. Openings along the *A T* give fine views north and west. (Hawksbill Mtn. in the foreground, Stony Man Mtn. farther away and, in the distance, Knob Mtn., the Neighbor, and, across the Page Valley can be seen Signal Knob at the north end of the Massanutten range.)

17.6 Swamp Nature Trail leaves *A T*, right. (Swamp Tr. leads 0.8m. to junction with the Dark Hollow Trail, then continues back through Big Meadows to its end near the amphitheatre. See Big Meadows inset on back of PATC map #10.) 50 ft. to left of *A T* at the trail junction is *David Spring. A T* now descends. Pass through beautiful hemlock grove.

18.4 Pass to left of split rock.

18.5 Spur trail leads right 100 ft. to Fishers Gap Parking Overlook on the Skyline Drive.

18.6 Intersection with Red Gate Fire Road, 350 ft. west of the Skyline Drive, just north of the Fishers Gap Parking Overlook, SDMP 49.3, el. 3061 ft. (To left, fire road (gated) leads 4.8m. down the mountain to VA. Sec. 611 at a point about 4m. from Stanley. Across the Drive, the Dark Hollow Falls Fire Rd. (also gated) leads down 1.0m. to the creek in Dark Hollow crossing it a few hundred feet below the main falls. Also here is the northern end of the Copper Mine-Dark Hollow Falls Loop Trail. See Chap. 5: "Side trails," Central Section. Also refer to PATC map #10 and PATC publication, *Circuit Hikes in the Shenandoah National Park*.)

SUBSECTION:
FISHERS GAP TO SKYLAND
SOUTH TO NORTH

6.3 miles (10.1 kilometers)   (PATC map No. 10:I-26)

General description:

Most of the Blue Ridge in this area was at one time covered by a series of lava flows. Today this lava, in its present form of greenstone, is the rock seen in the various rock outcrops along the Skyline Drive and along the Appalachian Trail in this section. On the west side of the ridge, where the slope is very steep the old layers of lava show as a series of vertical cliffs, one above another. The route of the *A T* at Franklin Cliffs, along Hawksbill, below Crescent Rocks, (and farther north along Stony Man Mtn.), follows along shelves below one series of cliffs and above another, thus affording a very rugged and photogenic section of Trail.

Hawksbill Mtn. is the highest in the Park. The *A T* slabs along the northwestern slope of Hawksbill but side trails lead to the summit, el. 4050'. Red spruce and balsam fir are native at high elevations from Hawksbill to Stony Man Mtn. just north of Skyland. They do not grow along the *A T* north of this area until one reaches Vermont! (They do grow farther south but at much higher elevations and are found along the *A T* in SW Virginia on Mt. Rogers, el. 5729', and White Top nearby.)

Side trails:

The summit of Hawksbill Mtn. can be reached by several routes. The lovely Whiteoak Canyon-Cedar Run circuit hike is in this area. East of the main ridge of the Blue Ridge the rock-sculptured top of Old Rag Mountain beckons hikers. For details of these and other side trails see Chap. 5: "Side Trails", Central Section.

Accommodations:

The Big Meadows Developed Area, SDMP 51.2, (see map #10, inset on the back), just south of Fishers Gap, offers meals and lodging for 200 persons. It also contains a wayside, stables, the Byrd Visitor Center, and a tremendous camping area with the standard facilities for campers—store, laundry, showers, etc. Big Meadows is the only campground in the Park open year-round. Public accommodations are also available at Skyland (See map No. 10, inset on back) from mid-April to early November. The lodge and cottages can accommodate 350 persons. A stable is maintained here and a network of horseback trails are in the area. For information and lodging reservations write to the ARA Virginia Sky-Line Co., Inc., Box 727, Luray, Va. 22835.

There are two open-faced shelters available for *AT* hikers, but for camping only during inclement weather: Byrd's Nest #2, (trails at both 2.2m. and 3.2m. lead about 1m. to the shelter which is located near the top of Hawksbill), and Hawksbill Gap Shelter, 3.2m. (across the Skyline Drive and 0.3m. from the *AT*). Considerably east of the Drive are two additional shelters, Byrds Nest #1, on the western ridge of Old Rag Mtn. and the Old Rag Shelter, 0.4m. SE of the junction of the Old Rag Rd. and Weakley Hollow Rd. via the Saddle Tr. up Old Rag Mtn. (See PATC map No. 10 and Chap. 5: "Side Trails", Central Section.)

One locked cabin, Rock Spring, 1.2m. (spur trail to cabin 0.2m.) is also available. Reservations for its use must be obtained in advance from PATC Headquarters. (See Chap. 6: "Shelters and Cabins")

Detailed Trail data:

0.0 Intersection of the *AT* and the Red Gate Fire Road in Fishers Gap. (To the west, the fire road leads 4.8m. down the mountain to VA. Sec. 611 about 4m. east of Stanley. To the right of the *AT* the road leads 350 ft. to the Skyline Drive at a point just north of Fishers Gap Parking Overlook, SDMP 49.3, el. 3061 ft. The road through Fishers Gap was once the Gordonsville Turnpike. Across the Drive the road, now called the Dark Hollow Falls Fire Rd. on the east side of the Drive, leads 1.0m. to the creek in Dark Hollow, crossing it a few hundred feet below the falls. Also at Fishers Gap is one end of the Copper Mine-Dark Hollow Falls loop trail. See Chap 5: "Side Trails," Central Section; also PATC map #10 and PATC publication, *Circuit Hikes in the Shenandoah National Park.*)

0.2 Pass post marking spur trail, right, leading uphill 0.1m. to the south end of Franklin Cliffs Overlook, SDMP 49.0, el. 3135 ft. From here *AT* passes below the Franklin Cliffs, along a ledge above more cliffs. (Cliffs, composed of altered basaltic rock, are the result of the erosion of ancient lava beds, laid down in layers 100 to 250 ft. thick for a total thickness of two to three thousand feet and later tilted about 90°.)

0.5 Post marks obscure trail, right of the *AT*, which leads 0.3m. to the north end of the Franklin Cliffs Overlook. 100 ft. farther along the *AT* there is a wet weather spring 15 ft. to the left of the Trail. *AT* continues to slab along the west side of the ridge.

1.3 Spur trail, right, marked by post, leads 150 ft. uphill to Skyline Drive at Spitler Knoll Parking Overlook, SDMP 48.1, nearest parking spot for users of Rock Spring Cabin. *AT* now gradually ascends, passing old road at 1.5m. Trail soon levels off, then descends gently.

1.9 *AT* comes into a slightly open area. Here post marks spur trail which leads left 0.2m. downhill to Rock Spring Cabin, a locked building. (For its use, reservations must be obtained in advance from PATC Headquarters. See Chap. 6: "Shelters and Cabins." A spring is 150 ft. north of the cabin. Twenty feet farther along the *AT* an old road, which serves as Park access road to the cabin, leads 0.2m. to the Drive, SDMP 47.8. The *AT* passes along an old field rapidly being overgrown with pine and locust.

2.2 Reach sag between Hawksbill Mtn. and Nakedtop. (To right, trail leads 0.9m. to top of Hawksbill Mtn., highest point in the SNP., el. 4050 ft. Byrds Nest No. 2, an open-faced shelter, is located just below the summit.) A few feet farther along the *AT* a side trail leads left 0.4m. to the summit of Nakedtop. (Two viewpoints have been cleared.) From the sag the *AT* slabs along the northern face of Hawksbill, passing below steep cliffs. Note balsam fir growing here. There are good views north of Ida Valley and Luray, and views ahead of Crescent Rock, Stony Man and Old Rag Mountain.

3.2 Reach Hawksbill Gap and a trail intersection. (To left, Buracker Hollow FFT leads down the mountain passing spring in 450 ft. To right, a trail leads uphill 300 ft. to Hawksbill Gap Parking Area on the Drive, SDMP 45.6, el. 3361'. On the east side of the Drive here is the start of the Cedar Run Trail. To reach Hawksbill Gap Shelter, follow this trail for 0.2m., then take spur trail on right for 250 ft.) (From the Hawksbill Gap Parking Area, the Hawksbill Trail leads steeply uphill 0.8m. to Byrd's Nest #2 and the summit, el. 4050', just beyond. From the summit, the Hawksbill Tr. descends southward to the Upper Hawksbill Parking Area on the Drive, SDMP 46.7. The Nakedtop Tr. also starts at the shelter and descends the west ridge of Hawksbill, intersecting the *AT* in 0.9m. and continuing on to Nakedtop. See Chap. 6: "Shelters and Cabins.")

3.7 The *AT* passes under the cliffs of Crescent Rock. These, like those of Franklin Cliffs, are the eroded remnants of ancient lava beds.

3.8 A side trail, marked by cement post, leads right, uphill, 0.1m. to near the north end of the Crescent Rock Parking Overlook, SDMP 44.4, coming into a short trail, 0.3m., leading from the Overlook north to Bettys Rock. (In crannies along the exposed rocks of Bettys Rock one may find the three-toothed cinquefoil, a northern plant, blooming in late spring and early summer.)

4.4 Pass piped spring 4 ft. right of the *AT*.

4.5 Spur trail, right, leads uphill 300 ft. to Timber Hollow Parking Overlook on the Drive, SDMP 43.3. From the trail junction the *AT* parallels the Drive, passing through a thicket of mountain laurel, blooming time early June. Trail then ascends by switchbacks toward Pollock Knob, el. 3560'. There are good views here of Hawksbill Mtn. and Ida Valley.

5.0 Reach top of ridge with splendid views of Hawksbill Mtn. and Ida Valley. Trail now follows cliffs along the west side of Pollock Knob, with fine views west. From here Trail ascends slightly, then follows the corral fence to Skyland stables.

5.7 Horse trail leads right to Skyline Drive and beyond to White Oak Canyon and on to Big Meadows. The *AT* continues ahead and crosses the paved road at the stables, then proceeds through woods.

6.1 At top of hill reach paved road on open Skyland grounds. At the road, 200 ft. left of the *AT* crossing, the Millers Head Trail goes left. (Excellent views are available at the end of the 0.8m. Millers Head Trail. It is well worth the side trip.)

6.3 Come into paved path, where sign board marks route of the *AT*. This is the end of the subsection. (*AT* continues straight ahead on paved path. To right, the path leads 75 ft. to Skyland Dining Hall.)

SUBSECTION:
SKYLAND TO THORNTON GAP
SOUTH TO NORTH

9.4 miles (15.1 kilometers)   (PATC map No. 10: G-7)

General description:

This section is especially scenic. From Skyland the Trail passes through beautiful woods of white pine and then hemlock. It then skirts the cliffs along the west edge of Stony Man, following the original Passamaquoddy Trail constructed by George Freeman Pollock, founder of Skyland. Along Stony Man, as at Franklin Cliffs, the cliffs were formed by the erosion of layer upon layer of ancient lava. Beyond, the *AT* swings around the head of Nicholson (Free State) Hollow paralleling the Skyline Drive. The Trail route crosses the edge of the Pinnacles Picnic Grounds, then passes below the Jewell Hollow Overlook. From here the Trail climbs over The Pinnacle, 3730 ft., then follows the narrow ridge crest to the southern end of the Marys Rock outcrop. Here the *AT* starts its long steady descent, 1200 ft., to Thornton Gap. A spur trail leads to the northern tip of Marys Rock with its outstanding panoramic views. *AT* passes below Panorama Restaurant in Thornton Gap reaching U.S. 211 about 0.1m. west of the Skyline Drive.

There are no dependable springs along the *AT* in this subsection. Piped water is available "in season" at the Byrd Shelter #3, the Pinnacles Picnic Area, and the Stony Man Mtn. Parking Overlook. The springs at Meadow Springs and Shaver Hollow Shelter are each 0.3m. downhill from the *AT*.

Side trails:

The Park is wide on the east side of the Drive in this area and there are many trails. In addition to the trails in the Skyland area including the very popular *AT*-Stony Man Trail loop, there is one network of trails centered around Nicholson (Free State) Hollow and Corbin Cabin and another one, overlapping the first, that covers the "Hazel Country", that section near the Hazel River and Hazel Mountain. For details see Chap. 5: "Side Trails," Central Section.

Accommodations:

Skyland has an excellent restaurant; also a lodge and cottages which can accommodate 350 guests. A stable is maintained here and there is a network of horse trails in the area. At Panorama, in Thornton Gap, there is also a restaurant, closed in winter. Gasoline is available here. Nearest public campground is at Big Meadows, SDMP 51.2 about 9 miles south of Skyland.

There are two open-faced shelters for use of *AT* hikers during inclement weather, Byrd Shelter #3, 3.0m., and Shavers Hollow Shelter, 6.5m. (follow spur trail 0.3m.) One and a half miles east of the Drive, SDMP 37.9, via the Corbin Cabin Cut-Off Tr., is Corbin Cabin, an old mountaineer cabin restored and maintained by the PATC. It is available for use by hikers but reservations must be made in advance at PATC Headquarters. See Chap. 6: "Shelters and Cabins."

Detailed Trail data:

0.0 This subsection of *AT* starts at wooden signboard at junction of paths about 75 ft. below the Dining Hall of Skyland (near Northern Entrance to Skyland, SDMP 41.7) At this junction the *AT,* coming from the south, comes into the paved Skyland path and follows it straight ahead. (To right, the paved path leads uphill to dining hall.) A few feet forward along the Trail, at a sharp bend to the left on the paved route, a spur trail leads right. (This trail leads to service road, in the dormitory area of Skyland. Road can be followed uphill toward north entrance of Skyland, to where the Stony Man Trail begins. From the *AT* via this route, the Stony Man Cliffs are 0.9m., and Little Stony Man 1.3m. This route has steeper grades than the

A T and is 0.2m. longer but must be taken if the summit of Stony Man, el. 4011 ft., is to be reached. Stony Man Trail rejoins the *A T* in 1.5m. at a point on the *A T* 1.3m. from start of the section.)

0.1 Turn sharp right away from paved path. Continue through woods.

0.2 Cross paved Skyland road and descend through grove of old white pines.

0.3 Turn right onto road at signpost. In 200 ft. turn into footpath. (Road, which was the original road to Skyland, continues, left, downhill, for 3m. to the "foot of the mountain". Road is gated at Park boundary, where it becomes VA. Sec. 672, about 8m. from Luray.) *A T* now passes through beautiful hemlock grove.

0.4 Pass Skyland power line and housed Furnace Spring 25 ft. to right of trail. From here the route of the *A T* as it skirts around Stony Man and Little Stony Man Mtns. is a slight relocation of George Freeman Pollock's original Passama-quoddy Trail built in 1932. ("Passamaquoddy" is a Maine Indian word signifying "abounding in pollock".) This bit of *A T* is exceptionally beautiful as it follows the base of rocky cliffs and passes by huge hemlock trees.

1.3 Stony Man Trail comes in on right. *A T* descends by switchbacks.

1.6 Spur trail, right, leads 150 ft. to Little Stony Man Parking Area on Skyline Drive, SDMP 39.1. *A T* drops well below the Drive, then parallels it, clinging to the steep western slopes of the main ridge. Trail route affords spectacular views of Page Valley, the Massanutten Range, New Market Gap and Luray. To the southeast is a near view of Little Stony Man Cliffs and the "profile" of Stony Man Mtn.

2.0 Spur trail, right, leads 200 ft. to south end of Stony Man Mtn. Parking Overlook in Hughes River Gap, SDMP 38.6, el. 3097 ft. Drinking water and toilets here. *A T* now ascends.

2.4 Trail junction. (To right, the blue-blazed Nicholson Hollow Trail leads 0.1m. to Skyline Drive, SDMP 38.4, then crosses it diagonally and continues down into Nicholson Hollow, passing Corbin Cabin in 1.9m. See Chap. 5: "Side

Trails", Central Section. Trail to left of *AT* here soon dead-ends.)

2.6 Intersection with the Crusher Ridge FFT. (The fire foot trail utilizes an old road known as Sours Lane. To left, the trail leads along Crusher Ridge, then descends into Shaver Hollow to near VA. Sec. 669. To right, the trail ends on the Nicholson Hollow Trail a few feet from the Skyline Drive.) *AT* descends, then passes over a slight rise and descends again.

3.2 Intersection with spur trail to Shaver Hollow Shelter. (The shelter is 0.3m. downhill to left of the *AT*. It is situated on a ridge crest between two valleys in an unusually attractive setting. The shelter may be used for camping only in very inclement weather. Spring is 300 ft. southwest of the shelter. To right of the *AT*, the trail leads 150 ft. to Skyline Drive at the Shaver Hollow Parking Area, SDMP 37.9. Across the Drive here the Corbin Cabin Cut-off Trail leads 1.5m. to Corbin Cabin and the Nicholson Hollow Trail. See Chap. 6: "Shelters and Cabins".) From the intersection, the *AT* ascends.

3.3 Where *AT* switchbacks sharply to the left there is an excellent viewpoint. The *AT* is immediately above the Skyline Drive here and offers an unobstructed view of Nicholson (Free State) Hollow and Old Rag Mountain beyond. (The mountaineers who once lived in Nicholson Hollow were reputed to be so mean they were a "law unto themselves" and the local sheriffs were afraid to enter the area, hence the name "Free State". See the book, *Skyland,* by George Freeman Pollock.)

3.6 Pass under power line. About 0.1m. farther, notice the impressive old white pine growing to the right of the *AT*. From here Trail ascends over knob, then descends to reach Pinnacles Picnic Grounds.

4.0 Come onto paved path in Picnic Grounds and bear left, following *AT* blazes. Turn left at drinking fountain (about 200 ft.), pass toilets and follow path between walls of laurel. Trail now follows picnic grounds path, paralleling the entrance road to the Pinnacles Area for about 0.1m.

4.3 Bear left, away from road. Descend gradually along narrow ridge crest. Fine views westward over Jewell Hollow.

4.4 Spur trail, right, leads 75 ft. to the Jewell Hollow Parking Overlook, SDMP 36.4. *AT* passes below the Overlook.

4.6 Pass a second spur trail leading back to the Overlook. Trail now ascends gently through some tall white pines.

4.7 Cross Leading Ridge FFT, yellow-blazed but its footway very obscure at the intersection. (To right trail leads 0.1m. to Skyline Drive. To left it climbs over Leading Ridge, then descends steeply toward the Shenandoah Valley and comes into VA. Sec. 669 outside the Park boundary, at a point about 2m. from U. S. 211 using the shortest route. See PATC map #10.) *AT* now ascends, passing through thick growth of mountain laurel.

5.4 Pass to the right of highest point of The Pinnacle, el. 3730 ft. Trail now leads for a short distance along the level ridge crest with excellent views. Pass, on left, the jagged rocks forming the north peak of The Pinnacle. From here Trail descends to a sag at base of The Pinnacle.

5.6 Pass obscure trail, left, leading 100 ft. to fine view north. *AT* descends by switchbacks along a rocky, picturesque ridge.

5.9 An obscure trail, right, leads down to Skyline Drive near Pinnacle Overlook. (This trail is useful for connecting the *AT* with the Hannah Run Trail for circuit hikes.)

6.4 Reach Byrds Nest #3. (Piped water available here during the warmer months. See Chap. 6: "Shelters and Cabins.") Beyond the shelter, *AT* follows access road for 180 ft., then turns left, away from the road. (Road leads 0.3m. to Skyline Drive, SDMP 33.9.) From road, *AT* ascends slightly by switchbacks on east slope of ridge, passing viewpoint at 6.7m, then bearing right along the ridge. Descend into slight sag.

7.0 Junction with Buck Hollow Trail. (Buck Hollow Trail leads right, downhill, passing Meadow Springs on its left in 0.3m. Buck Hollow Trail continues downhill crossing the Skyline Drive, SDMP 33.5, in 0.7m. and continuing down to reach U.S. 211 in 3.7m. at a point 3.4m. west of Sperryville.) From trail junction *AT* follows the ridge crest. Just before start of the large rock outcrop marking Marys Rock, swing to the right of the ridge and start to descend.

7.7 Spur trail leads left 0.1m. to the exposed northern tip of Marys Rock. (The view from this point is unsurpassed anywhere in the Park. Highest point, 3514 ft., is reached by climbing to the top of the rock outcrop (granodiorite). It can be dangerous in icy, wet, or windy weather. (Geologists believe the rock of Marys Rock is over one billion years old!) From trail junction the *AT* descends steadily all the way to Thornton Gap, at first through laurel and scrub oak. Here there are splendid views—of Hazel Mtn. to the southeast, of Oventop Mtn. with its many peaks to the northeast, and of the Blue Ridge as far north as Mt. Marshall.

8.6 At sharp bend in trail, the non-maintained Tunnel Trail leads down the mountain to the right. (About 0.2m. down, the Tunnel Trail forks, one branch leads to the south portal of the tunnel on the Skyline Drive, SDMP 32.2, and the other to the north portal. Footway is somewhat precarious near the tunnel portals and the Park Service no longer marks or maintains this trail.) *AT* continues its descent toward Thornton Gap. At 9.0m. it turns right along a ravine, then switches back twice under a power line.

9.3 Spur trail, right, leads into Panorama Upper Parking Area. The *AT* now passes to the left and below the Panorama Restaurant.

9.4 Junction with US 211, about 0.1m. west of the Skyline Drive in Thornton Gap. (Skyline Drive at Thornton Gap, SDMP 31.5, el. 2307'.)

SUMMARY OF DISTANCES ALONG THE *AT*
Section VII Central
(for Skyline Drive mileages, see N to S)

	Miles	**Kilometers**
Swift Run Gap and U.S. Rt. 33	0.0	0.0
South River Shelter	2.5 + 0.3	4.0 + 0.5
South River Falls Trail	3.0	4.8
Pocosin Cabin	6.3	10.1
Lewis Mtn. Campground	8.2	13.2
Bearfence Mtn. Shelter	9.1 + 0.2	14.7 + 0.3
Hazeltop Mtn. summit	12.5	20.1
Skyline Drive, *AT* crossing at Milam Gap	14.4	23.2
Lewis Spring Service Rd.	16.1	25.9
Big Meadows—Amphitheatre area	17.0	27.4
Fishers Gap	18.6	30.0
Rock Spring Cabin	20.5 + 0.2	33.0 + 0.3
Byrds Nest #2 and Hawksbill Mtn. summit via Nakedtop Trail from *AT*	20.8 + 0.9	33.5 + 1.4
Hawksbill Gap	21.8	35.1
Hawksbill Gap Shelter	21.8 + 0.3	35.1 + 0.5
Whiteoak Canyon Trail	24.3	39.1
Skyland (area of Dining Hall)	24.9	40.1
Little Stony Man Parking Area	26.5	42.7
Stony Man Parking Overlook	26.9	43.3
Nicholson Hollow Trail	27.3	44.0
Shaver Hollow Shelter	28.1 + 0.3	45.2 + 0.5
Pinnacles Picnic Grounds	28.9	46.5
Byrds Nest #3	31.3	50.4
Buck Hollow Trail	31.9	51.4
Marys Rock summit	32.6 + 0.1	52.5 + 0.2
Thornton Gap and U.S. 211	34.3	55.2

SECTION VI NORTHERN SHENANDOAH PARK
THORNTON GAP TO U.S. 522
SOUTH TO NORTH

27.5 miles (44.3 kilometers)   (PATC Map No. 9: I-18)

Section VI of the Appalachian Trail in Virginia begins at U.S. 211 in Thornton Gap. Through most of the section the Trail and Skyline Drive parallel closely and there are many intersections, so that the *AT* throughout this section is easily accessible. However the deep woods through which the Trail passes makes the Trail hiker feel remote from civilization. At Compton Gap the *AT* leaves the proximity of the Skyline Drive and continues north along the Blue Ridge crest following the old road from Compton Gap toward Chester Gap for a mile and three-quarters. It then descends the northwest side of the ridge, leaving the Shenandoah National Park near the top. It passes along easements first through private property in Harmony Hollow, then across land of the Northern Virginia 4 H Educational Center. For the last mile and a half before the end of the section at U.S. 522 the *AT* follows near the edge of property of the National Zoological Park Conservation Center.

Numerous side trails and fire roads in the northern area of the Park can be used in conjunction with the *AT* for a variety of walking trips including some circuit hikes.

For convenience, the trail description of this section has been divided into two subsections: Thornton Gap to Gravel Springs Gap and Gravel Springs Gap to U.S. 522.

Maps:
PATC trail map #9. Also available are the USGS map of Shenandoah Park, Northern Section, 1969, scale 1:62500 and 7½ min. quads for Front Royal, Bentonville, Chester Gap, Luray, Thornton Gap, and Washington, Va.

SUBSECTION:
THORNTON GAP TO GRAVEL SPRINGS GAP

14.6 miles (23.5 kilometers)   (PATC Map No. 9: I-18)

General description:

From Thornton Gap the Trail climbs Pass Mountain, then makes several other smaller ascents as it follows the crest of the Blue Ridge. From Elkwallow Gap the Trail climbs over a thousand feet to reach the highest elevation in the northern section of the Park, the summit of the Second Peak of the Hogback, el. 3475'. From the Hogback peaks the route is downhill all the way to Gravel Springs Gap. South of Pass Mtn. and also near Range View Cabin, the Trail passes through areas where large oak trees with low widespreading branches are being crowded by slender young forest trees. The old oaks remind the hiker that these areas were open fields in the pre-National Park days during which these oaks grew to maturity.

Side trails:

At 10.8m. the *AT* connects with the Big Blue-Tuscarora Trail at its southern terminus. This trail, when completed, will offer a 220 mile route west of the *AT*, rejoining it northeast of Carlisle, PA. From the junction in the SNP the Big Blue utilizes the Overall Run Trail for 4.5 miles, then forks to the right, crossing U.S. 340 just south of Bentonville. From there it crosses the two forks of the Shenandoah River and the Massanutten range which separates them, and continues on west as far as the VA.-W. VA. state line, whence it proceeds generally north-northeast, roughly paralleling the *AT* route far to the east. By 1974 approximately 55m. of the southern (Big Blue) portion had been completed, starting at the southern terminus on the *AT*. Another 25m. remains to be done to reach the Potomac River at Hancock, Md. The Tuscarora section, that part of the Big Blue-Tuscarora Trail north of the Potomac River, has been finished.

The Thornton Gap-Gravel Springs area is rich is side trails, too many to enumerate here. See Chap 5: "Side Trails," Northern Section; also the PATC publications: *Circuit Hikes in the Shenandoah National Park* and *Walkers' Chart #1.*

Accommodations:

Four open-faced shelters along this section are available for camping only during inclement weather: Pass Mtn. Shelter, 1.2m. (follow spur trail 0.2m. from *AT*), Byrds Nest #4, 4.0m., Elkwallow Shelter, 8.2m. and Gravel Springs Shelter, 14.4m. (follow Bluff Tr. 0.2m.). There is also one locked cabin, Range View Cabin, 9.5m. (follow spur trail right for 0.1m.). Reservations for the use of the cabin must be obtained in advance from PATC Headquarters. See Chap. 6: "Shelters and Cabins".

Matthews Arm Campground, SDMP 22.2, offers extensive camping facilities. Meals are available at Panorama Restaurant at Thornton Gap and lunches can be purchased at the Elkwallow Wayside, SDMP 24.0. None of these facilities are available during the cold months.

Detailed Trail Data:

0.0 Intersection with U.S. 211 at a point 0.15m. west of the Skyline Drive in Thornton Gap, SDMP 31.5, el. 2307'. Trail leads uphill through woods.

0.1 Cross to right side of Skyline Drive and follow service road for a few feet; then turn left, up the bank, into woods.

0.4 *AT* turns left onto service road, follows it about 150 ft., then turns left, away from the road. Trail now ascends gradually.

1.2 Spur trail leads right 0.2m. to Pass Mtn. Shelter. (See Chap. 6: "Shelters and Cabins".)

2.0 Reach wooded summit of Pass Mtn., el. 3052'.

2.4 The *AT*, descending, passes through rocky area with wintertime views west of Kemp Hollow, Neighbor Mtn. and Knob Mtn.

3.1 Trail crosses to left of the Skyline Drive, SDMP 28.6, at Beahms Gap.

3.3 A spur trail leads right 0.1m. to Beahms Gap Parking Overlook on the Skyline Drive, SDMP 28.5.

3.5 *AT* intersects the Kemp Hollow A FFT. (This fire foot trail leads left 0.4m. to the Park boundary but is closed to the public outside the Park.) Immediately beyond this intersection a trail on the left leads down 100 ft. to a spring.

3.6 Cross access road to Byrd's Nest #4. In the next 0.3m. the Trail crosses the access road several times.

4.0 Pass the shelter, Byrd's Nest #4, to right of the *AT*. Piped water is available mid-May through October. At knob above the shelter short trails from the *AT* lead to observation points. (The viewpoint on the right is now badly overgrown with scrub oak.) The *AT* now descends to a slight sag, then climbs again.

4.4 Reach top of rise. Two hundred feet farther reach junction with the Neighbor Trail. (There are two forks about 50 ft. apart. The Neighbor Tr. follows a side ridge almost along a contour line as far as the peak of "The Neighbor", 1.9m., and then descends steeply to Jeremys Run Trail, 4.6m)

4.8 Spur trail leads right 0.1m. to unofficial parking area on Skyline Drive, SDMP 26.8. On the *AT*, a short distance farther, cross Jeremys Hollow FFT. (This trail leads right 300 ft. to the Skyline Drive; to left it leads downhill 1.2m. to the Jeremys Run Trail.) Beyond this junction the *AT* continues along the crest of a long narrow ridge for over two miles, then descends.

7.9 There is a spring 5 yds. to the left of the *AT*, shortly after a sharp turn to the right. The Trail continues to descend.

8.1 Cross creek. 100 ft. beyond, where the *AT* turns sharply right, is intersection with the Jeremys Run Trail. (Jeremys Run Tr. leads left 6.5m. to Va. Sec. 611 at a point 3.5m. from Big Spring on U.S. 340. See Chap. 5: "Side Trails" for details of this trail and circuit hikes that can be made in this area; also see PATC publication: *Circuit Hikes in the Shenandoah National Park*.) *AT* now ascends.

8.2 Cross access road to Elkwallow Shelter. (See Chap. 6: "Shelters and Cabins.") To the left, road leads 150 ft. to the shelter. To the right road is about 0.5m. from the Skyline Drive. Also at this intersection, sharply to the right, is a short trail to spring.

8.3 Spur trail, left, leads 150 ft. to the shelter.

8.4 A trail straight ahead leads 200 ft. to Elkwallow Picnic Grounds. *AT* turns sharply to the left here, to swing around the developed area of the Elkwallow Picnic Grounds and Wayside.

8.6 Intersect the Elkwallow Trail. (To the left this trail leads 1.9m. to Matthews Arm Campground; to the right it leads 0.1m.

to the Elkwallow Wayside. Lunches may be obtained here from mid-May through October.) At 250 ft. farther the *AT* crosses to right of Skyline Drive, SDMP 23.9. Trail now ascends gently.

9.5 Cross service road to Range View Cabin. (To right road leads down 0.1m. to the cabin. About 100 ft. down this road the Piney Ridge Trail leads off to the right. See Chap. 5: "Side Trails." To the left road leads 0.6m. to Piney River Ranger Station and the Skyline Drive, SDMP 22.1.) 200 ft. farther along the *AT*, a spur trail leads right 0.1m. to Range View Cabin, a locked structure. (See Chap. 6: "Shelters and Cabins")

9.6 Pass under power line. A trail to right follows power line 0.1 m. to the cabin.

9.9 Turn right into access road and follow it a few feet before leaving it again as road bends to the left. Immediately ahead is junction with Piney Branch Trail which leads right from *AT*. (See Chap. 5: "Side Trails;" also see publication: *Circuit Hikes in the Shenandoah National Park*.)

10.2 Cross to left side of Skyline Drive, SDMP 21.9, Rattlesnake Point is to left of Trail as you reach the Drive. (50 yds. right of the *AT*, on the Drive, is Rattlesnake Point Overlook, el. 3105'., with views east over Piney Branch. 0.2m. to left of the *AT*, along the Drive, is the entrance road to Matthews Arm Campground.) *AT* now ascends.

10.5 Spur trail on left leads 50 ft. to summit of Sugarloaf.

10.8 Junction with Big Blue-Overall Run Trail. (This is the southern terminus of the Big Blue-Tuscarora Trail which, when completed, will provide a 220m. route connected to the *AT* at each end. 5.6m. of the Big Blue Tr. lies within the Shenandoah Park. From the junction with the *AT* the Big Blue-Overall Run Trail descends to the left. At 0.7m. a trail leads left from it to Matthews Arm Campground. The trail passes near Overall Falls at 2.7 m. At 4.5m. the Big Blue parts from the Overall Run Tr. and at 6.6m. reaches U.S. 340 at a point 2.6m. south of Bentonville. See Chap. 5: "Side Trails.")

10.9 Side trail leads right 30 ft. to summit of the Fourth Peak of Hogback, el. 3440 ft., with fine view south. Continue along ridge, descending slightly.

11.2 Cross to right of Skyline Dirve, SDMP 21.1. Ascend

over the Third Peak of Hogback, 3440'. Just beyond the top a side trail leads 15 ft. to a spot offering a splendid view north over Browntown Valley and Dickey Ridge. (Skyline Drive is directly below; there are enormous rocks here.) Descend.

11.5 Cross to left of Skyline Drive, SDMP 20.8. Follow tower access road a few feet, then bear right off the road. (A spur trail leads right, here, 300 ft. to Skyline Drive.) In 400 ft. *AT* crosses to left of access road.

11.7 Trail follows road across its turn-around area, reaching the summit of the Second Peak of Hogback, el. 3475', highest point in northern section of the SNP; antenna towers are to left of Trail. Descend.

11.8 Graded trail to right leads 0.2m. downhill to a walled-in spring which is within sight of the Skyline Drive. *AT* now ascends.

12.0 Pass a few feet to the right of the First Peak of Hogback, el. 3420'. Continue along ridge crest, then descend steeply, by switchbacks, down the east face of the mountain.

12.7 Spur trail, at signpost, leads right 50 ft. to Little Hogback Parking Overlook on the Skyline Drive, SDMP 19.7. *AT* veers left here, and climbs.

12.8 Reach top of Little Hogback where there is a fine outlook from ledge 30 ft. to left of Trail. *AT* now descends gradually.

13.1 Spur trail to right leads 100 ft. to Skyline Drive, SDMP 19.4, at junction of the Jinney Gray Fire Road on east side of Drive. (Jinney Gray Fire Rd. leads south along the east slopes of the Blue Ridge, passing the point known as "Four-Way" in 1.0m. See Chap. 5: "Side Trails", also the booklet, *Circuit Hikes in the Shenandoah National Park*.)

13.3 Cross to right side of Skyline Drive, SDMP 18.9. Trail passes along an almost level area.

14.4 Junction with the Bluff Trail. *AT* turns sharply left, paralleling the old Browntown-Harris Hollow Rd. from here to the Drive. (Bluff Tr. starts here, descends by switchbacks to Gravel Springs, 0.2m., where it crosses the old Harris Hollow Rd. It continues on, slabbing the east sides of South and North Marshall Mtns. ending at the Mt. Marshall Fire Rd., 4.7m.

Gravel Springs Shelter is 50 ft. from Gravel Springs, to the right of the Bluff Trail. See Chap. 6: "Shelters and Cabins")

14.6 Cross to the left side of the Skyline Drive, SDMP 17.7, el. 2665', at its intersection with the old Browntown-Harris Hollow Rd., (Harris Hollow Rd., right of the Drive and of the *AT*, is utilized as a service road to the Gravel Springs Shelter for 0.3m., beyond which it continues, as a fire foot trail, to VA. Sec. 622 reaching it at a point 5.0m. from Washington, VA. The Old Browntown Rd., left of the Drive, leads northwest down the mountain 3.4m. to VA. Sec. 631 reaching it at a point about 1m. south of Browntown.)

SUBSECTION:
GRAVEL SPRINGS GAP TO U.S. 522

12.9 miles (20.8 kilometers)   (map 9: G-10)

General description:
From Gravel Springs Gap the Trail ascends South and North Marshall Mtns., then descends about 1000 ft. to Jenkins Gap. After a climb to Compton Peak and descent to Compton Gap the *AT* leaves the proximity of the Skyline Drive, which here swings to the west, and follows along the old Compton Gap Rd. toward Chester Gap still following the crest of the Blue Ridge. In one and three-quarter miles it turns left off the road and descends the northwest slopes of the ridge into Harmony Hollow, leaving the Shenandoah Park near the top. The *AT* comes into VA. Sec. 601 in 1 mile, then leaves it again immediately. Members of the PATC have constructed a small, primitive campground, the Tom Floyd Wayside, along the *AT* about halfway between the Park boundary and Rt. 601. A quarter of a mile north of Rt. 601 the trail enters the property of the Northern Virginia 4 H Educational Center and continues through this property until it reaches VA. Sec. 602 which it crosses. Beyond this point the *AT* is on property of the National Zoological Park Conservation Center all the way to U.S. 522 and beyond.

Viewpoints along the Trail in the northern section of the Park are limited to occasional rock outcrops. Fields on the 4H and on the Zoological Park land offer nice vistas. Water is obtainable at several springs on or near the Trail along this 12.9 mile stretch.

Side trails:

The Bluff Trail, the Dickey Ridge Trail, the Mt. Marshall Fire Rd., the Lands Run Fire Rd., and the old Browntown-Harris Hollow Rd. (that part west of the Skyline Drive) offer good walking; so do the two short but interesting trails, Big Devils Stairs Tr. and The Peak Tr. The old Compton Gap Rd. north of its junction with the *AT*, together with Va. Sec. 610 from the Park boundary down to Chester Gap and a blue-blazed trail along the mountain north of the gap to Mosby Shelter (the former route of the *AT*; see PATC map #8) can be used with the *AT* for a circuit hike. For details on side trails see Chap. 5: "Side Trails". Also refer to the PATC publications: *Circuit Hikes in the Shenandoah National Park* and *Walkers' Chart #1.*

Accommodations:

Two open-faced shelters, Gravel Springs Shelter, 0.0m. (follow the Harris Hollow Rd. east 0.3m. from Gravel Springs Gap) and Indian Run Shelter, 7.5m. (follow spur trail 0.5m. downhill to right of *AT*) can only be used for camping in inclement weather.

South of Gravel Springs Gap, at SDMP 22.2, the Matthews Arm Campground with extensive camping facilities is open during the warmer months. There are many motels and restaurants in Front Royal, 4 miles northwest of the Trail intersection with U.S. 522; there are also a number of private campgrounds in the Front Royal area.

The Tom Floyd Wayside, a primitive camping area for through hikers with a few tent sites and a rain shelter, is located on the *AT* about one-half mile north of the Park boundary (and 0.5m. south of VA. Sec. 601).

Detailed Trail Data:

0.0 West side of the Skyline Drive at its intersection with the Browntown-Harris Hollow Road, SDMP 17.7, el. 2666'. (The old Browntown Rd., leads northwest down the mountain for 3.4m. entering VA. Sec. 631 at a point about 1m. south of Browntown. East of the Drive the Harris Hollow Rd. serves for 0.3 m as the service road to Gravel Springs Shelter. Below the shelter the old road continues as a fire foot trail to VA. Sec. 622 at a point about 5m. from Washington, VA.) *AT* follows Browntown Rd. for a few feet, then turns right and ascends gradually. Ledges on left, near top of mountain, afford splendid views.

1.0 Reach summit of South Marshall, el. 3212'.

1.6 Cross to the right of the Skyline Drive, SDMP 15.9, el. 3087'. Ascend North Marshall by switchbacks. Near top, where Trail jogs sharply left, the high cliffs on right are worth a scramble. At the next bend of the Trail there is an excellent view of the Blue Ridge to the south. (The cliffs of North Marshall are quite visible from the Skyline Drive south of the mountain.)

2.1 Reach crest of ridge. Cliffs to left of the trail offer many good views to the west.

2.2 Reach summit of North Marshall, el. 3368 ft. (The name of this mountain grows out of the fact that these lands were formerly a part of the Blue Ridge holdings of John Marshall, the noted Chief Justice of the United States from 1801-1835. See "Manor of Leeds" by Jean Stephenson in the April, 1934 PATC Bulletin.) Trail now descends gradually.

3.1 Pass Hogwallow Spring, 30 ft. on right. Continue to descend, very gently, through Hogwallow Flat.

3.7 Cross to left of Skyline Drive at Hogwallow Gap, SDMP 14.2, el. 2739'. For half a mile the *AT* proceeds across relatively level terrain. Foundations of an old building can be seen on right at 3.9m. Trail now climbs unnamed mountain, passing through an area of old orchard, with many of the old fruit trees persisting, although now topped by black locust trees.

5.3 Cross abandoned road diagonally. (The old road leads left 0.1m. to an old quarry.)

5.4 Cross gravel road in Jenkins Gap. (To left road leads 100 ft. to former dump. Below dump area are old roads, one the Jenkins Gap FFT, which descend the mountain to VA. Sec. 634 at a point 2.2m. east of Browntown. Road leads right 150 ft. to

Drive, SDMP 12.3. Some parking space available at Jenkins Gap, more at the Jenkins Gap Overlook, SDMP 12.4. The Mt. Marshall Fire Rd. can be reached by walking south along the Skyline Drive for about 0.2m.) Trail now passes through a level area containing an extensive growth of mountain laurel (bloom, early June) and pink azalea (bloom, late May). Beyond, trail ascends fairly steeply.

6.2 Pass Compton Springs. One spring is about 15 ft. to the left and below the *A T,* another is 50 ft. uphill on the right.

6.6 A sign post at top of climb marks short blue-blazed trails leading left and right to viewpoints. Though ungraded and offering only rough footing, both trails are worthwhile. (Trail on right leads down 0.2m. to an interesting outcrop of columnar basalt. To see the columnar structure it is necessary to climb down below the rocks. The top of the outcrop affords a good view east. Trail on left leads over the crest of Compton Mtn., 2909', and down 0.2m. to a rocky ledge offering excellent views to west and north.) *A T* continues along the ridge of Compton Mtn. for about 0.2m., then descends, passing several large boulder-like outcrops of basalt. There is at least one clump of yellow lady-slipper (bloom in mid-May) and some white clintonia (bloom early June) along this stretch of Trail.

7.4 In Compton Gap cross to the right side of the Skyline Drive, SDMP 10.4, el. 2415'. The *A T* now follows the old Compton Gap-Chester Gap Road, continuing along the Blue Ridge crest. (The Skyline Drive swings northwest here along Dickey Ridge down which it descends to Front Royal.)

7.5 A cement post on the right marks trail to Indian Run Shelter, 0.5m. from this junction. (See Chap. 6: "Shelters and Cabins")

7.7 Intersection with the Dickey Ridge Trail (left) and service road (right) to Indian Run Shelter. (Dickey Ridge Tr. begins here and leads northwest 9.2m. to the entrance to the Skyline Drive at the Front Royal town limits. Fort Windham Rocks are 0.2m. from the *A T* along this trail. The service road leads 0.4m. to the Indian Run Shelter, the northernmost shelter in the SNP. There is a spring 250 ft. to the left of the service road about 0.1m. before reaching the shelter.)

8.0 An old road leads left from the *AT* for 0.7m. coming into the Dickey Ridge Trail at a point 0.6m. north of its *AT* junction.

9.1 Turn left from the Compton Gap Rd. onto footpath. (Compton Gap Rd., blue-blazed beyond this point, continues 0.5m. downhill to VA. Sec. 610 at the Park boundary. It is 1.8m. farther, via Rt. 610, to U.S. 522 at Chester Gap. This was the route of the *AT* until 1974.)

9.3 Leave Shenandoah National Park. The *AT* now follows a narrow easement over private property; STAY ON TRAIL! *AT* descends by switchbacks.

9.7 Enter Tom Floyd Wayside, an area for primitive camping. No open fires permitted. A spur trail leads left 150 ft. to a rain shelter.

9.8 Spur trial leads left 800 ft. to Ginger Spring. Leave Wayside.

10.2 Bear right, diagonally, across old road. In 200 ft. cross small creek and pass through gap in rock wall.

10.3 Come into VA. Sec. 601 at a sharp corner of the road. (It is 0.4m. down Rt. 601 to a PATC parking area and 0.3m. farther to the main road through Harmony Hollow, VA. Sec. 604.) Immediately turn right onto farm road passing a white house on the right side of the *AT*. Follow farm road for about 750 ft., then turn left onto footpath. (Property to the left of the farm road and *AT* here belongs to the PATC.)

10.5 A trail leads left from the *AT* 0.2m. to a parking area, PATC owned, on VA. Sec. 601.

10.7 Cross through narrow gap in fence onto property of the Northern Virginia 4 H Educational Center.

11.0 Come into field. There is a good view of Harmony Hollow and its fruit orchards from the center of this field.

11.3 Turn sharply right into woods and immediately cross wet weather creek.

11.5 Cross small creek, Moore's Run, and then dirt road, VA. Sec. 602. *AT* enters the property of the National Zoological Park Conservation and Research Center here. Trail now ascends.

12.0 Reach summit of hill. 100 ft. beyond, cross stile.

12.5 Enter field. From this vantage point and with the help of field glasses, the hiker may be able to spot various zoo animals in the fenced-in areas across the highway. The *AT* descends along the edge of fields, passing below the dam of Lake Front Royal.

12.9 Cross bridges over Sloan Creek swamp and reach U.S. 522 at a point 3.2m. SE of its junction with U.S. 55 in Front Royal. (The *AT* crosses the highway here and continues through property of the National Zoological Park Conservation and Research Center.)

SUMMARY OF DISTANCES ALONG THE *AT*
Section VI Northern

	Miles	Kilometers
Thornton Gap (U.S. 211)	0.0	0.0
Pass Mtn. Shelter	1.2 + 0.2	1.9 + 0.3
Pass Mtn.	2.0	3.2
Skyline Drive crossing,		
Beahms Gap	3.1	5.0
Byrds Nest #4	4.0	6.4
The Neighbor Trail	4.5	7.2
Jeremys Run Trail	8.1	13.0
Elkwallow Shelter	8.2	13.2
Skyline Drive crossing,		
Elkwallow Gap	8.7	14.0
Range View Cabin	9.5 + 0.1	15.2 + 0.2
Piney Ridge Trail	9.5	15.2
Piney Branch Trail	9.9	15.9
Big Blue Trail	10.8	17.4
Summit of Hogback, 2nd Peak	11.7	18.8
Gravel Springs Shelter	14.4 + 0.2	23.2 + 0.3
Gravel Springs Gap	14.6	23.5
Summit of North Marshall	16.8	27.0
Jenkins Gap	20.0	32.2
Compton Gap	22.0	35.4
Indian Run Shelter	22.1 + 0.5	35.6 + 0.8
U.S. 522	27.5	44.3

For summary of distances by Skyline Drive to points on the *AT*, see end of write-up for "North to South, Section VI."

CHAPTER 5

SIDE TRAILS

Contents

Southern Section:

INTRODUCTION TO SIDE TRAILS

Trails developed by the Potomac Appalachian Trail Club are marked by blue paint blazes. Horses are not allowed on most blue-blazed trails. Trails constructed by the National Park Service for public use are indicated by signs and by the dug footway but are not paint-blazed. Horseback riding is permitted on these except where specifically prohibited. The Park Service also has a large number of fire foot trails marked with yellow blazes. Some of these are good trails, often old roads; some are valuable for use as links to connect other trails. Generally, however, these trails should be used with caution; they may be difficult to follow (some give out entirely) and no hiker should use them unless fully prepared to bushwhack. In addition to the foot trails, the fire roads (and service roads) which are chained at the Skyline Drive and at Park boundaries can be used for walking.

The Park Service has placed cement signposts at most trail junctions giving mileages to nearby roads or other trails. The termini of the fire foot trails are marked with yellow metal posts.

Trail descriptions have been grouped according to area to facilitate the planning of hikes. The PATC publications, *Circuit Hikes in the Shenandoah National Park* and *Walkers' Charts 1, 2 & 3* will also be found useful in hike planning. The three PATC maps of the Shenandoah Park: #9 Northern Section, #10 Central Section, and #11 Southern Section are valuable for use in conjunction with this Guide. USGS 7½ min. quadrangle maps are available but are chiefly of value for bushwhacking and exploring.

In giving detailed trail data in this section, description is given in one direction only. The distances indicated on the left are those in the direction indicated. Those on the right are the distances in the reverse direction.

NORTHERN SECTION

DICKEY RIDGE TRAIL
(DICKEY HILL TR.)

9.2 miles (14.8 kilometers)   PATC map No. 9: B-1

This is a very popular trail because of its accessibility and gentle grade. The northern end is at the northern entrance to the Skyline Drive. The trail parallels the Drive much of the way, crossing it at SDMP 2.1, again at Low Gap, and yet again at Lands Run Gap. The southern terminus is on the Appalachian Trail just north of Compton Gap, SDMP 10.4. Most of the climb along Dickey Ridge is between the northern end and the summit of Dickey Hill and involves a change in elevation of about 1700 ft. The remainder of the route consists of gentle ups and downs.

There are few views from this trail. Where it climbs nearly to the top of Dickey Hill there are glimpses west of the Shenandoah Valley. Outstanding views can be had by scrambling a few feet to the cleared summit of Dickey Hill. (Summit has been cleared because of a federal navigational installation, Vortac.) Near the southern end of the trail, the Fort Windham Rocks are of considerable interest.

Detailed trail data:

(N to S.) Front Royal to the *AT* near Compton Gap

0.0-9.2 Southern side of U.S. Rt. 340, at the southern limits of Front Royal. Trail cuts across open area of the Shenandoah Park's northern entrance and crosses to the right side of the Skyline Drive at the Entrance Parking Area, SDMP 0.0. From here trail ascends very gently along a small creek. Although close to the Drive here, it is effectively isolated from it by trees and a jungle of Japanese honeysuckle. At about 1.4m. it turns sharply right away from the creek and climbs more steeply.

1.9-7.3 Cross to left of Skyline Drive, SDMP 2.1. Continue to ascend. In about one-half mile the trail comes quite close to the Drive at the Shenandoah Valley Overlook from where there is a good view of Front Royal and Signal Knob in the Massanuttens.

There is a large patch of Virginia Bluebells right on the trail in this area, probably planted by a long ago resident of the area. Expect to find the bluebells in bloom the latter part of April.

4.0-5.2 The Skyline Drive is slightly above and to the right of the trail here. Cleared areas allow glimpses of Dickey Ridge Visitor Center and several side trails lead up to it. Among these is a new Park circuit trail, the Fox Hollow Tr., which cuts across the Dickey Ridge Tr. directly below the visitor center, descends about one-half mile to the former Fox Farm, then returns to the Dickey Ridge trail and follows it south about 0.2m. before turning up to the Drive. The 4th trail, the Fox FFT, also continues left of the Dickey Ridge Trail and follows an old road, down to Va. Sec. 645 which is parallel to and very near the Skyline Drive at the Pay Station. (The Dickey Ridge Trail-Fox FFT makes a nice circuit hike.)

4.5-4.7 Cross dirt road, Snead Rd. (To right the road leads a few feet to the Drive, just opposite the exit road of the Dickey Ridge Picnic Grounds, SDMP 5.1. To left, road leads into old apple orchard. An intersecting road leads to the Vortac installation atop Dickey Hill.)

5.3-3.9 Trail skirts along the ridge, just below the summit of Dickey Hill. Summit can be reached by a short scramble and offers sweeping views. From here trail descends gently.

7.0-2.2 Reach Low Gap, SDMP 7.9. Cross to right of the Skyline Drive.

8.0-1.2 Reach Lands Run Gap, SDMP 9.2 and cross to left of the Drive. (To the right, and south, Lands Run Fire Rd. leads 2.0m. to Park boundary and Va. Sec. 622 at a point about 2 miles east of Browntown. To left and north, the Harmony Hollow (Hickerson Hollow) FFT leads 1 m. down beyond the Park boundary to Va. Sec. 600 at a point about 3.5m. from U.S. 522.)

8.6-0.6 An old road leads left for 0.7m. to join the Compton Gap Rd. and *A T* at a point 0.3m. north of where the Dickey Ridge Tr. itself joins the *A T*.

9.0-0.2 Pass Fort Windham Rocks on the left. They are interesting to climb upon.

9.2-0.0 Junction with the *A T*, which is here coincident with the Compton Gap Rd, at a point on the *A T* 0.3m. from Compton Gap, SDMP 10.4. (To left, *A T* follows the road for 1.5m. then turns left and descends into Harmony Hollow reaching U.S. 522 in 3.8 additional miles. Compton Gap Rd. itself leads down to the Park boundary. As Va. Sec. 610 it continues to U.S. 522 at Chester Gap. Distance from Dickey Ridge Tr. to Chester Gap via this route, 3.7m.)

FOX FFT

approx. 2 miles (3 km.)   (PATC map No. 9: C-3)

This fire trail follows an old road down the mountain. Its upper end is on the Skyline Drive, just north of the entrance to the Dickey Ridge Picnic Grounds. It intersects the Dickey Ridge Trail in a few hundred feet. It is easy walking. The trail ends on Va. Sec. 645 at the Park boundary. It is easy to follow down Rt. 645 a short distance, then cut through the woods (SNP property) to the Skyline Drive just above the Pay Station. A spur trail, across the Drive, leads down to the Dickey Ridge Trail at a point about a half-mile from its lower end, thus making a circuit hike possible.

LANDS RUN FIRE RD.

2.0 miles (3.2 kilometers)   (PATC map No. 9: F-4)

Lands Run Fire Rd. leaves the Skyline Drive, SDMP 9.2, in Lands Run Gap and descends the west side of the Blue Ridge to the Park boundary where it connects with Va. Sec. 622, a narrow graveled road, at a point on the latter about 2m. NE of Browntown. About a half-mile from the Skyline Drive the road crosses Lands Run. The creek immediately below the road here is very pretty, falling rapidly in a series of cascades.

To reach the Lands Run Fire Rd. from below, drive to Browntown (which is about 6 miles east of Bentonville via Va. Sec. 613 and 7 miles SW of Front Royal on Va. Sec. 649). Turn east in Browntown onto Va. Sec. 634. In 1 mile turn left onto Va. Sec. 622. Reach fire road in 1 mile from this junction.

HARMONY HOLLOW (OR HICKERSON HOLLOW) TRAIL

1 mile (1.6 kilometers)   (PATC map No. 9: F-4)

This trail leads from Lands Run Gap, SDMP 9.2, northward down one of the branches of Happy Creek into Harmony Hollow. It ends outside the Park where it meets Va. Sec. 600 at a point on the road about 0.5m. from Va. Sec. 604, the main road through Harmony Hollow. (The land is posted along the stretch of trail between the Park boundary and Va. 600.) A circuit hike could include the *AT* from Va. Sec. 601 in Harmony Hollow uphill to its junction with the Dickey Ridge Trail, that trail to Lands Run Gap, and the Harmony Hollow Tr. back down the mountain, then a road walk down Rts. 600 and 604, and up 601 to the start, for a total distance of about 7 miles.

JENKINS GAP FFT

approx. 1 mile (1.6 kilometers)   (PATC map No. 9: G-6)

From the Skyline Drive, SDMP 12.3, follow the service road 0.2m. to a former landfill area. Below the landfill two old roads lead down into the hollow, the one on the right is the fire trail and is blazed, but not very well. The trail itself is not hard to follow. It passes through an area with much mountain laurel. Outside the park the trail continues another 0.2m. through private property (but presently open to hikers) to reach Va. Sec. 634 at a point 2.2m. from Browntown.

OLD BROWNTOWN RD. (western part of OLD BROWNTOWN-HARRIS HOLLOW RD.)

3.4 miles (5.5 kilometers)   (PATC map No. 9: F-9)

This old road runs down the west side of the Blue Ridge from Gravel Springs Gap, descending in switchbacks. There are frequent glimpses of Hogback Mtn. and Gimlet Ridge through the trees.

Access:

The road intersects the Skyline Drive in Gravel Springs Gap, SDMP 17.7. In 50 ft. it intersects the *AT*.

The lower end of the road can be reached by driving to Browntown (6m. east of Bentonville via Va. Sec. 613 and 7m. SW of Front Royal via Va. Sec. 649.) From Browntown follow Va. Sec. 631 for about 1 mile. Here, where Rt. 631 turns sharply right, the old Browntown Rd. is straight ahead. There is room for two cars to park. Do not drive up the old Browntown Rd. but start hiking here.

Detailed trail data:

From Rt. 631 to Skyline Drive

0.0-3.4 Junction with Va. Sec. 631. Follow old road along creek, Phils Arm Run. Land is posted on both sides of road so stay on road.

0.2-3.2 Take right fork and immediately cross creek. (Left fork leads through a gate into field.)

0.8-2.6 Where road forks, take right fork straight ahead. In a few yards road forks again and again take right fork straight ahead. (Avoid other roads to right which are gated.) Road soon begins to climb.

1.1-2.3 Cross into SNP. Road is gated here. Continue to climb. Road soon begins a series of switchbacks. There are occasional views of Hogback Mtn. and Gimlet Ridge.

3.4-0.0 Pass gate. In a few feet intersect the *AT* and a few feet farther reach the Skyline Drive, SDMP 17.7. (The road continues east of the Skyline Drive, passing the Gravel Springs shelter; then, as the Harris Hollow FFT, it descends into Harris Hollow reaching Va. Sec. 622. in about 2.6 miles from the Drive.)

COMPTON GAP FIRE ROAD—VA. SEC. 610

4.0 miles (6.4 kilometers)　　　　　(PATC map No. 9: G-4)

This fire road leads NE along the Blue Ridge crest from Compton Gap, SDMP 10.4, for 2.2 miles. Here it leaves the Park and becomes Va. Sec. 610. which continues another 1.8m.

to Chester Gap where U.S. 522 crosses the mountain; (the last 350 ft. of road is Va. Sec. 665.) The *AT*, until 1974, followed this route from Compton Gap to Chester Gap and continued across U.S. 522 following at first near the mountain crest, then on through woods to reach Mosby Shelter in another 2.5m. The present route of the *AT* follows the fire road from Compton Gap for 1.7m., then turns north away from it. The old route of the *AT*, from the *AT*-fire road junction down to Chester Gap and on to Mosby Shelter is now blue-blazed. Both loop hikes and a circuit hike can be made using combinations including the *AT* and the blue-blazed route.

Detailed description:
   Compton Gap to U.S. 522
   0.0-4.0 Junction with Skyline Drive, SDMP 10.4, el. 2415 ft. *AT* hikers traveling north will cross the Drive at this junction after descending Compton Mtn. From here the *AT* and fire road are coincident for the next 1.7m.
   0.1-3.9 Post on right marks trail to Indian Run Shelter, 0.5m. from this intersection. (See Chap. 6: "Shelters and Cabins")
   0.3-3.7 Intersection with Dickey Ridge Trail (left) and service road (right) leading to Indian Run Shelter. (Dickey Ridge Tr. leads north 9.2m. to entrance to Skyline Drive at Front Royal town limits. Fort Windham Rocks are 0.2m. from the fire road along this trail. Access road leads 0.4m. to Indian Run Shelter. Spring is 250 ft. from the service road, on the left, about 0.1m. before reaching the shelter.)
   0.6-3.4 Old road leads left 0.7m., coming into the Dickey Ridge Trail at a point 0.6m. north of its junction with the fire road.
   1.7-2.3 The *AT* turns left, away from the fire road here. Beyond this junction the road is blue-blazed.
   2.2-1.8 Pass gate and leave Park. Beyond this point road is Va. Sec. 610 and is paved. Blue blazes continue.
   3.9-0.1 Take left fork of road, Va. Sec. 665, and descend a short distance.
   4.0-0.0 Reach U.S. 522 in Chester Gap. (Blue-blazed trail continues along the ridge and through woods for another 2.5m. to rejoin the *AT* at Mosby Shelter.) To the left along U.S. 522 it is

1.5m. to the *A T* crossing and 3.2m. farther to the junction of U.S.
522 with Va. Rt. 55 in Front Royal.

SIDE TRAILS IN THE NORTH AND
SOUTH MARSHALL MOUNTAINS AREA

This group of trails includes the Mt. Marshall Fire Rd., the
Bluff Trail, the Peak Trail, the Big Devil Stairs Tr. and the
Harris Hollow FFT (part of the old Browntown Harris Hollow
Rd.)

Access:

From *Skyline Drive* there are two points of access. The Mt.
Marshall Fire Rd. enters the Drive at milepost 12.5, just south
of Jenkins Gap Overlook. At, Gravel Springs Gap, SDMP 17.7,
the Old Browntown-Harris Hollow Rd. descends eastward
paralleling the *A T* for a short distance and, in 0.3m., intersects
the Bluff Trail at Gravel Springs. One can also follow the *A T*
from Gravel Springs Gap 0.2m. to the start of the Bluff Trail.

From the *east,* access to the area is through the town of
Washington, Va. From the main corner of the town go north
one block on Va. Sec. 628, then turn left on Va. Sec. 622. *To
reach the Mt. Marshall Fire Rd.,* follow Rt. 622 for 2.4m., then
turn right onto Va. Sec. 625 and follow for 0.5m. to sign
indicating parking area. On foot continue along Rt. 625 for
another 0.5m. to sign marking blue-blazed trail which leads
over stone wall at right. Follow trail 250 yds. to reach Mt.
Marshall Fire Rd. Turn left onto road. (Road to east here is
closed to hikers) *To reach bottom of Big Devil Stairs Tr.* follow
Va. Sec. 622 4.0 miles from Washington, Va. and 0.1m. west of
stream crossing. *To reach bottom of the Harris Hollow FFT*
follow Va. Sec. 622 for about 5 miles to the head of Harris
Hollow. Trail starts just before reaching the highest elevation of
Rt. 622.

MT. MARSHALL FIRE RD.

5.7 miles (9.1 kilometers)   (PATC map No. 9: G-6)

The fire road is valuable in providing access to the Bluff Tr.

and the Peak Tr.; also for use in several circuit hikes. The upper 4 miles are almost level. The lower end of the road has been closed shortly below the Park boundary, but a blue-blazed access trail has been constructed so that the lower portion of road is again available to the hiker.

Detailed trail data:

Skyline Drive to Harris Hollow

0.0-5.7 Intersection with Skyline Drive, SDMP 12.5, just south of Jenkins Gap Overlook. Road contours along eastern slopes of the Blue Ridge for 2 miles, then descends slightly.

2.4-3.3 Junction with Bluff Trail. (To right, Bluff Tr. leads 3.1m. to junction with Big Devils Stairs Trail and 1.6m. farther to the *A T* near Gravel Springs Gap.)

3.9-1.8 Intersection with the Peak Trail in the Peak Saddle, Thorofare Gap.

5.0-0.6 Pass chain across road near **Park boundary**.

5.3-0.4 Pass through wooden gate.

5.5-0.2 Turn right off road onto blue-blazed trail.

5.7-0.0 Trail junction with Va. Sec. 625. From here it is a 0.5m. walk to left along Rt. 625 to parking area and another 0.5m. to the junction of Rt. 625 with the main road through Harris Hollow, Va. Sec. 622.

BLUFF TRAIL

4.7 miles (7.6 kilometers)   (PATC map No. 9: G-10)

"Bluff" was a local name for Mt. Marshall. The trail slabs around the southern and eastern slopes of the mountain with a very gentle grade. It provides access to the Big Devils Stairs Trail and the Peak Trail and is also useful in circuit hikes.

Detailed trail data:

From *A T* to Mt. Marshall Fire Rd., S to N

0.0-4.7 Junction with *A T*, 0.2m. south of Gravel Springs Gap, SDMP 17.7

0.2-4.5 Intersection with old Browntown-Harris Hollow Rd. at Gravel Springs. Gravel Springs Shelter is 100 ft. to right. See Chap. 6: "Shelters and Cabins." (Old Harris Hollow Rd., now a fire foot trail, leads down about 2.2 miles to Va. Sec. 622.)

1.6-3.1 Junction with Big Devil Stairs Trail which leads right, downhill.

3.4-1.3 Junction with the Peak Trail which leads right, crossing the Mt. Marshall Fire Rd. in 0.3m.

4.7-0.0 Reach Mt. Marshall Fire Rd. (To left, road is 2.4m. to Skyline Drive, SDMP 12.5; to right, it is 3.3m. to Va. Sec. 625.)

THE PEAK TRAIL

1.8 miles (including loop) (2.9 km.)   (PATC map No. 9:I-8)

A short but steep climb to summit of "The Peak", el. 3020 ft.

0.0 Junction with Bluff Tr. at a point 3.4m. from the *AT* near Gravel Springs Gap.

0.3 Cross Mt. Marshall Fire Rd. in Thorofare Gap. (To left on road it is 3.9m. to Skyline Drive; to right, 1.8m. to Va. Sec. 625 in Harris Hollow.) From this intersection trail ascends steeply.

0.7-1.8 Reach trail fork where loop begins, (description given in clockwise direction) Ascend left fork, being careful of loose rock.

1.1-1.4 Reach wooded summit of The Peak. (Side trail on left leads to viewpoint.) Continue along crest of ridge, then bear right descending.

1.4-1.1 Turn sharp right downhill onto old road. (To left old road leads 250 ft. to excellent viewpoint.)

1.8-0.7 Reach end of loop.

BIG DEVILS STAIRS TRAIL

1.9 miles (3.0 kilometers)   (PATC map No. 9: H-9)

The Big Devils Stairs canyon is one of the most impressive features of the Shenandoah Park. The trail is rough and calls for considerable exertion and some caution, especially in wet or icy weather. The canyon offers exceptional opportunities for rock climbing. Description given from the Bluff Trail to Harris Hollow.

0.0-1.9 Junction with Bluff Trail, 1.6m. from the *AT* near Gravel Springs Gap.

0.2-1.7 Enter canyon area. Trail descends steeply, along the creek edge. (Creek is a branch of the Rush River.) Trail crosses the creek several times and is quite rough.

1.2-0.7 Pass Park boundary. From here trail remains on the southwest side of the creek, gradually leaving it.

1.9-0.0 Junction with Va. Sec. 622 in Harris Hollow at a point about 0.1m. west of the creek and 4.0m. from Washington.

HARRIS HOLLOW FFT
(eastern portion of the Old Browntown-Harris Hollow Rd.)

2.5 miles (4.0 kilometers)   (PATC map No. 9: G-10)

The fire foot trail is useful for circuit hikes when used with either the Mt. Marshall Fire Rd. or the Big Devils Stairs Trail. Trail description is from Skyline Drive to Va. Sec. 622.

0.0-2.5 Skyline Drive at Gravel Springs Gap, SDMP 17.7.

0.3-2.2 Reach Gravel Springs. The Gravel Springs Shelter is on the right.

1.0-1.5 Reach Park boundary.

1.7-0.8 Cross small stream near its head.

2.5-0.0 Reach Va. Sec. 622 in Harris Hollow at a point 5m. from Washington, Va. To left, on Rt. 622, it is 1.2m. to the foot of the Big Devils Stairs Trail and 5 miles to Washington. To the right, it is between six and seven miles via Va. Sec. 622, 623, and 614 to the foot of Little Devils Stairs Trail and Keyser Run Fire Rd.

TRAILS IN THE RANGE VIEW CABIN AREA—
EAST OF THE SKYLINE DRIVE

The Jinney Gray Fire Road and the Piney Branch Trail are the major routes in the area. Trails that intersect one or both of these include the Piney Ridge Tr., the Little Devils Stairs Tr., the Pole Bridge Link, the PLD Rd., Keyser Run Fire Rd., and the North Fork Rd. There are also in the area some fire foot trails that are usable by experienced hikers—the Fork Mtn. FFT, Thornton Hollow FFT and Hull School FFT (the former Beahms Gap Road). Range View Cabin is ideally situated for campers who wish to hike in this area or in the adjacent Matthews Arm-Elkwallow area. Cabin reservations must be made in advance at PATC Headquarters; see Chap. 6: "Shelters and Cabins".

Access to the area:

I. From the Skyline Drive there are four points of access:

a. *SDMP 19.4:* Here is the upper end of the Jinney Gray Fire Road. Also at this mile post, but across the Drive from the fire road, a spur trail goes west to connect with the *AT* in 100 ft. One mile down the fire road is "Four-Way", the point where the Little Devils Stairs Trail goes off to the left (east) and the Pole Bridge Link Trail goes to the right.

b. *SDMP 22.1:* Here a service road (gated) leads by Piney River Ranger Station and on east to Range View Cabin, intersecting the *AT*. Both the Piney Branch Trail and the Piney Ridge Trail have their upper ends on this road (and on or near the *AT*).

c. *SDMP 21.9:* The *AT* crosses the Drive here, just south of the Rattlesnake Point Overlook. Follow the *AT* south for 0.4m. to reach the upper end of the Piney Branch Trail and another 0.4m. to reach the intersection with the service road to Range View Cabin. The upper end of the Piney Ridge Trail is a few feet down the road from this intersection.

II. From the Piedmont north of Sperryville there are three points of access:

a. *Lower end of Jinney Gray Fire Road:* To reach this point turn northwest from U.S. 522-211 onto Va. Sec. 612 at a point just north of the Thornton River bridge north of the town. In 1.3m. continue ahead on Va. Sec. 600 following the Piney River. Reach a junction with Va. Sec. 653, which enters from the left, when 3.3m. from U.S. 522-211. Park car near this junction. Continue along Rt. 600 on foot to its end, about 0.1m. Here the Jinney Gray Fire Rd. leads left, crossing the Piney River, then continuing up the river for 0.6m. before entering the Park.

The lower ends of the Piney Branch Trail and Piney Ridge Trail can be reached from the Jinney Gray Fire Rd. The fire road also connects with the old North Fork Rd., the PLD Road, and the Keyser Run Fire Rd. Fords of the Piney River along the lower stretch of the Jinney Gray Fire Rd. may be difficult in wet weather.

   b. *Lower end of the North Fork Road:* Turn off U.S. 522-211 as described above but continue on Va. Sec. 612 where it forks left at its junction with Va. Sec. 600. About 3.2m. from the junction reach the end of state maintenance and park. Continue up the road on foot and, in 0.1m., enter the Park. This road, the old North Fork Road, continues up the North Fork of the Thornton River for 1.4m.; then it turns sharply right, climbs over the Fork Mtn. ridge in a sag and descends to the Piney River where it ends at the Jinney Gray Fire Rd. There are no fords on the North Fork Rd. (but one just beyond its end on the Jinney Gray Fire Rd.) The Hull School FFT and the Thornton Hollow FFT come into this old road and the Fork Mtn. FFT crosses it.

   c. *Lower ends of the Little Devils Stairs Trail and Keyser Run Road:* From U.S. 522-211 at the southwest side of the bridge over the Covington River, about 2.5m. north of Sperryville, turn west onto Va. Sec. 622. Follow Rt. 622 for 2.0m. to just past the bridge over the Covington River. There take the left fork which is Va. Sec. 614 and follow it about 3.0m. to the start of the Little Devils Stairs Trail. *Do not park on private land* at the trail entrance. On weekends one can park about 0.2m. back where sign indicates a schoolbus stop (across from a house). Keyser Run Fire Rd. is a continuation of Va. Rt. 614 and is gated at the Park boundary.

JINNEY GRAY FIRE ROAD

6.4 miles (10.3 kilometers)   (PATC map No. 9: G-11)

   This is a pleasant road to hike with an easy gradient most of the way. It is also an important route as it offers access to the Little Devils Stairs Tr., Pole Bridge Link, Piney Branch Tr., and other trails in the area. Across the Drive from its upper end

a short spur trail leads west to the *AT*, thus extending the
number of circuit hikes for which the fire road can be used.

Access:

The upper end starts at the Skyline Drive, SDMP 19.4, at the
east base of Little Hogback Mtn. A short spur trail (100 ft.)
between the *AT* and a point on the Drive directly opposite the
fire road gives access from the *AT*. The lower end can be
reached from VA. Sec. 600 on the Piney River. (See details in
previous section.)

Detailed trail data:

From Skyline Drive to Va. Sec. 600

0.0-6.4 From south or "east" side of the Skyline Drive,
SDMP 19.4, the fire road drops very gradually, passing around
the head of the hollow containing Little Devils Stairs.

1.0-5.4 Reach "Four-Way". To left the Little Devils Stairs
Tr. leads 2.0m. down to Va. Sec. 614. To right Pole Bridge Link
leads 1.0m. to Piney Branch Trail.

3.0-3.4 Keyser Run Fire Rd. leads left 1.7 to Va. Sec. 614 and
the lower end of Little Devils Stairs Tr.

3.9-2.5 The PLD Road comes in from the left. (The PLD
Road leads 0.4m. to the Keyser Run Fire Rd.) Just before
reaching the junction there is a sheltered spring to the right of
the Jinney Gray Fire Rd.

4.3-2.1 Junction with the Piney Branch Trail which enters
the road from the right.

4.5-1.9 Road junction just beyond ford of Piney River. To
the right the old North Fork Rd. leads over the sag in Fork Mtn.
to the North Fork of the Thornton River, then down it. Jinney
Gray Fire Rd. continues straight ahead. Below the junction
there are two more fords of the Piney River.

5.7-0.7 Road is gated at the Park boundary.

6.3-0.1 Turn left across bridge, blocked to cars by cable.

6.4-0.0 Reach the junction of Va. Sec. 600 and 653.

LITTLE DEVILS STAIRS TRAIL

2.0 miles (3.2 kilometers)   (PATC map No. 9: H-12)

This trail follows up Keyser Run into the canyon known as Little Devils Stairs. The canyon area is steep, wild and picturesque. Its sheer cliffs are outstanding; they offer a challenge to rock climbers. The trail's upper end is at "Four-Way" on the Jinney Gray Fire Road, 1.0m. from the Skyline Drive and the *A T*. The lower end is reached via Va. Sec. 622 and 614 from U.S. 522-211. (See "Access to Trails in the Range View Cabin area")

The trail route is dangerous in wet or icy weather and even in good weather must be negotiated with care. For a circuit hike it is wise to ascend the Little Devils Stairs Trail, and to descend via the Jinney Gray and Keyser Run Fire Roads.

Detailed trail data:

From Va. Sec. 614 to Jinney Gray Fire Rd. at "Four-Way"

0.0-2.0 Start at road, Va. Sec. 614, and follow blue-blazed route which goes north from the road and shortly crosses Keyser Run. (Rt. 614 west of the trailhead is known as the Keyser Run Fire Rd. It enters the Park in 0.3m. and reaches the PLD Rd. in about 1.3m, and the Jinney Gray Fire Rd. in 1.7m.)

0.6-1.4 Take trail to left and continue into canyon. Trail crosses Keyser Run frequently as it climbs steeply along the creek.

1.7-0.3 Reach small waterfall at the head of the canyon. Trail bears left from the creek, still ascending steeply.

2.0-0.0 Reach Jinney Gray Fire Rd. at "Four-Way", a point 1.0m. from the Skyline Drive (and *A T*) along the fire road and 1.0m. from the Piney Branch Trail via the Pole Bridge Link straight across the road. A short circuit hike starting at the end of Va. Sec. 614 would include ascending the 2.0m. of Little Devils Stairs, then descending the Jinney Gray Fire Rd. 2.0m. to the Keyser Run Fire Rd., then descending that road 1.7m. to reach the start of the circuit.

KEYSER RUN FIRE ROAD

1.7 miles (2.7 kilometers)   (PATC map No. 9: H-12)

PLD ROAD

0.4 miles (0.6 kilometers)   (PATC map No. 9: H-13)

The name, Keyser Run Rd., is generally applied to Va. Sec. 614 for the 0.3m from the Little Devils Stairs Trailhead to the Park boundary as well as to the road's continuation within the Park. Access from U.S. 522-211 is via Va. Sec. 622 and 614. (See "Access to Trails in the Range View Cabin area").

About 1.3m. up the road from the Little Devils Stairs Tr. the road forks; the left fork, straight ahead, is the PLD Road (PLD originally stood for *P*iney Branch-*L*ittle *D*evils Stairs); the right fork continues as the Keyser Run Fire Rd. On the right, just beyond the fork, is the old Bolen Cemetery. In another 0.4m. the Keyser Run Rd. ends on the Jinney Gray Fire Rd. at a point on the latter 3.0m. from the Skyline Drive and 0.9m. above its junction with the PLD Rd.

The PLD Rd., the left fork mentioned above, descends southward for 0.4m. and ends also on the Jinney Gray Fire Rd. at a point on the latter 3.9m. from the Drive and 0.4m. above its junction with the Piney Branch Trail.

POLE BRIDGE LINK

1.0 miles (1.5 kilometers)   (PATC map No. 9: F-12)

This trail links the Jinney Gray Fire Rd. and Little Devils Stairs Trail with the Piney Branch Trail.

Detailed trail data:
     Jinney Gray Fire Rd. to Piney Branch Trail
     0.0-1.0 "Four-Way" intersection on Jinney Gray Fire Rd., 1.0m. from Skyline Drive (and the *AT*). Little Devils Stairs Trail also starts here, from the opposite side of the fire road.
     0.8-0.2 Take less-worn left fork. (Right fork is a cut-off trail, about a quarter mile in length, which reaches Piney Branch

Trail about 0.2m. up from the Pole Bridge Link-Piney Branch Trail intersection.)

1.0-0.0 Intersection with Piney Branch Trail. (To right, via Piney Branch Trail, the *AT* is 1.4m. and Range View Cabin 0.4m. farther. To left the Jinney Gray Fire Rd. is 2.8m. and the lower end of the Piney Ridge Trail is 2.4m.)

PINEY BRANCH TRAIL

4.2 miles (6.8 kilometers)   (PATC map No. 9: E-13)

This trail, with the Piney Ridge Trail, provides a circuit hike from Range View Cabin. Another circuit could include this trail, the Pole Bridge Link and Jinney Gray Fire Rd. A somewhat longer circuit would be Little Devils Stairs, Pole Bridge Link, this trail, a little stretch of Jinney Gray Fire Rd., the PLD Rd., and Keyser Run Rd. Yet another circuit trip could be the *AT* between the Piney Ridge Tr. junction and Jinney Gray Fire Rd., the Jinney Gray Fire Rd. down to "Four-Way", then the Pole Bridge Link, and back up Piney Branch Trail to the start.

Access:

The upper end of the trail starts at the *AT* and the service road leading to Range View Cabin. (See PATC Map #9, insert of Range View Cabin area) Start of the trail is 0.4m. north of Range View Cabin and 0.4m. from the Skyline Drive at Rattlesnake Point, SDMP 21.9, via the *AT*. (and about 0.3m. from the Drive via the service road at Piney River Ranger Station, SDMP 22.1.) The lower end of the trail is on the Jinney Gray Fire Rd. 2.1m. from its lower end on Va. Sec. 600. See "Access to Trails in the Range View Cabin area" for details.

Detailed trail data:

From *AT* to Jinney Gray Fire Rd.

0.0-4.2 Intersection with *AT*, 0.4m. north of Range View Cabin and 0.4m. south of Skyline Drive at Rattlesnake Point. Trail leads east at signpost. It follows an old road down the mountain, through overgrown fields and woods. Follow blue blazes.

1.2-3.0 Take less-worn right fork, downhill. (Left fork is a cut-off trail, about a quarter mile in length, to the Pole Bridge Link Trail.)

1.3-2.9 Cross Piney Branch at site of the former Pole Bridge.

1.4-2.8 Junction with Pole Bridge Link Tr. which comes in from the left. (Via Pole Bridge Link it is 1.0m to "Four-Way" on Jinney Gray Fire Rd.) Turn right at this junction. Trail now follows stream, crossing it at 2.7m., 3.0m. and 3.5m.

3.8-0.4 Junction with Piney Ridge Trail which enters from right. (Range View Cabin is 3.4m. from this junction via Piney Ridge Tr.)

4.1-0.1 Cross Piney Branch.

4.2-0.0 Junction with Jinney Gray Fire Rd. at a point on the latter 2.1m. from the junction of Va. Sec. 600 and 653.

PINEY RIDGE TRAIL

3.3 miles (5.3 kilometers)   (PATC map No. 9: F-13)

This blue-blazed trail used along with the Piney Branch Trail, provides a circuit hike from the Range View Cabin.

Access:

The upper end of the Piney Ridge Trail may be reached by following the service road from the Skyline Drive (SDMP 22.1) past the Piney River Ranger Station south about 0.7m., crossing the *AT* a few feet before reaching the start of the Piney Ridge Trail which leads right from the road. (The trailhead is within sight of the Range View Cabin at the road's end.) One can also start at Rattlesnake Point Overlook and follow the *AT* south for 0.8m. to its intersection with the service road, then turn left onto the road toward the cabin and, in a few feet, reach the start of the Piney Ridge Trail. See inset map of area, on back of PATC map #9. The lower end of the Piney Ridge Trail is on the Piney Branch Tr. 0.4m. on that trail from its lower end on the Jinney Gray Fire Rd.

Detailed trail data:

From Range View Cabin Service Rd. (near *AT*) to Piney Branch Trail

0.0-3.3 Junction with service road, just west of Range View Cabin. Trail bears south, descending along crest of the ridge.

2.0-1.3 Pass old cemetery to right of the trail; a few feet beyond take left fork (east) at trail intersection. (Straight ahead the yellow-blazed Fork Mtn. FFT continues along the ridge, crossing the North Fork Rd. in about 1.2m.) As one descends one may find traces of an old homesite.

2.5-0.8 Where the main trail turns to the left an unmarked trail leads right to connect with the Fork Mtn. FFT.

3.3-0.0 Reach Piney Branch Trail at a point on that trail 0.4m. from its lower end on the Jinney Gray Fire Rd.

NORTH FORK ROAD

3.3 miles (5.4 kilometers)   (PATC map No. 9: J-15)

This old road follows up the North Fork, Thornton River, then leads over Fork Mtn. to the Jinney Gray Fire Rd. on the Piney River. It links the Hull School FFT (formerly the Beahms Gap Rd.), the Thornton Hollow FFT, and the Fork Mtn. FFT with the trails farther north. Access to the Park via this route is particularly useful when wet weather causes fording problems along the lowest portion of the Jinney Gray Fire Rd. See "Access to Trails in the Range View Cabin area".

Detailed trail data:

From junction of Va. Sec. 612 and 653 to Jinney Gray Fire Rd. Rd.

0.0-3.3 From junction of Rts. 612 and 653 continue up Rt. 612 on foot.

0.6-2.7 State road maintenance ends.

0.7-2.6 Road gated at Park boundary. There is a spring to right of the road just beyond the gate.

2.0-1.3 Junction with Hull School FFT. Here the road turns sharply to the right away from the river. In a few feet the Thornton Hollow FFT comes in from the left.

2.7-0.6 Reach top of the Fork Mtn. ridge in a deep sag. Fork Mtn. FFT crosses road here.

3.3-0.0 Junction with the Jinney Gray Fire Rd. at a point on that road 2.0m. from the junction of Va. Sec. 600 and 653, and

0.2m. below the Piney Branch Tr.-Jinney Gray Fire Rd. junction.

FORK MTN. FFT

2.2 miles (3.5 kilometers)   (PATC map No. 9: G-14)

This yellow-blazed trail leads along the Fork Mtn. ridge from the Piney Ridge Trail, southeastward to the Park boundary. The old trail is no longer followable outside the Park. The 1.2m. stretch between the Piney Ridge Trail and its intersection with the old North Fork Rd. can be useful in circuit hikes but should not be used by inexperienced hikers.

HULL SCHOOL FFT (formerly the Beahms Gap Rd.)

approx. 2 miles (3 kilometers)   (PATC map No. 9: G-16)

This trail, most of it following the old road, leads from the Skyline Drive at Beahms Gap, SDMP 28.1, down to the North Fork Rd. on the Thornton River, joining the road at the site of the former Hull School. The trail is only sporadically cleared or blazed and is difficult to follow, especially in summer. It should be used by experienced hikers only.

THORNTON HOLLOW FFT

approx. 3 miles (5 kilometers)   (PATC map No. 9: F-15)

The fire trail leaves the Skyline Drive, SDMP 25.2, and descends into Thornton Hollow. It comes into the old North Fork Rd. at a point on the road 2 miles above the junction of Va. Rts. 612 and 653 and a few feet from the road's junction with the Hull School FFT. Both ends of the Thornton River FFT are marked by yellow posts. The trail is badly overgrown and there are many "false" trails in the area, confusing to a novice. It should be used only by the experienced hiker prepared to bushwhack.

TRAIL NETWORK IN THE MATTHEWS ARM-
ELKWALLOW AREA (WEST OF SKYLINE DRIVE)

This trail network includes the Big Blue Trail, the Overall Run Trail, Matthews Arm Fire Rd., Knob Mtn. Tr. (part of it fire road), Jeremys Run Tr., Elkwallow Trail, the Knob Mtn.-Jeremys Run Cut-off Tr., Neighbor Mtn. Tr., the Traces Tr. (a nature trail at Matthews Arm Campround), and a number of fire foot trails.

Historical note: Mat(t)hews Arm was part of a grant of land made by Lord Fairfax to Israel Mathews. Many of Israel's decendents still live in Warren County.

BIG BLUE TRAIL

(Description of the section of this major trail which lies between the Appalachian Trail in the Shenandoah Park and U.S. Rt. 340.)

7.5 miles (12.0 kilometers)   (PATC map No. 9: E-12)

OVERALL RUN TRAIL

(This trail follows the same route as the Big Blue Trail for 4.5 miles of its length.)

5.6 miles (9.0 kilometers)   (PATC map No. 9: E-12)

The Big Blue-Tuscarora Trail, when completed, will extend about 220 miles, with its southern terminus at the Appalachian Trail on Hogback Mountain in the SNP and its northern terminus also on the *AT* near Duncannon, Pa. Much of the route has been completed but, at the time of the printing of this edition, one large gap remains—from near Capon Springs, West Virginia, south of U.S. Rt. 50, to Hancock, Md. It is complete from Capon Springs south to the *AT* on Hogback Mtn., a stretch of 50 trail miles. West of U.S. Rt. 340 the route crosses the south branch of the Shenandoah River at the Bentonville Low Water Bridge, then climbs west over the ridges of the Massanutten, crosses the main Shenandoah Valley in the area of Toms Brook, climbs Little North Mountain and zigzags its way west to the Va.-W. Va. State line from where it runs generally northeast.

Within the SNP the Big Blue utilizes the route of the Overall Run Trail for much of the distance. Below the point where they separate, the Overall Run Tr. continues on down the creek as far as the Park boundary. The landowner has closed that portion of trail outside the Park.

Just off the Big Blue-Overall Run Trail, at a point 2.8m. from the *AT* and 4.6m. from Rt. 340 via the Big Blue Tr., is the beautiful cascade, Overall Run Falls. This is one of the prettiest spots in the northern section of the Park. The falls here is considered the highest in the Park. Caution: The Big Blue Tr. is extremely steep near here and the side trail to the base of the falls is very rough.

Access:

To reach the southern end of the Big Blue Trail, follow the *AT* south for 0.4m. from the *AT* crossing of the Skyline Drive at SDMP 21.1, or follow the *AT* north 0.6m. from the crossing of the Drive at SDMP 21.9, just south of Rattlesnake Point Overlook which provides parking space. Cement post on the *AT* identifies the trail here as the Big Blue Tr. and the Overall Run Tr.

To reach the NW end of this section of the Big Blue Tr., drive along U.S. Rt. 340 to a point about 1.5m. south of Bentonville (and 300 yds. south of Va. Sec. 628) and 1.1m. north of Overall. There is room for parking on the west side of Rt. 340 here. Directly across the highway the Big Blue Trail heads eastward along a farm road.

Detailed trail data:

From the *AT* to U.S. 340

0.0-7.5 Junction with *AT*. The Big Blue-Overall Run Tr. descends to the west.

0.7-6.8 Turn sharply right. Straight ahead a short, connecting trail leads 250 ft. to Matthews Arm Nature Tr. (Traces Tr.), and beyond to the northern part of the Matthews Arm Campground. (Follow the Nature Trail to the left for 0.5m. to reach parking area and the entrance road to the Campground.) The Big Blue-Overall Run Tr. continues to descend gently, skirting a swampy area known as Bearwallow.

2.3-5.2 Come into Matthews Arm Rd. at its junction with the Gimlet Ridge FFT. Continue ahead on the road (left fork) for 250 ft., then turn left from it and descend steeply.

2.4-5.1 At trail junction turn sharply right. (To left is old Overall Run Trail route.) Continue descent. Several spur trails lead left to views of Overall Run Falls and the valley below. Beyond these, the trail becomes very steep.

2.8-4.7 Blue-blazed spur trail leads left 0.2m. to foot of Overall Falls. (Spur trail is very rugged; dangerous in icy weather.) Beyond the junction the main trail continues to descend steeply.

3.2-4.3 About here the trail levels out and approaches Overall Run.

3.4-4.1 Trail crosses to south side of the creek.

3.8-3.7 Trail recrosses creek (to north bank)

4.5-3.0 Concrete post marks separation point of Big Blue and Overall Run Trails. (Description of the lower part of the Overall Run Trail follows after description of the Big Blue Tr.) The Big Blue turns sharply right here and ascends.

4.7-2.8 Turn 90° to left. (Old Thompson Hollow FFT continues straight ahead.) Big Blue now follows the trace of an old road.

5.2-2.3 Take left fork of the old road, heading northwest. Then bear around or over several hills with relatively little change in elevation.

6.0-1.5 Begin descent.

6.2-1.3 Make a sharp right turn. (An old trail continues ahead, reaching Park boundary in about 100 ft.) Trail now descends along the Park boundary, crossing in and out several times.

6.4-1.1 Cross creek and turn left. 200 ft. farther, leave Park. Ascend gradually along old road.

6.5-1.0 Turn back sharply to the right while continuing to climb.

6.6-0.9 Again turn right, returning to the Park boundary and following it a short distance. Then descend gradually through pines, passing a pasture on the left.

7.0-0.5 Cross gate and turn sharply left, following the southwest edge of pasture. At lower corner of pasture, nearly under power-line, bear right downhill, heading directly toward railroad underpass in the hollow. (Trail through meadow is marked with stakes, blue-blazed)

7.3-0.2 Reach farm road and turn left onto it. Pass through railroad underpass.

7.5-0.0 Reach U.S. 340. at a point on the highway 1.5m. south of Bentonville and 1.1m. north of Overall.

Overall Run Trail:
East to West

0.0-5.6 Junction with *A T*. Trail coincident with the *A T* here. (For the first 4.5m. of the Overall Run Tr. see description of the Big Blue Tr.)

4.5-1.1 Concrete post marks separation point of Big Blue and Overall Run Trails. Overall Run Tr. continues straight ahead along creek. (Big Blue turns sharply right here away from creek.)

4.6-1.0 Spur trail leads a few hundred feet to the left to the lower falls.

5.1-0.5 Beecher Ridge FFT enters from the left.

5.4-0.2 Trail crosses to south side of the creek.

5.6-0.0 Reach Park boundary. Trail below this point is on private property and is closed to the public.

JEREMYS RUN TRAIL

6.2 miles (10.0 kilometers)   (PATC map No. 9: E-14)

Jeremys Run Trail is one of the most delightful routes in the park. From the park boundary at the base of the western slope of the Blue Ridge, it leads up Jeremys Run in a deep gorge between two projecting spurs, Knob Mtn. and Neighbor Mtn., to the Appalachian Trail at a point 0.3m. from the Elkwallow Picnic Grounds. The whole of this valley is beautifully forested; the run itself is a continual series of cascades and pools. The hiking is generally easy, with a gentle rise in elevation and numerous rockhopping crossings of the stream. The exceptions are two very steep stretches—the lowest 0.5m. and the uppermost 0.8m. The valley abounds with wild life. Deer are frequently seen, beaver-felled saplings are common, and bear scat can be found on the trail, though the bears themselves are seldom sighted. Jeremys Run is considered one of the fine trout streams in the park.

Access:

The upper or northeast end of the trail can be reached by following the *A T* south 0.6m. from the Skyline Drive crossing in Elkwallow Gap, SDMP 23.9, or by following a short spur trail from the Elkwallow Picnic Grounds to the *A T* and then down the *A T* 0.3m.

To reach the lower or southwestern end of the trail turn east from Rt. 340 at Big Spring (5 m. north of Luray) onto Va. Sec. 654. In 1.4m. turn left onto Va. Sec. 611. Follow Rt. 611 for about 1 mile to Jeremys Run but do not cross bridge. Turn right onto a farm road. At first fork bear left, fording Jeremys Run. Continue up road, passing through gate into farmyard of Mr. Clarence Deaver. Parking is a problem. Deaver, at times, permits parking on his ground for a small fee, but it is perhaps best to park back on 611. The Park Boundary and start of Jeremys Run Trail are about 100 yds. beyond this property.

Detailed trail data:

From *A T* downhill

0.0-6.2 Junction with *A T*, 0.3m. south of Elkwallow Picnic Grounds (and 0.6m. south of the Skyline Drive at Elkwallow Gap via the *A T*) Trail descends steeply.

0.8-5.4 Junction with Knob Mtn. Cut-Off Trail. (A possible circuit hike of about 6m. would include the 0.8m. of Jeremys Run Tr., the Knob Mtn. Cut-Off Tr., the upper portion of the Knob Mtn. Tr., the Elkwallow Tr. and the 0.6m. stretch of *A T*.) One hundred yards beyond the junction, cross the first of the many fords of Jeremys Run.

3.1-3.1 Cross the 11th ford of the creek at the halfway point of the trail.

4.8-1.4 Pass the largest of the waterfalls on Jeremys Run.

5.4-0.8 Junction with the Neighbor Trail which enters from the left. 50 ft. farther the Knob Mtn. Trail enters from the right.

5.5-0.7 Cross the 16th and final ford.
6.2-0.0 Reach park boundary.

KNOB MTN. TRAIL—KNOB MTN. FIRE RD.

7.6 miles (12.2 kilometers)   (PATC map No. 9: E-12)

The trail and fire road are coincident for the first 4.3m. from Matthews Arm Campground to where the roadway ends. Beyond, the trail route follows a footpath, passing over the peak of Knob Mtn., descending along the ridge crest, then dropping down to Jeremys Run. This section is unmarked but the graded footway is unmistakable.

Access:
To reach the upper end of trail and road turn west from the Skyline Drive, SDMP 22.2, onto the entrance road to Matthews Arm Campground and drive a half-mile to the parking area at the entrance station. (In winter the entrance road to the campground is closed so it is necessary to walk down from the Drive. One can avoid the paved road by following an abandoned section of the Matthews Arm Fire Rd. which parallels the entrance road a few feet to the south.) From the parking area follow on foot the paved road leading left to the trailor sewage disposal area. Knob Mtn. Tr. (and Fire Rd.) starts at the far side of the paved road's turnaround loop. (See inset map of Matthews Arm area, back of PATC map #9.) Start of trail is 0.9m. from the Skyline Drive.
The lower end is reached via the Jeremys Run Trail. See description of that trail.

Detailed trail data:
From Matthews Arm Campground to Jeremys Run
0.0-7.5 From loop in paved campground road, follow graveled road beyond chain.
0.4-7.1 Heiskell Hollow FFT junction. (The fire trail leads right 3.3m. down to the Park boundary near the town of Compton. Another fire trail, the Molden Hollow (or Dry Run) FFT branches left from the Heiskell Hollow FFT, and more or

less parallels the Knob Mtn. Tr. Both follow old wood roads, now somewhat overgrown.)

2.1-5.2 Faint trail on right leads down to the Molden Hollow Tr.

2.2-5.3 To left, the Knob Mtn. (Jeremys Run) Cut-Off Trail, marked with yellow blazes, leads 0.5m. steeply down to Jeremys Run Tr. at a point on the latter 0.8m. from the *AT*. (A six mile circuit hike would include the 2.2m. of Knob Mtn. Tr., the Knob Mtn. Cut-Off Tr., the upper portion of Jeremys Run Tr., the *AT* back to Elkwallow Gap, then the Elkwallow Tr. back to Matthews Arm Campground.)

4.3-3.2 The roadway ends here, just short of the highest peak of Knob Mtn. The trail continues as a much narrower footway, immediately climbing over the peak, 2865 ft., then descending along the ridge crest, finally dropping steeply toward Jeremys Run.

7.5-0.0 Cross Jeremys Run and, 50 ft. beyond, reach the Jeremys Run Trail. (From this junction it is 0.8m, right, down the Jeremys Run Tr. to the park boundary. To the left, the Jeremys Run Tr. intersects the Neighbor Tr. in 50 ft. The *AT* is 5.4m. from this junction via the Jeremys Run Tr. and 4.6m. via the Neighbor Tr. See PATC map #9.)

KNOB MTN. (JEREMYS RUN) CUT-OFF TRAIL

0.5 miles (0.8 kilometers)   (PATC map No. 9: D-14)

This is a short, very steep trail, yellow-blazed, that connects the Jeremys Run Trail to the Knob Mtn. Trail. It is useful in circuit hikes. One end is on the Knob Mtn. Trail 2.2m. from the Matthews Arm Campground;, the other is on the Jeremys Run Trail, 0.8m. from its upper end on the *AT* near Elkwallow Picnic Grounds.

ELKWALLOW TRAIL

2.0 miles (3.2 kilometers)   (PATC map No. 9: E-14)

This short trail leads from the Elkwallow Wayside over to the Registration Area (and parking area) of the Matthews Arm

Campground, roughly paralleling the Skyline Drive. It crosses the *AT* near the edge of the Wayside area. It is not marked except at the ends and caution is needed in following it around the upper end of Jeremys Run. It is useful in circuit hikes. One such hike, about 5m., would include the *AT* from Elkwallow Gap north 2.1m. to its junction with the Big Blue (Overall Run) Trail. Descend the Big Blue for 0.7m. Turn left on spur trail toward Matthews Arm Campground. Bear left along nature trail, entering paved entrance road to the campground at the upper end of the parking area. The beginning of the Elkwallow Trail, with sign post so indicating it, is directly across the entrance road here. Follow this back to Elkwallow Wayside. Another possible circuit would include the upper portions of the Jeremys Run and Knob Mtn. Trails, the Knob Mtn. Cut-Off Tr. and a short stretch of *AT*.

MATTHEWS ARM FIRE ROAD

5.3 miles (8.5 kilometers)   (PATC map No. 9: E-12)

This old road, most of which is now classified by the Park as trail, leads north from the Matthews Arm Campground. After crossing Overall Run it continues along the long ridge, Matthews Arm, from which the campground takes its name. Beyond the Park, the road is closed to the public, including foot-travelers.

Access:

From the Skyline Drive, SDMP 22.2, drive down paved entrance road to the Matthews Arm Campground and park in the lot near the registration station. Note large map at the station indicating the camp layout and select any route desired to Tent Area B. (Distance from Drive to Tent Area B is 1.1m. When campground is closed one must walk the full distance. One can follow the abandoned section of the Matthews Arm Rd. from the Drive to the Registration station and avoid some of the paved road walking.) Trail description below starts at the camp road in Tent Area B.

Detailed trail data:

0.0-5.3 Matthews Arm Road is gated as it leaves paved camp road in Tent Area. B. Descend gently.

0.1-5.2 The "Traces" Nature Trail intersects the road here.

0.9-4.4 Beecher Ridge Fire Foot Trail leads left down the Beecher Ridge. This connects with the Overall Run Tr. near the Park boundary.

1.3-4.0 Cross Overall Run.

1.4-3.9 Intersection with Big Blue-Overall Run Trail, right at junction with Gimlet Ridge FFT. (From this junction it is 2.3m. right, via the Big Blue Tr. to the *AT*; to the left via the Big Blue Tr. it is 5.2m. to Rt. 340.)

2.7-2.6 Road descends steeply. In 0.6m. turn sharp left off the ridge crest.

4.4-0.9 Reach Park boundary.

5.3-0.0 Reach Va. Sec. 630.

THE NEIGHBOR TRAIL

4.6 miles (7.4 kilometers)   (PATC map No. 9: F-17)

The upper half of this trail is gently undulating and makes an ideal short hike for novice hikers. The trail starts at the *AT* at a point easily reached from the Skyline Drive and follows the ridge of "The Neighbor" mountain west. Beyond the peak of "The Neighbor" the trail descends steeply to Jeremys Run where it connects with the Jeremys Run Trail and Knob Mtn. Trail, offering a choice of circuit hikes.

Access:

From Skyline Drive, SDMP 26.8, follow spur trail a few feet to *AT*. Follow *AT* south (left) 0.3m. to the junction with The Neighbor Trail. (Via the *AT* this junction is 3.9m. south of Elkwallow Picnic Grounds and 1.4m. north of Beahms Gap)

Access at the bottom or western end is via Jeremys Run Trail. Refer to description of that trail.

Detailed trail data:

From *AT* west to Jeremys Run Trail

0.0-4.6 Junction with *AT*, Trail follows the ridge crest of The Neighbor Mtn. with almost no changes in elevation.

1.0-3.6 Pass curious rocks known as "The Gendarmes".

1.9-2.7 Reach peak of "The Neighbor". Trail now descends steeply with switchbacks. The Three Sisters FFT enters from the left about 0.1m. below the peak.

3.7-0.9 Spur trail leads right 50 ft. to Dripping Spring.

4.6-0.0 Junction with Jeremys Run Trail. (To left Jeremys Run Tr. leads 0.8m. to Park boundary, passing junction with Knob Mtn. Tr. in 50 ft. To right Jeremys Run Tr. continues uphill 5.4m. to its junction with *AT* at a point 3.6m. from the upper end of The Neighbor Trail, thus offering a 13.6m. circuit hike.)

THE TRACES NATURE TRAIL (MATTHEWS ARM CAMPGROUND)

1.7 miles (2.8 kilometers)   (PATC map No. 9: E-12)

This trail, which loops around the Matthews Arm Campround, emphasizes the traces that remain of the pre-Park days of this land. It starts at the upper end of the parking area (near the Entrance Station) and circles the campground in a counter-clockwise direction.

Detailed trail data:

0.0 Sign at edge of parking area.

0.5 Cement post marks spur trail to campground. 50 ft. farther a second post marks spur trail which leads right 0.1m. to the Big Blue (Overall Run) Trail.

0.9 Unmarked trail crosses the "Traces" Tr.

1.1 The nature trail intersects the Matthews Arm Rd. at a point on the latter about 0.1m. from the northern end of the campground.

1.3 There is a viewpoint on right.

1.6 Reach camp road at lower end of parking area.

1.7 Completion of loop at trail's start.

GIMLET RIDGE FIRE FOOT TRAIL

1.3 miles (2.1 kilometers)   (PATC map No. 9: D-11)

This trail follows an old road from the Matthews Arm Road (at a point 1.4m. from the northern end of the Matthews Arm

Campground) out Gimlet Ridge to just beyond the high point of the ridge. There is no problem following this fire trail as the roadway is well defined.

HEISKELL HOLLOW FIRE FOOT TRAIL
3.9 miles (6.3 kilometers)   (PATC map No. 9: D-13)

MOLDEN HOLLOW (OR DRY RUN) FIRE FOOT TRAIL
1.1 miles (1.8 kilometers)   (PATC map No. 9: D-13)

The area west of Matthews Arm Campgrounds is full of criss-crossing old roads. The two designated as fire foot trails are not well blazed (and yellow blazes can be found on some of the other roads!) so none but the experienced hiker should try them.

The Heiskell Hollow FFT goes all the way to the valley (but the last 0.2m. is on private land.) ending at Va. Sec. 697 about a mile from U.S. 340 at Compton. The lower half of the trail is quite lovely as it follows a branch of Compton Creek through a narrow gorge. To reach the upper end of this trail follow the Knob Mtn. Tr. 0.4m. from its upper end at Matthews Arm Campground.

About 0.5m. down the Heiskell FFT the old road forks. An old sign (fallen) identifies the left fork as the Molden Hollow FFT, the right one as the Heiskell Hollow FFT. The Molden Hollow FFT, also called the Dry Run FFT, parallels the Knob Mtn. Ridge and ends at a "corner" of the Park boundary, at a considerable distance from any state road.

BEECHER RIDGE FFT
approx. 3 miles (5 kilometers)   (PATC map No. 9: D-11)

The fire foot trail leaves the Matthews Arm Road at a point 0.9m. from the northern end of the Matthews Arm Campground and descends along the crest of Beecher Ridge. After about 2½ miles the trail turns right and descends a side ridge to Overall Run. It comes into the Overall Run Trail at a point on the latter 0.6m. below its junction with the Big Blue and 5.1m. from the *AT*. The fire foot trail is kept open through heavy use but it is not well blazed (when last checked) so should be used only by the experienced hiker. It does provide a nice circuit when used in conjunction with the Overall Run Trail.

THREE SISTERS FFT

2.4 miles including 1.8m. within the Park   (PATC map
                                                            No. 9: E-18)

The upper end of the Three Sisters FFT is on "The Neighbor" Trail. Starting at a point just below (0.1m) the peak of "The Neighbor", it descends southwestward along a ridge, passing over or around each of the "Sisters". The blazing of this trail is very poor at present and the footway vague so this trail is not recommended for any but hikers prepared to bushwhack. The trail continues outside the Park but gives out abruptly before reaching any road.

JEREMYS HOLLOW FFT

1.2 miles (1.9 kilometers)   (PATC map No. 9: F-16)

This trail leads from the Skyline Drive, SDMP 26.8, down to the Jeremys Run Trail and is useful in circuit hikes; however, like many of the fire foot trails, it should be used only by experienced hikers. Its upper end, marked by a yellow post, is at the parking area for "The Neighbor" Trail. (Two trails lead west from the post here, the fire foot trail is the more northerly one; the other is a spur trail to the *AT* used by hikers of "The Neighbor" Trail.) The fire foot trail crosses the *AT* in 300 ft. and continues down into Jeremys Hollow where it meets the Jeremys Run Trail at a point on the latter about 1¼ miles upstream from "The Neighbor" Trail junction.

PASS MTN. FFT

2.2 miles (3.5 kilometers)   (PATC map No. 9: H-18)

OVENTOP MTN. FFT

2 miles (within the Park)   (PATC map No. 9: I-16)

BUTTERWOOD BRANCH FFT

approx. 2 miles (3km.)   (PATC map No. 9: I-17)

The Pass Mtn. FFT starts from the service road to Pass Mtn. Shelter at a point on the road about 0.4m. south of the shelter. The trail first heads northeast. In 0.3m. a spur trail, also yellow blazed, comes in on the left from the Pass Mtn. Shelter. The fire foot trail ends in the deep sag between Pass Mtn. and Oventop Mtn. at a trail intersection where it meets the Oventop Mtn. FFT and the Butterwood Branch FFT.

The Oventop Mtn. FFT starts where the Pass Mtn. FFT ends, in the sag between Pass Mtn. and Oventop Mtn. This fire foot trail leads eastward along the ridge of Oventop Mtn. and offers many good viewpoints and plenty of rocks for scrambling upon. The trail continues outside the Park through private land. Easiest approach to the Oventop FFT is via the Butterwood Branch FFT from U.S. 211.

The Butterwood Branch FFT leaves U.S. 211 at a point directly across from the Piedmont Picnic Area (approx. 4½ miles west of Sperryville and 2½ miles east of Thornton Gap) and goes north, crossing the Pass Mtn.-Oventop Mtn. FFT in the sag between Oventop and Pass Mtns. in about 0.5m. Beyond the trail intersection it descends the Butterwood Branch to Va. Sec. 612. The southern half-mile of this trail has a well-defined footway so is a useful access trail to the Oventop Mtn. FFT. The section north of the trail intersection may be badly overgrown so is recommended for exploration only.

KEMP HOLLOW A FFT

0.4 miles (0.6km.)   (PATC map No. 9: G-16)

KEMP HOLLOW B FFT

0.9 miles (1.5km.)   (PATC map No. 9:G-18)

The Kemp Hollow A FFT descends west from Beahms Gap. Its lower end is inaccessible from the valley at present as it runs through land that is posted "No Trespassing".

The Kemp Hollow B FFT descends to the west from the Skyline Drive, SDMP 29.8, but there is no post marking it and the trail is difficult to find from the Drive because its start is below a steep embankment. To reach its lower end, turn off U.S. 211 just below Shenandoah Park Headquarters onto Va. Sec. 674. Turn right in 0.2m. onto Va. Sec. 658; then, in 0.4m., turn left onto Va. Sec. 612. In 1.3m. turn right onto Va. Sec. 666 and follow it to the end of the drivable road and park. Continue along the road on foot, passing chain across road in 0.1m. (Road follows Park boundary.) Near the highest point on the road, turn right onto a clearly visible old road; this is the fire foot trail. The trail is not marked with the customary yellow post, but it is blazed well most of the way. The trail utilizes old roads as it zigzags up the mountain to reach the Skyline Drive at SDMP 29.8. This trail is recommended only for experienced hikers.

CENTRAL SECTION

BUCK HOLLOW TRAIL

3.7 miles (6.0 kilometers)   (PATC map No. 10: 1-1)

This trail starts from U.S. Rt. 211 at a point about 3½ m. west of Sperryville, climbs to the Skyline Drive in 3m., crossing it near the junction of the Hazel Fire Rd. with the Drive. Continuing to climb, the trail reaches the *AT* on the crest of the Blue Ridge, for a total gain in altitude of 2270 ft. Two fire foot trails, on Buck Ridge and Skinner Ridge, parallel the Buck Hollow Trail below the Drive. They are hard to find and to follow at their lower ends but can be used by the adventurous for circuit trips.

Detailed trail data:

U.S. 211 to *AT* (north to south)

0.0-3.7 U.S. 211, at a point 3.4 west of its junction with U.S. 522 in Sperryville and 4.6m. east of Thornton Gap. From U.S. 211 trail passes through overgrown field.

0.1-3.6 Cross Thornton River. 200 ft. farther cross Buck Hollow stream.

1.3-2.4 Again cross Buck Hollow stream. In 150 ft. an old road leads off to left. For the next 0.3m. the trail is close to stream and is particularly attractive.

1.6-2.1 Old road, mentioned above, comes back into trail. Trail continues along stream here with falls and large boulders. There are some splendid trees along the trail.

3.0-0.7 Intersection with Skyline Drive, SDMP 33.5. (Parking area on west side of Drive here. Hazel Mt. Fire Rd. junction is just south of here. Buck Ridge FFT leads off the fire road in 1/3m. Skinner Ridge FFT leaves the Skyline Drive about a mile north of here.) Trail crosses Drive diagonally; then climbs, quite steeply at first.

3.4-0.3 Pass Meadow Spring, to right of trail. (Here was site of former PATC's Meadow Spring Cabin which burned in 1946.)

3.7-0.0 Reach Appalachian Trail. (Via the *AT* it is 2.4m. right to Thornton Gap, and 0.6m. left to Byrds Nest #3.)

TUNNEL SPUR TRAIL

0.2 miles (0.3 kilometers)   (PATC map No. 10: H-2)

This trail, no longer maintained, climbs from the Skyline Drive at the tunnel 3/4m. south of Thornton Gap to the Appalachian Trail. This is the shortest foot route, 1.3m., to Marys Rock. There are two branches of this trail at the bottom, one from the north portal of the tunnel, one from the south portal. There is ample parking space at the latter at the Tunnel

Overlook. The trail is not marked at present but is easy to find.
The southern spur starts on the east side of the Drive at the
north end of the Tunnel Overlook which is right at the tunnel.
From the junction with the *AT*, follow the *AT* to the left for
about a mile to reach the short side trail, right from the *AT*,
leading to Marys Rock. Both Marys Rock and the rock through
which the tunnel passes are composed of granodiorite, believed
to be over a billion years old. At the north end of the tunnel
there is exposed a 15 ft. dike of greenstone, showing columnar
jointing.

SKINNER RIDGE FFT

1.7 miles (2.7 kilometers)   (PATC map No. 10:I-2)

This trail is infrequently cleared and is not recommended for
any but bushwhackers. It leads from the Skyline Drive about a
tenth mile north of the Buck Hollow Overlook, SDMP 32.9,
down Skinner Ridge to U.S. 211, joining it at a point about
0.6m. above the Buck Hollow Trailhead. For the adventurous
who wish to use this trail along with the Buck Hollow Trail for a
circuit hike, it is recommended that one climb via the Buck
Hollow Trail and descend via the Skinner Ridge Trail as the
latter is most vague at its lower end.

BUCK RIDGE FFT

2.4 miles (3.9 kilometers)   (PATC map No. 10: I-1)

This trail is infrequently cleared and is especially vague at its
lower end. It should be used only by those prepared to
bushwhack. It has its lower end on the Buck Hollow Trail about
0.2m. from the lower end of the latter on U.S. 211. Its upper end
is on the Hazel Mtn. Fire Rd. about 0.4m. from the Skyline
Drive, SDMP 33.5. In using this trail along with the Buck
Hollow Trail for a circuit hike it is recommended that one
ascend the Buck Hollow Trail and descend the Buck Ridge
FFT.

LEADING RIDGE FFT

1.3 miles (2.1 kilometers)   (PATC map No. 10: H-4)

This trail is recommended only for experienced hikers. It leads from the Skyline Drive, SDMP 36.2, and crosses the *AT* in a few hundred feet. The footway of the fire foot trail is vague at this crossing but there are fresh yellow blazes. The trail climbs to a small knob about 0.1m. west of the *AT* intersection, then descends along a ridge, finally coming into Jewell Hollow and reaching Va. Sec. 669. The trail route near the knob is quite vague but beyond the knob, along the ridge, it can be followed more easily. To reach the trail from the valley turn south from U.S. 211 at a point about 1.0m. east of Park Headquarters and 2½m. west of Panorama. In 0.5m. turn left onto Va. Sec. 669 and drive about 0.8m. to the Leading Ridge FFT trailhead.

CRUSHER RIDGE FFT

approx. 2½ miles (4 kilometers)   (PATC map No. 10: H-6)

This trail, recently reblazed, is suitable for exploring. The fire foot trail starts on the Nicholson Hollow Trail a few feet "west" of the Skyline Drive and heads north along Crusher Ridge following an old road once known as Sours Lane. It crosses the *AT* about 0.1m. from the Drive. In about 1½m. it leaves the ridge and descends into Shaver Hollow and then goes out of the Park.

PINNACLE RIDGE FFT

1.6 miles (2.6 km.)   (PATC map No. 10: I-4)

This is an old trail, now overgrown but followable, that leads from the Skyline Drive between SDMP 35 and 36 out to the end of Pinnacle Ridge. It does not connect with any other trail. The fire foot trail is yellow-blazed.

NICHOLSON HOLLOW—HAZEL COUNTRY
TRAIL NETWORK

3.7 miles (6.0 kilometers)   (PATC map No. 10: I-1)

This area was well populated before the creation of the
Shenandoah National Park. Now most of the old cabins are
gone, but a few, in ruins, can be seen along the trails. There is
one cluster, still quite interesting, along the Hannah Run Trail;
two can still be seen along the Broad Hollow Trail and another
on the Hot-Short Mtn. Trail. Corbin Cabin, on the Nicholson
Hollow Trail, has been restored and is maintained in good
condition by the PATC. It is available for use by hikers but
reservations must be made in advance at PATC Headquarters.
Its location is ideal for anyone wanting to explore the many
trails of the area. Most of the present trails were originally roads
that served the mountain community. There are many other
signs of the formerly well-populated area—small orchards,
rock walls and the remains of chestnut rail fences, walled
springs, even bits of rusting metal. Sometimes one discovers an
old family cemetery with the only markers thin slabs of local
rock, set vertically into the ground. Very often periwinkle was
planted around the graves and its bright shiny greenery helps
one spot the cemetery plots today.

Nicholson Hollow was named after the Nicholson clan that
had homes along the Hughes River. It was also called "Free
State" Hollow, reputedly because law enforcement officers
avoided entering the hollow because of its ill-tempered and
lawless inhabitants. George F. Pollock, in his book, *Skyland*,
gives a vivid description of some of the Nicholsons who lived
here. The old USGS Stony Man Quadrangle map, surveyed in
1927, indicated the location of many of the mountain cabins. A
series of articles by H.T. Dockerty, published in the
Washington Times and preserved in the PATC scrap books,
recorded many legends of the "Free State" Hollow.

Three major trails cross through the area—the Nicholson
Hollow Trail which leads up the Hughes River, the Hannah
Run Trail, and the Hazel Mtn. Fire Rd. Other trails in the area
include the Catlett Mtn. Trail, the Hot-Short Mtn. Tr., the

Sams Ridge Tr., the Broad Hollow Tr., and the Corbin Cabin Cut-Off Tr., all blue-blazed. In addition to these are several Park trails—the Old Hazel Road Tr., White Rocks Trail, Hazel-Catlett Spur FFT, Hazel River FFT, Pine Hill Gap FFT, Indian Run FFT, Corbin Mtn. FFT, Jenkins Hollow FFT, Hazel Hollow FFT, and the Pinnacle Ridge FFT. See PATC map #10 and the PATC booklet, *Circuit Hikes in the Shenandoah National Park.*

Access:

The upper ends of the Corbin Cabin Cut-Off Tr., Hannah Run Tr., Pinnacle Ridge FFT, and Hazel Mtn. Fire Rd. are on the Skyline Drive. The Nicholson Hollow Tr., which starts on the *A T,* crosses the Drive at SDMP 38.4. Parking for this trail is in the Stony Man Overlook-Hughes River Gap Parking Area 0.2m. farther south. The Corbin Cabin Cut-Off Tr. begins at the Drive, SDMP 37.9, just opposite the Shaver Hollow Parking Area. Pinnacle Ridge FFT starts at about SDMP 35.6. The Hazel Mtn. Fire Rd. leaves the Drive at SDMP 33.5, diagonally opposite the Meadow Spring Parking Area. The upper ends of the Buck Ridge FFT, the Old Hazel Rd. Tr., Sams Ridge Tr., Broad Hollow Tr., Hazel River FFT, and Pine Hill Gap FFT are all on the Hazel Mtn. Fire Rd., as are the lower ends of the Catlett Mtn. Tr. and the Hazel-Catlett Spur FFT. The Buck Hollow-Meadow Spring Tr. crosses the Drive at the entrance of the Hazel Mtn. Fire Rd.

From the east, access is primarily from Va. Rt. 231 south of Sperryville. To reach the lower ends of Sams Ridge Trail, Hazel River FFT, Broad Hollow Tr. and Pine Hill Gap FFT turn west from Rt. 231 onto Va. Sec. 681. (The road junction is about 4m. south of the U.S. 522-Va. Rt. 231 junction and is just north of the bridge over the Hazel River.) In about 1m. reach road fork. For Broad Hollow and Pine Hill Gap Trails go left on Rt. 681. Reach lower end of Broad Hollow Trail in about 1½m. Beyond this point road is not passable by car so continue on foot another ½m. to start of Pine Hill Gap Tr. For Sams Ridge Trail, Hazel River FFT and White Rocks Tr. take right fork which is Va. Sec. 600. In about 1m., where Rt. 600 crosses the Hazel

River, is start of Sams Ridge Tr. which leads to the Hazel River FFT's lower end at the Park boundary. The White Rocks FFT is on up Rt. 600 another mile to a point 0.1m south of its junction with Va. Sec. 608.

The Old Hazel Road Tr. starts on U.S. 211 about 3m. west of Sperryville at the Beech Spring Church. The Buck Hollow (and Buck Ridge) Trail takes off from U.S. 211 about 0.7m. farther west.

NICHOLSON HOLLOW TRAIL

5.9 miles (9.3 kilometers)   (PATC map No. 10: H-6)

This trail leads down through the hollow formed by the Hughes River. Reputedly, the mountaineers, mostly members of the Nicholson clan, who once lived in cabins scattered through the hollow, were so feared by the valley folks that the Madison Co. sheriffs and their deputies avoided entering the hollow, hence the name "Free State Hollow". Corbin Cabin, located on the Nicholson Hollow Trail, was the pre-Shenandoah Park home of George Corbin. It has been restored and is now maintained by the PATC. Reservations for its use must be made with PATC Headquarters. See Chap. 6: "Shelters and Cabins." From the *AT* west of the Drive the Nicholson Hollow Trail, blue-blazed, soon crosses the Skyline Drive, SDMP 38.4, near Hughes River Gap and continues in generally southwest direction to Va. Sec. 600 at its junction with the old Weakley Hollow Rd. (This is where the Brokenback Run joins the Hughes River.) Difficulty may be experienced in crossing Brokenback Run and the numerous fords of the Hughes River when the water is high. Trails connecting with the Nicholson Hollow Trail include the Hannah Run Tr., Hot-Short Mtn. Tr., and the Corbin Cabin Cut-Off Tr., all blue-blazed, and the Indian Run FFT.

Detailed trail data:

From the *AT* to Va. Sec. 600 (west to east)

0.0-5.9 Trailhead, marked by a cement signpost, is at a point on the *AT* 7.0m. south of Thornton Gap and 0.3m. north of Stony Man Mtn. Overlook. The Nicholson Hollow Trail, blue-blazed, leads southeast toward the Skyline Drive.

0.1-5.8 To left of the trail a yellow post marks the start of the Crusher Ridge FFT which leads north, crossing the *A T* in 0.1m. In a few feet reach the Skyline Drive and cross it diagonally to the left. The Nicholson Hollow Trail here is marked with a cement post. Descend bank and turn left along an old road which leads through an area of scrub oak and soon descends.

0.5-5.4 To right of trail is good walled-in Dale Spring.

1.7-4.2 Cross a creek.

1.8-4.1 Here the Indian Run FFT leads right. (The fire foot trail leads uphill for 1.6m. to the Thorofare Mtn. FFT. The latter trail comes into the Old Rag Fire Rd. in another 0.6m. Although these fire foot trails can be used for a circuit hike they were poorly blazed when last checked and not well cleared so should not be used by the inexperienced hiker.) Nicholson Hollow Tr. continues downhill, soon following the Hughes River.

1.9-4.0 Junction with the Corbin Cabin Cut-Off Tr. which leads left, climbing 1.4m. to the Skyline Drive, SDMP 37.9. To the right of the trail here is Corbin Cabin, operated by the PATC for the use of campers. There are accommodations for 8 persons. Reservations must be made at PATC headquarters in advance. See Chap. 6: "Shelters and Cabins."

2.0-3.9 Pass overgrown field on right. This was once the site of Madison Corbin's cabin. 250 ft. farther, on left of trail, is a marked spring.

2.1-3.8 Old road leads left to the Hughes River. Just below the road, across the river, are the ruins of Aaron Nicholson's cabin. An unmarked path here connects with the Corbin Cut-Off Tr.

3.5-2.4 Cross to left side of the Hughes River at base of deep pool.

4.0-1.9 Junction with Hannah Run Trail which leads left 3.7m. to Skyline Drive at SDMP 35.0. There are some giant hemlock near the junction.

4.1-1.8 Cross Hannah Run.

4.2-1.7 Junction with Hot-Short Mtn. Trail which follows an old road, to the left, up a valley between Short Mtn. and Hot Mtn. and comes into the Hazel Mtn. Fire Rd. in 2.1m.

5.1-0.8 To left of trail is a walled-in spring.

5.6-0.3 Leave SNP.

5.8-0.1 Cross to right of Hughes River. 150 ft. farther cross Brokenback Run. Beyond, turn left onto dirt road.

5.9-0.0 Reach Va. Sec. 600 at point where Weakley Hollow Rd. leads right toward Old Rag Mtn. There is automobile parking here and a SNP parking lot up the Weakley Hollow Rd. Both areas may be crowded on weekends. The Park Service has recently opened an Overflow Parking Area 0.5m. east of the trail on Rt. 600.

HANNAH RUN TRAIL

3.7 miles (6.0km.)   (PATC map No. 10: I-4)

This blue-blazed trail extends from the Skyline Drive down to the Nicholson Hollow Trail on the Hughes River, with a descent of about 2000 ft. It passes by the ruins of several old mountain cabins. The Catlett Mtn. Tr. serves as a link between Hannah Run Tr. and the Hazel Mtn. Fire Rd. (Hazel-Catlett Spur FFT also links the same trails) The Hot-Short Mtn. Trail, with its lower end just a short distance, 0.2m., down the Nicholson Hollow Tr. from the lower end of the Hannah Run Tr. also connects with the Hazel Mtn. Fire Rd. so that an easy circuit hike can be made. One other circuit hike might be mentioned here. Leaving the car at the Pinnacle Overlook, walk 0.1m. north to the Hannah Run Tr., follow the trail down to the Nicholson Hollow Tr., then follow up this trail to Corbin Cabin, a distance of 2.1m., then take the Corbin Cabin Cut-Off Tr. 1.5m. to the Drive. Directly across the Drive a short spur trail (to Shaver Hollow Shelter) connects with the *AT* Follow the *AT* north for 1.2m., turning off on a spur trail which leads a few feet to the Jewell Hollow Parking Overlook. From here it is about 1.3m. along the Drive back to your car, for a total distance of just under 10 miles.

Detailed trail data:

Skyline Drive to Nicholson Hollow Tr.

0.0-3.7 East side of Skyline Drive, SDMP 35.0, about 0.1m.

"north" of the Pinnacles Overlook Parking Area. Trail descends steeply with switchbacks. There are wintertime views to the east over Hazel Country, with Hazel Mtn. as the dominant feature.

1.2-2.5 Reach trail intersection in deep sag, with low knob ahead. Here the Catlett Mtn. Tr. leads 1.2m. to the Hazel Mtn. Fire Rd. (A short distance along the Catlett Mtn. Tr. the Hazel-Catlett Spur FFT leads left from it and also joins the Hazel Mtn. Fire Rd. but 1½m. farther north.) At the intersection the Hannah Run Tr. turns sharply right and again descends.

1.6-2.1 Here trail is exceedingly steep, dropping 500 ft. in 0.2m.

1.8-1.9 Cross Hannah Run. After climbing out of ravine, pass ruins of a cabin on the left.

2.2-1.5 Pass between ruins of cabins. There is a spring on the right and an old apple orchard. Trail descends along Hannah Run but does not cross it.

3.7-0.0 Cross small stream; 200 ft. farther, reach Nicholson Hollow Tr. Left from this junction via the Nicholson Hollow Tr. it is 0.2m. to the Hot-Short Mtn. Trail, and 1.7m. farther to its lower end at Va. Sec. 600. To the right it is 2.1m. to Corbin Cabin and 1.8m. farther to Skyline Drive (but only 1.5m. to the Drive via the Corbin Cabin Cut-Off Tr.)

HAZEL MTN. FIRE RD.

5.2 miles (8.4km.)   (PATC Map No. 10: I-3)

This old road is gated where it leaves the Skyline Drive, SDMP 33.5, diagonally across from the Meadow Spring Parking Area. The road might well be called the hemlock trail for it passes through hemlock for much of the way; many of the trees are quite young but in the low areas, along the headwaters of the Hazel River, there are much larger trees, so that it is a veritable "limberlost". For the first two miles the road or trail descends gently along one branch of the Hazel River. It then heads southward and climbs along another branch of the river. From here is passes through a broad level area for another 2 miles before dipping into a sag, then climbing along the Hot Mtn. ridge where it dead-ends.

At the Drive, a signpost just north of the road marks the Buck Hollow Tr. In about 0.3m. the Buck Ridge FFT leads north from the fire road. A mile or so farther along the road there is a fork. The left fork, leading northward is the old Hazel Rd., now classified as trail. The White Rocks Tr. takes off from the Old Hazel Rd.. Still farther along the Hazel Mtn. Fire Rd. are the junctions with Sams Ridge Tr., Broad Hollow Tr., Hot-Short Mtn. Trail, Hazel River FFT, and Pine Hill Gap FFT. The old Hazel School which served the area in pre-Shenandoah Park days was situated near the junction of the Hazel Mtn. Fire Rd. with the Sams Ridge-Broad Hollow Trails.

Detailed trail data:
    Skyline Drive to Hot Mtn.
    0.0-5.2 Road leaves Skyline Drive, SDMP 33.5, at a point diagonally across from the Meadow Spring Parking Area. (Buck Hollow Tr. crosses the Drive here and is marked by cement post.) Road is gated at the Drive.
    0.4-4.8 Where road turns sharply to the right, the Buck Ridge FFT leads east down Buck Ridge and comes into the Buck Hollow Tr. a short distance from that trail's lower end on U.S. 211. (Caution: the lower part of the Buck Ridge FFT is vague and hard to follow.)
    1.6-3.6 Reach road fork. Take right branch. (Left fork is the Old Hazel Road (trail) which leads down Beech Spring Hollow to U.S. 211. About a mile along this road is junction with the White Rocks Tr. Also at this junction a short, very steep trail leads south to Hazel Cave. On the Hazel River, just above the cave, is a waterfall.)
    1.7-3.5 Cross bridge over a branch of the Hazel River.
    2.2-3.0 Hazel-Catlett Spur FFT leads right 1.1m. to come into the Catlett Mtn. Tr. just short of the latter's junction with the Hannah Run Tr. Immediately beyond fire trail, ford creek. Then in 250 ft. ford a second creek; both are branches of Hazel River. The old road now climbs, paralleling the last creek. Hemlocks are lovely here.

2.9-2.3 Hazel River FFT leads left 2.8m. to park boundary and junction with Sams Ridge Tr. at a point about 0.4m. west of Va. Sec. 600. Beyond the fire trail, the road passes to the right of the bulk of Hazel Mtn.

3.1-2.1 Cement post marks junction with the Sams Ridge-Broad Hollow Trail which are coincident here. (The Sams Ridge Tr. leads 2.2m. east down to Va. Sec. 600 where the Hazel River crosses that road. The Broad Hollow Tr. leads 2.4m. southeastward, coming into Va. Sec. 681.)

3.4-1.8 Unmarked trail on left leads 0.2m. to Broad Hollow Tr.

3.6-1.6 Junction with Catlett Mtn. Tr. (Catlett Mtn. Tr. leads right 1.2m. to junction with Hannah Run Tr. at a point on the latter 1.2m. from its junction with Skyline Drive.)

4.1-1.1 Junction with Hot-Short Mtn. Tr. (The Hot-Short Mtn. Tr. leads 2.1m. to the Nicholson Hollow Tr. at a point on the latter 0.2m. below its junction with the Hannah Run Tr.)

4.5-0.7 To left, the Pine Hill Gap FFT leads to Park boundary and beyond to Pine Hill Gap where old road, not passable by auto, but a continuation of Va. Sec. 707 to the south and Rt. 681 to the NE crosses the Gap. Trail now follows ridge of Hot Mtn.

5.2-0.0 Reach end of road, near summit of Hot Mtn.

CORBIN CABIN CUT-OFF TRAIL

1.4 miles (2.3km.)   (PATC map No. 10: H-5)

This is the shortest route from the Skyline Drive to Corbin Cabin. It is an old, old trail used by the mountain folk in Nicholson Hollow long before there was a Skyline Drive. Parking space is available directly across the Drive from the trail's start, at the Shaver Hollow Parking Area, SDMP 37.9. Trail is quite steep, descending 1000 ft. in the 1.5m.

Detailed trail data:
   Skyline Drive to Corbin Cabin
   0.0-1.4 From Skyline Drive, SDMP 37.9, directly opposite Shaver Hollow Parking Area, descend along blue-blazed trail.

0.5-0.9 Trail turns sharply to the left here.

0.7-0.7 Trail here switchbacks to right. The footway is rough and rocky for the next 250 ft.

1.1-0.3 Ruins of one of the Nicholson cabins to the left of the trail here.

1.3-0.1 A path leads right 180 ft. to a graveyard. Only unmarked, upended stones mark the graves, as is true of most of the old family cemeteries in the Park.

1.4-0.0 Cross Hughes River. Beyond come into Nicholson Hollow Trail just below Corbin Cabin which is to the right. (Corbin Cabin was once the home of George Corbin, and is typical of the mountain cabins which were once numerous in the hollows. It has been restored and may be rented by hikers. It is equipped for 8 persons. Reservations for its use must be made in advance at PATC Headquarters. See Chap 6: Shelters and Cabins.)

SAMS RIDGE TRAIL

2.2 miles (3.5km.)   (PATC map No. 10: L-2)

This blue-blazed trail is one of the trails leading into Hazel Country from east of the mountains. It can be used with one of the others—the Broad Hollow Trail, also blue-blazed, or the Hazel River FFT or the Pine Hill Gap FFT—for a relatively short circuit hike, for all these trails have upper ends on the Hazel Mtn. Fire Rd. and all have their lower ends on either Va. Sec. 681 or Va. Sec. 600 which forks from Rt. 681.

Detailed trail data:
   Va. Sec. 600 to Hazel Mtn. Fire Rd. (east to west)

0.0-2.2 Junction with Va. Sec. 600. (To reach this point by car, turn west off of Va. Rt. 231 onto Va. Sec. 681 at a point just north of the bridge over the Hazel River. Follow Rt. 681 for about 1m. to road fork. Take right fork which is Va. Sec. 600 and continue to where Rt. 600 crosses Hazel River. Trail begins here.) Follow old road up the south side of the Hazel River.

0.4-1.8 Reach Park boundary. Trail turns left away from road. (Road, within Park, becomes the Hazel River FFT.) Trail now tends away from the Park, climbing the slope of the ridge through private property. It then follows up the crest of the ridge.

0.6-1.6 Enter SNP, continuing up Sams Ridge.

1.5-0.7 Pass site of mountaineer home. The stone foundation, scattered apple trees, and rose bushes are the only evidences of former habitation. Here is a good view to the north of the Hazel River Valley. There is a spring 200 ft. to left of the trail.

2.0-0.2 Junction with Broad Hollow Trail which comes in from left. From here the two trails are coincident.

2.2-0.0 Junction of Sams Ridge-Broad Hollow Tr. with Hazel Mtn. Fire Rd. (To left via the Hazel Mtn. Fire Rd. it is 0.5m. to the Catlett Mtn. Tr., 1.0m. to Hot-Short Mtn. Tr., and 1.4m. to Pine Hill Gap FFT. To right it is 0.2m. to Hazel River FFT and 1.5m. to Old Hazel Road.) The old Hazel School was located near this junction. There is a spring 200 ft. to right of junction down abandoned Sams Run Tr.

HAZEL RIVER FFT

2.8 mile (4.5km.)   (PATC map No. 10: L-2)

This yellow-blazed trail offers yet another route into Hazel Country from the east. Its lower end is on the Sams Ridge Trail. Where that trail turns left away from the old road following the Hazel River, the road itself continues within the SNP as the Hazel River FFT. It crosses Sams Run, then follows up the Hazel River for over a mile before swinging left up a subsidiary creek and climbing over a shoulder of Hazel Mtn. to reach its upper end on the Hazel Mtn. Fire Rd. at a point on the latter 0.2m. NW of the Sams Ridge-Broad Hollow Tr. junction and 1.3m. south of the junction with the Old Hazel Rd. About 2/3 the way up the Hazel River FFT, the Hazel Hollow FFT (unblazed and not recommended) leads north to connect with the White Rocks Tr. There is little difficulty in following the Hazel River FFT. as the footway is clear and it is well blazed.

BROAD HOLLOW TRAIL

2.4 miles (3.8km.)   (PATC map No. 10: L-4)

Like the Sams Ridge Trail this blue-blazed trail offers access
into Hazel Country from the east and can be used in
combination with that trail or with the Pine Hill Gap FFT or
the Hazel River FFT for a circuit hike. The Broad Hollow Tr.
ascends about 1400 ft., with its lower end on Va. Sec. 681 and its
upper end coincident with the Sams Ridge Trail end on the
Hazel Mtn. Fire Rd. It passes several abandoned cabins along
its route.

Detailed trail data:
Va. Sec. 681 to Hazel Mtn. Fire Rd. (east to west)
0.0-2.4 Junction with Va. Sec. 681. (To reach this point by
car, turn west off Va. Rt. 231 onto Va. Sec. 681 at a point just
north of the bridge over the Hazel River. Follow Rt. 681 for
about 2½m. Trailhead on the right of the road.) In about 50 ft.
trail crosses Broad Hollow Run. 250 ft. farther an old road
takes off to the right of the trail.
0.3-2.1 Trail crosses run.
0.5-1.9 Trail recrosses run, continuing up the hollow for
some distance farther.
0.7-1.7 Two old trails, about 250 ft. apart, lead left to the
remains of two log buildings. Continue to ascend steadily, with
several sharp turns in the trail.
1.0-1.4 Pass a rocked-up spring and, 150 ft. beyond it, a
ruined cabin with shingled sides.
1.5-0.9 Pass a roofless cabin here, and another in about a
quarter mile.
2.1-0.3 Unmarked trail leads left about 0.2m. to the Hazel
Mtn. Fire Rd. coming into the latter at a point about 0.2m. north
of the Catlett Mtn. Tr. junction.
2.2-0.2 Junction with Sams Ridge Trail which comes in from
the right. The two trails coincide for the next 0.2m.
2.4-0.0 Junction with Hazel Mtn. Fire Rd. near the site of the
old Hazel School. (To left via the Hazel Mtn. Fire Rd. it is 0.5m.
to the Catlett Mtn. Tr., 1.0m. to the Hot-Short Mtn. Tr., and
1.4m. to Pine Hill Gap FFT. To the right it is 0.2m. to Hazel

River FFT and 1.5m. to the Old Hazel Road. There is a spring 200 ft. to right of junction, down abandoned Sams Run Tr.)

PINE HILL GAP FFT

about 1.4m. (2.2km.)   (PATC map No. 10: L-4)

This yellow-blazed trail leads from Pine Hill Gap to the Hazel Mtn. Fire Rd., coming into that trail at a point 0.4m south of the Hot-Short Mtn. Trail junction. To reach the lower end of the trail at Pine Hill Gap either drive up Va. Sec. 681 as far as is passable by car or follow Va. Sec. 707 from Nethers as far as is drivable; by either route continue on foot to the Gap, where trail starts. This trail is followable and is useful for circuit hikes.

HOT-SHORT MTN. TR.

2.1 miles (3.4km.)   (PATC map No. 10: K-6)

This is an interesting stretch of trail, blue-blazed, along the valley between Hot and Short Mountains. It connects the Nicholson Hollow Trail with the Hazel Mtn. Fire Road. From its lower end this trail involves a considerable climb with a change in elevation of about 1300 ft. It follows up a stream much of the way, utilizing old roads and passing several old homesites.

Detailed trail data:
Nicholson Hollow to Hazel Mtn. Fire Rd.
0.0-2.1 This trail begins on Nicholson Hollow Trail at a point 1.7m. from the latter's intersection with Va. Sec. 600 where it is joined by the Wcakley Hollow Rd.
0.1-2.0 Turn left and follow trail between stone walls. From here trail ascends.
0.4-1.7 Continue to ascend, along a road, with ravine to left.
0.7-1.4 Reach an outcropping of rocks where there is a splendid view of Corbin and Robertson Mtns. across Nicholson Hollow.
0.9-1.2 Notice old farmhouse across stream to left. In 200 ft. cross stream and follow up it. 250 ft. farther, turn sharp left and

ascend steeply. Then turn right and cross overgrown clearing.

1.3-0.8 Cross stream and continue to ascend.

1.4-0.7 Trail leads through overgrown field with apple trees. To right is view of Hot Mtn.

1.6-0.5 Cross stream again.

1.9-0.2 There is an old chimney worthy of notice about 100 ft. to right of trail.

2.0-0.1 Enter old road and continue through level section.

2.1-0.0 Junction with Hazel Mtn. Fire Rd. (To left on Hazel Mtn. Tr. it is 0.5m. to Catlett Mtn. Tr., 1.0m to Broad Hollow— Sams Ridge Trails, and 4.1m. to the Skyline Drive; to right it is 0.4m. to the Pine Hill Gap FFT.)

CATLETT MTN. TR.

1.2 miles (1.9km.)   (PATC map No. 10: J-4)

This blue-blazed trail connects the Hannah Run Trail with the Hazel Mtn. Fire Road. It affords a pleasant, easy walk along the north slope of Catlett Mtn. through woods, abandoned orchards, and small clearings. A good 10 mile hike could start at the end of Va. Sec. 600 west of Nethers. From here follow the blue-blazed Nicholson Hollow Tr. for 1.7m., then the Hot-Short Mtn. Tr. for 2.1m. Turn left on Hazel Mtn. Fire Rd. and follow 0.5m. to the Catlett Mtn. Tr. Then follow this trail over to the Hannah Run Tr., 1.2m. and take the Hannah Run Tr. down 2.5m. to the Nicholson Hollow Tr., then 1.9m. down this trail back to the start at Va. Sec. 600.

Detailed trail data:

Hannah Run Tr. to Hazel Mtn. Fire Rd.

0.0-1.2 Junction with Hannah Run Trail at a point on the latter 1.2m from the Skyline Drive. Follow old road, descending slightly. In 200 ft. turn right off road into pine grove still descending. (Straight ahead, on road, is the Hazel-Catlett Spur FFT marked by yellow post. This spur trail leads to Hazel Mtn. Fire Rd. 1.4m. nearer the Skyline Drive than the Catlett Mtn. Tr. junction with the Hazel Mtn. Fire Rd.)

0.1-1.1 Bear right around a pit; remnants of old stone wall to right of trail. Climb gently.

0.3-0.9 Cross worn road. For some distance trail is level; summit of Catlett Mtn. is to the right of trail.

0.7-0.5 Trail crosses over the shoulder of Catlett Mtn. From here it descends gradually through pine and abandoned orchard.

1.0-0.2 Cross stream and ascend.

1.2-0.0 Junction with Hazel Mtn. Fire Rd. at a point on the latter 0.5m. north of the Hot-Short Mtn. Tr. and 0.5m. SW of the junction with the Sams Ridge-Broad Hollow Trs.

HAZEL-CATLETT SPUR FFT

1.1 miles (1.8km.)   (PATC map No. 10: J-4)

This yellow-blazed trail connects the Hazel Mtn. Fire Road with the Hannah Run Trail. At the sag, where the Hannah Run Trail turns sharply right descending (1.2m. from Skyline Drive), follow the Catlett Mtn. Trail along an old road for 200 ft. Here a yellow post marks the Hazel-Catlett Spur Tr. which continues straight ahead along the old road. It descends gently along one of the Hazel River tributaries, coming into the Hazel Mtn. Fire Rd. at a point 2.2m. east of the Skyline Drive. This end of the fire trail is 1.4m. from where the Catlett Mtn. Tr. joins the Hazel Mtn. Fire Rd.

OLD HAZEL ROAD (a trail)

about 2.4 miles (3.8 kilometers)   (PATC map No. 10: J-1)

This old road, no longer drivable by car, leads from U.S. 211 at Beech Spring Church to the Hazel Mtn. Fire Road. Crossing of the Thornton River may be difficult. (Beech Spring Church is about 3m. west of Sperryville.) The old road follows up Beech Spring Hollow for about a mile, then climbs toward the White Rocks Ridge. It then heads west along this ridge which separates the Beech Spring Hollow and the upper valley of the Hazel River. The old road comes into the Hazel Mtn. Fire Rd. at a point on the latter 1.6. from the Skyline Drive and 1.5m. from the junction with the Sams Ridge—Broad Hollow Trails.

Where the Old Hazel Rd. first reaches the ridge crest there is a
trail junction. (The Old Hazel Rd. is blazed as a fire foot trail up
to this point.) To the left the White Rocks FFT, yellow blazed as
far as the Park boundary, follows the ridge east, then drops
down toward Va. Sec. 600. Ahead, a short trail leads straight
down to Hazel Cave. Just up the Hazel River from the cave is a
waterfall. Old Hazel Rd. itself turns right and is distinctly
roadlike from this junction all the way to the Hazel Mtn. Fire
Road.

WHITE ROCKS FFT

1.7 miles (2.7km.)   (PATC map No. 10: J-2)

This yellow-blazed trail leads east from the Old Hazel Road
(trail) following a ridge crest for about a mile before descending
to the Park boundary. Outside the Park an unblazed path
follows an old roadbed down to Va. Sec. 600, joining the latter
just 0.1m. south of the junction of Rt. 600 with Rt. 608. To reach
the lower end of this trail by car turn west off Rt. 231 about
1-3/4m. south of Rt. 231's junction with U.S. 522 just SE of
Sperryville, onto Va. Sec. 608. At road junction turn left onto
Rt. 600. Trail, unmarked, leads uphill on right of road, through
a gap in a fence. It is not marked. This trail should be used only
by experienced hikers prepared to bushwhack. The lower end of
this trail is 1.1m. north of Sams Run via Rt. 600.

HAZEL HOLLOW FFT

0.8 miles (1.3km.)   (PATC map No. 10: K-2)

JENKINS HOLLOW FFT

1.1 miles (1.8 km.)   (PATC map No. 10: K-2)

These fire foot trails are shown on the maps but were badly
overgrown when last checked and neither is blazed. They are
suitable only for exploring. The Hazel Hollow FFT links the
Hazel River FFT with the White Rocks Trail. The Jenkins
Hollow FFT leads from the White Rocks Tr. down Jenkins

Hollow to the Park boundary near Va. Sec. 600 about 1 mile south of U.S. 211 west of Sperryville.

TRAILS IN THE SKYLAND-OLD RAG AREA

Skyland is situated almost in the center of the Shenandoah Park. The story of Skyland's early days, from about 1890 to the formation of the SNP in the 1930's, and of its charismatic founder, George Freeman Pollock, has given the whole area around Skyland a romantic aura. Who can help smiling at the thought of Pollock's guests, elegant Washingtonians, rubbing elbows with rough mountain characters such as those who lived in the hollow once known as "Free State"? But what is Skyland today? A lodge and dining hall, some cottages and dormitories, a recreation room and stables—all these but much, much more. At the northern entrance to Skyland the Skyline Drive reaches its highest elevation, 3680 ft. Surrounding Skyland is as great a variety of fascinating places to explore as one could ask for. To start, listing them in clockwise order, there is that "Free State" Hollow (Nicholson Hollow), once home of the reputedly fierce and lawless Corbins and Nicholsons: then the unique Old Rag Mountain with its ragged top; next, the magnificent Whiteoak Canyon with its series of cascades; Hawksbill Mtn. that towers over the rest of the Park; then fearsome Kettle Canyon, immediately below Skyland; and, lastly, Stony Man Mtn. whose "profile" is so visible when travelling south along the Drive. Small wonder that the Shenandoah Park's most popular trails are here.

STONY MAN MTN. NATURE
TRAIL—LITTLE STONY MAN TRAIL

1.0 miles plus 0.5 mile loop   (PATC map No. 10: Skyland Inset)

The Park Service has constructed a Nature Trail leading from the Parking Area near the northern entrance to Skyland to Stony Man Mtn., where the trail loops around the summit and offers a view from the top of the cliffs that form the Stony Man's profile. Branching from the Nature Trail is another trail that leads on to the cliffs of Little Stony Man, then descends to the *AT*. By returning to Skyland via the *AT*, which follows a shelf below the cliffs, a good circuit hike can be made.

The cliffs of Stony Man and Little Stony Man are the weathered remnants of ancient beds of lava. (See Chap. 3, Geology of the SNP) From 1845 to the turn of the century a copper mine operated near the top of Stony Man Mtn. Overgrown culm banks and tree-masked workings on the cliff-face, with green rock showing the presence of copper, mark the place. The ore was smelted at Furnace Spring, the site of which is on the *AT* just north of Skyland. After operations were discontinued the mine was still a spot of much interest to visitors. The shaft, however, became a hazard and was filled up. There is now no trail to the spot.

Detailed trail data:

0.0 Nature Trail Parking Area, near the northern entrance to Skyland, SDMP 41.7.

0.4 Trail junction. Straight ahead the Nature Tr. continues and in 250 ft. starts a 0.4m. loop around the summit of Stony Man Mtn. To left, a spur trail connects with the Skyland-Stony Man Mtn. Horse Trail. Turn right here to continue on toward Little Stony Man.

0.8 Reach the cliffs of Little Stony Man. The *AT* is directly below the cliffs here. From here trail descends steeply by switchbacks.

1.0 Reach *AT* at a point 0.3m. south of the Little Stony Man Parking Area, SDMP 39.1. From this point it is 1.2m. via the *AT* to paved Skyland Rd. (which leads uphill to Nature Trail Parking Area) and 1.3m. to where a short spur trail leads to paved service road which also can be followed to the Parking Area.

MILLERS HEAD TRAIL

0.8 miles (1.3 kilometers)   (PATC map No. 10: Skyland Inset)

This short but rewarding trail leads over Bushytop Mtn. and on out the ridge to a lower peak known as Millers Head. This ridge forms the southern wall of the deep Kettle Canyon. A stone platform on Millers Head offers a superb view of the Shenandoah Valley, the Massanuttens and mountains farther west, Kettle Canyon, the buildings of Skyland, and, to the southwest, Buracher Hollow.

Access:
   Park at the southern entrance to Skyland, SDMP 42.5, and walk up the Skyland road toward the stables (left fork) only a few feet to reach the *AT*. Follow *AT* to the right to where it crosses the paved Skyland Rd. Turn left along the road for 200 ft. Sign indicates start of Millers Head Trail.

Detailed trail data:
   0.0 Trail sign on paved Skyland Road. (The gravel road to left of trail here rejoins trail on summit of Bushytop, where it ends.)
   0.2 Summit of Bushytop. (There is a microwave installation here.) 100 ft. farther along the trail is an excellent viewpoint on the right, with Kettle Canyon below and the Skyland buildings quite visible above the canyon.
   0.8 Reach the Millers Head.

SKYLAND ROAD

3.2 miles (5.2 kilometers)   (PATC map No. 10: F-7)

   As one walks this road it is fun to imagine what a trip to the "top of the mountain" was like in Pollock's day when it was only just barely usable for horse-drawn vehicles. The road climbs 2000 ft. following up the ridge between Kettle Canyon and Dry Run Hollow and is gated at the Park boundary and again just below Furnace Spring, located at the head of Dry Run and close by the *AT*. To reach the upper end follow down the north entrance road to Skyland, keeping to the right at each fork, until reaching the graveled road. Or one can follow the *AT* from the south entrance road down to Furnace Spring and there connect with the road. To reach the lower end from Luray, head south on U.S. 340. Just south of the town turn left onto Va. Sec. 642. Follow Rt. 642 for about 1.6m., then turn right onto Va.

Sec. 689 which follow for another 2 miles. Turn left on Va. Sec. 668 for 0.9m., then right on Va. Sec. 672. State maintenance ends in 0.6m. and road continues as the Skyland Rd. soon entering the Park.

WHITEOAK CANYON TRAIL

5.1 miles (8.2 kilometers)   (PATC map No. 10: H-8)

Whiteoak Canyon is one of the scenic gems of the Shenandoah National Park. Whiteoak Run gathers waters from a number of streamlets gushing from as many springs located just below the Skyline Drive in the Skyland area. The broad area where these headwaters gather is covered with a virgin hemlock forest and is still called the "Limberlost", the name given to it by Mr. Pollock as it reminded him of the locale of Gene Stratton Porter's novel, *Girl of the Limberlost*.

Below the Limberlost Whiteoak Run has cut a deep canyon in its rush to Old Rag Valley far below. There are six cascades, each more than 40 ft. high, along its route (See Waterfall chart.) The falls occur between layers of the ancient lava beds, now tilted vertically, because the less resistant rock could withstand the creek's erosive powers much less than the basaltic rock. From the start of the Whiteoak Canyon Trail to the base of the sixth or lowest cascade there is a loss in altitude of 2000 ft. The trail drops another 350 ft. before reaching the Berry Hollow Rd. (Va. Sec. 600). The canyon is lined with towering trees—white oak, hemlock, tulip and ash.

A few miles to the south Cedar Creek forms a canyon paralleling Whiteoak Canyon. A very popular hike includes a trip down one canyon and up the other with the stretch of the *AT* between Skyland and Hawksbill Mtn. completing the circuit.

Access:

The Whiteoak Canyon Trail starts at the Parking Area directly across the Skyline Drive from the south entrance to Skyland. To reach the lower end of the trail by car, follow Va. Rt. 231 to about 5m. north of Madison and turn west on Va. Sec. 670 which passes through the community of Criglersville.

Five miles beyond Criglersville, at Syria, turn right on Va. Sec. 643. In about 1 mile turn left on Va. Sec. 600 and follow the Robinson River on up into Berry Hollow to start of trail which is marked by a concrete post. (4.8m. by car from Syria). Another valley approach is up the Hughes River following Va. Rts. 602, 707 and 600 to the Weakley Hollow Fire Rd. where parking is available just inside the Park boundary. One must then walk 2.5m. up Weakley Hollow Fire Rd. and down Berry Hollow another 1.6m. to the Whiteoak Canyon trailhead.

Detailed trail data:
  Skyline Drive at Skyland to Old Rag Valley
  0.0-5.1 Trail begins at parking area, east of the Drive and almost directly across from the southern entrance to Skyland, SDMP 42.5. Trail descends. (*AT* is 0.1m from trailhead, on west side of Drive.)
  0.5-4.6 Cross a branch of Whiteoak Run.
  0.6-4.5 Cross Old Rag Fire Rd. (to right road leads 0.2m. to a parking area and 0.1m. farther to the Skyline Drive. To left it leads down the mountain 4.7m to the Old Rag Valley at the top of the rise where the Weakley Hollow Fire Rd. and Berry Hollow Fire Rd. come together.) Trail soon enters the Limberlost area.
  0.8-4.3 At trail junction the Limberlost Trail leads right 0.8m. to the parking area near the beginning of the Old Rag Fire Rd. To the left a spur trail leads 0.1m. over to Old Rag Fire Rd. Whiteoak Canyon Tr. descends more and more steeply from here.
  2.2-2.9 Turn sharp left and cross footbridge over Whiteoak Run. (Just below the present bridge is the location of Mr. Pollock's "Middle Bridge". This was the side of his famous barbeques in the old "Skyland Days" and a favorite spot of his Skyland guests.) A few feet farther the trail intersects the Skyland-Big Meadows Horse Trail. (Horses must ford the Run. West of the Run the horse trail follows the Whiteoak Fire Rd. up the mountain. Hikers making the Cedar Run Canyon-Whiteoak Canyon circuit may "short cut" the climb up Whiteoak Canyon from here by following this Fire Rd. 1.8 miles to the Skyline Drive, SDMP 45.0, at a point on the Drive

only 0.6m. from the upper end of the Cedar Run Trail.)

2.3-2.8 To right is excellent viewpoint over the Upper Whiteoak Falls, the first of the six cascades in the canyon. From here the trail descends very steeply.

2.4-2.7 A spur trail on the right leads back 250 ft. along Whiteoak Run to near the base of the Upper Falls. The canyon trail continues its steep descent, remaining on the northeast side of the Run. There are occasional views of the various falls as the trail switchbacks down the canyon.

3.7-1.4 Cross side creek, Negro Run. (There is a falls on this creek visible from the trail.) Trail now comes quite close to Whiteoak Run at a point just below the lowest or sixth cascade.

4.3-0.8 Junction with Cedar Run Trail which leads to the right, fording the Whiteoak Run, then continuing almost level until it reaches Cedar Run, where it then climbs to the Drive. (It is 3.5m. from the junction to the Skyline Drive at Hawksbill Gap, SDMP 45.6, via Cedar Run Tr.)

4.9-0.2 Reach Park boundary. Beyond, at top of slight rise, pass house on left.

5.1-0.0 Cross Berry Hollow Run and in a few feet reach the road through Berry Hollow, Va. Sec. 600, at a point 4.8m. northwest of Syria and 1.6m. southwest of the gap where the Berry Hollow, Weakley Hollow and Old Rag Fire Rds. come together. (Whiteoak Run, Cedar Run and Berry Hollow Run come together to make the Robinson River.)

CEDAR RUN TRAIL

3.5 miles (5.7 kilometers)   (PATC map No. 10: I-10)

Cedar Run flows southeast, paralleling Whiteoak Run which it joins near the Berry Hollow Rd., Va. Sec. 600. The two canyons are separated by a high ridge along which the former Half-Mile Cliffs Trail extended. The Cedar Run Canyon is deep and wild with tall trees. While the stream has a lesser flow of water than Whiteoak Run, it has several high falls, sheer cliffs and deep pools.

The Cedar Run Trail is often used in conjunction with the Whiteoak Canyon Trail. The full circuit, starting at Hawksbill

Gap, would be to descent the Cedar Run Tr., ascend the White-oak Canyon Tr. all the way to the Drive, cross to the *AT* and follow the *AT* back to Hawksbill Gap, a distance of 10.5m. A shorter circuit which would still include the deep canyon area of the Whiteoak Canyon Trail would be to descend as before, then to ascend the Whiteoak Tr. to just above the Upper Falls, then to turn left across the Run and follow the Whiteoak Fire Road up the mountain to the Drive, then walk along the Drive the 0.5m. back to Hawksbill Gap, for a total distance of 7.8m. (If starting from Va. Sec. 600 it is necessary to add 1.6m. to the total distances.)

The Hawksbill Gap Shelter, 0.2m. down the Cedar Run Trail, is available for camping in inclement weather. See Chap. 6: Shelters and Cabins.

Access:

The upper end of the Cedar Run Tr. is directly across from the Hawksbill Gap Parking Area, SDMP 45.6. The lower end of the trail is reached from Old Rag Valley by following the Whiteoak Canyon Trail uphill from Va. Sec. 600 for 0.8m. to its junction with Cedar Run Trail.

Detailed trail data:

From Hawksbill Gap to Old Rag Valley

0.0-3.5 East side of the Skyline Drive at Hawksbill Gap, SDMP 45.6, across from Parking Area. Reach gate in 200 ft. Here trail forks. Left fork is Cedar Run Tr. (Right fork leads directly downhill to Hawksbill Shelter.) Just east of the gate the Skyland-Big Meadows Horse Trail crosses both forks.

0.2-3.3 Spur trail leads right 250 ft. to Hawksbill Gap Shelter. From this junction Cedar Run Trail descends, with the stream close to it on the right.

1.1-2.4 To the right is the uppermost cascade of Cedar Run.

1.6-1.9 Cross to the right of Cedar Run and swing away from it.

1.8-1.7 Trail again comes near Cedar Run at a point near its highest falls. Across the creek here tower the sheer Half Mile Cliffs.

2.6-0.9 Here trail turns left and fords the run. (Old road which follows down the right side of the run passes through private property to reach Va. Sec. 600.)

3.5-0.0 Reach junction with Whiteoak Canyon Trail immediately after crossing Whiteoak Run. (To left via Whiteoak Canyon Tr. it is 4.3m. to Skyline Drive, SDMP 42.5; to right it is 0.8m. to Va. Sec. 600 in Berry Hollow, Old Rag Valley.)

WEAKLEY HOLLOW FIRE ROAD

2.5 miles (4.0 kilometers)   (PATC map No. 10: L-6)

BERRY HOLLOW FIRE ROAD

0.8 miles (1.3 kilometers)   (PATC map No. 10: K-8)

Prior to the establishment of the Shenandoah National Park, Old Rag Valley was an extensive mountain community. The state road that is now Va. Sec. 600 went from the village of Nethers through this valley and on out to Syria. A log building, the Old Rag Post Office, was located at the highest spot on this road, at its junction with a road coming down the Blue Ridge from Skyland. The section of the old highway, now in the Park, that lies northeast of the junction is now known as the Weakley Hollow Fire Rd., whereas southwest of the junction it is called the Berry Hollow Fire Rd. These two fire roads along with their extensions outside the park (Va. Sec. 600 in both directions) are very valuable for access purposes; both the Ridge Trail and Saddle Trails up Old Rag mountain start from here, the lower termini of the Whiteoak Canyon Tr. (and access to the Cedar Run Trail) and Nicholson Hollow Trail are on this road, as is the Old Rag Fire Rd. Two fire foot trails, the Robertson Mtn. FFT and the Corbin Hollow FFT, also have their lower ends on this road.

The Weakley Hollow Fire Rd. is an important link for completing a circuit of Old Rag Mtn. The Park Service has constructed a parking area on this road just within the Park! There is also an "overflow" parking area 0.8m. back on Va. Sec. 600. The Berry Hollow Rd. is often used to complete a circuit along with the Whiteoak Canyon Trail and the Old Rag Fire Rd.

Access:

To reach the Weakley Hollow Fire Road turn west off Va. State Rt. 231 (south of Sperryville) onto Va. Sec. 602 at a point just south of the bridge over the Hughes River. Continue up the river, on Va. Sec. 707 where Rt. 602 ends. About 4 miles from Rt. 231, where Rt. 707 turns right and crosses the river, continue on the paved road, Rt. 600, which follows on up the river. In one mile the road turns sharply to the left uphill. 0.3m. farther reach the Park boundary and parking area just beyond.

To reach the Berry Hollow Rd., turn west off Va. State Rt. 231 onto Va. Sec. 670 at a point about 5 miles north of Madison. Continue on Rt. 670 through Criglersville and on to Syria, about 3.5m., then turn right onto Va. Sec. 643, and very shortly turn left onto Va. Sec. 600. Rt. 600 follows up the Robinson River and Berry Hollow 4.8m. to the Park boundary. Parking space is very limited on this road.

Detailed Trail data:

NE to SW

0.0-3.3 Parking area just beyond end of Rt. 600. (Nicholson Hollow Trailhead is 0.3m. down Rt. 600 from here.) Ridge Trail over Old Rag Mtn. leads south from here.

1.2-2.1 Corbin Hollow FFT leads right, crossing Brokenback Run then following up the creek.

1.3-2.0 To the right the Robertson Mtn. FFT leads up the ridge.

2.5-0.8 Road junction. To the right the Old Rag Fire Rd. leads northwest to the Skyland Drive joining it just south of Skyland at SDMP 43.0. Berry Hollow Fire Rd. is straight ahead here. To the left, the Saddle Trail leads 1.9m. to the summit of Old Rag Mtn., passing the Old Rag Shelter in 0.4m. and the Byrds Nest #1 in 1.5m. From the junction the Berry Hollow Fire Rd. descends.

3.3-0.0 Reach Park boundary and Va. Sec. 600. (0.8m. farther, down Rt. 600, is the lower end of the Whiteoak Canyon trail and access to the Cedar Run Trail.)

OLD RAG FIRE RD.

5.0 miles (8.0 kilometers)   (PATC map No. 10: H-8)

In pre-Shenandoah Park days, a road led from Skyland down the east slope of the Blue Ridge to the Old Rag Valley, coming into the road thru the valley at its highest point. The Old Rag Post Office was located at this junction. Now the building that served as post office is gone, as is the community it served. But the lower 4 miles of the present fire road follows pretty much the route of the old road down the mountain. Above Comer's Deadening, the present road continues almost due west and reaches the Skyland Drive about a mile SW of where the original road crossed the Drive.

The Old Rag Fire Rd. can be used in conjunction with the Whiteoak Canyon Trail and the Berry Hollow Fire Rd. for a circuit trip of about 11.5m. From the Skyline Drive, the fire road is the shortest route to the start of the Saddle Trail up Old Rag Mtn. The fire road also serves for access to the Thorofare Mtn. FFT (and via the latter to the Indian Run FFT), the Corbin Hollow FFT and the Robertson Mtn. FFT.

Detailed trail data:

0.0-5.0 Skyline Drive, SDMP 43.0, el. 3360 ft. Fire road leads eastward.

0.1-4.9 Parking area to left of road. To right of road is upper end of Limberlost Trail which leads 0.8m. through the area of virgin hemlocks to its end on the Whiteoak Canyon Trail. Ahead the fire road is gated. Just beyond the gate the Skyland-Big Meadows Horse Trail enters the road from the left and follows down it.

0.3-4.7 Whiteoak Canyon Trail crosses the fireroad. (To the left it is 0.6m. to the Skyline Drive at the southern entrance to Skyland, SDMP 42.5. To the right it is 0.2m. to the lower end of the Limberlost Trail, 1.6m. to the viewpoint above the upper falls and 4.5m. to Va. Sec. 600 in Berry Hollow.)

0.5-4.5 Spur trail leads right 0.1m. to Whiteoak Canyon Tr. entering at the junction of the Whiteoak Canyon and Limberlost Trails.

0.7-4.3 Cross Whiteoak Run.

1.0-4.0 Reach the area known as Comer's Deadening. Here the Skyland-Big Meadows Horse Trail turns right leaving the fire road, and in 1.7m. reaches the Whiteoak Run just above the Upper Falls. 100 ft. farther along the fire road a trail, marked by cement post, comes in from the left. (This was the former Skyland-Old Rag Rd. It leads about 1m. to the Skyline Drive, at a point just opposite the northern entrance to Skyland.)

1.1-3.9 Pass Ranger cabin on right. Beyond here the fire road descends steadily.

1.8-3.2 Thorofare Mtn. FFT enters from the left. (This fire trail follows an old road down to a sag, then up Thorofare Mtn. In 0.6m. the Corbin Mtn. FFT leads right from it, also following an old road. The blazes on the latter are faded and the trail now gives out completely in approx. 1 mile, before reaching Corbin Mtn. A few feet beyond the Corbin Mtn. FFT junction the Indian Run FFT leads left from the Thorofare Mtn. FFT and connects with the Nicholson Hollow Tr. just above Corbin Cabin.

2.3-2.7 Corbin Hollow FFT leads left for 2.0m., following down Brokenback Run to reach the Weakley Hollow Fire Rd. at a point 1.2m. above the parking area at Va. Sec. 600.

2.4-2.6 Robertson Mtn. FFT leads left for 2.4m. climbing over Robertson Mtn., el. 3296 ft., then descending to Old Rag Valley entering the Weakley Hollow Fire Rd. at a point 1.3m. above the parking area on that road, at the start of Va. Sec. 600.

5.0-0.0 Junction with the Weakley Hollow and Berry Hollow Fire Roads, at the top of the gap between Old Rag Mtn. and the main Blue Ridge (elevation here 1913 ft.). Directly ahead is the start of the Saddle Trail. (Via the Saddle Trail it is 0.4m. to the Old Rag Shelter, 1.5m. to Byrds Nest #1, and 1.9m. to the summit of Old Rag.) From the junction of the fire roads it is 2.5m. via the Weakley Hollow Fire Rd. to the parking lot at the Park boundary and 0.3m. farther, via Va. Sec. 600, to the lower end of the Nicholson Hollow Trail. To the right, via the Berry Hollow Fire Rd. it is 0.8m. to the Park boundary and 0.8m. farther along Va. Sec. 600 to the lower end of the Whiteoak Canyon Trail.

LIMBERLOST TRAIL

0.8 miles (1.3 kilometers)   (PATC map No. 10: H-8)

This trail leads through a very beautiful forest of virgin hemlock and some spruce, called by George Freeman Pollock the "Limberlost" because of its supposed similarity to the woods in the novel by Gene Stratton Porter entitled *Girl of the Limberlost.* There is little change in elevation on this trail.

From the Limberlost Trail Parking Area on Old Rag Fire Rd. 0.1m. east of Skyline Drive, SDMP 43.0, the trail leads gently down, toward the south, for 0.4m. Here at a trail junction the Crescent Rock Tr. leads right for 1.1m. to the Skyline Drive at Crescent Rock Overlook. From the trail junction the Limberlost Tr. swings to the east and ends on the Whiteoak Canyon Trail in another 0.4m.

For a short circuit hike, follow the Limberlost Tr. down to the Whiteoak Canyon Tr.; turn left and follow the Whiteoak Canyon Tr. up for 0.2m. to its intersection with the Old Rag Fire Rd., then follow the fire road left for 0.2m. back to the parking area.

Another circuit, about 4m. in length, would include the upper 0.4m. of the Limberlost Tr., the Crescent Rock Tr., the *A T* back to Skyland, and the short section of the Skyland-Big Meadows Horse Tr. between the *A T* and the Limberlost Parking Area. See write-up of the Crescent Rock Tr. for a slightly different circuit. (Note: The Crescent Rock Tr. does not show on PATC map #10, 12th ed.)

THOROFARE MTN. FFT

0.6m. (1.0 kilometers)   (PATC map No. 10: I-7)

CORBIN MTN. FFT

1 mile (1½ kilometers)   (PATC map No. 10: I-7)

INDIAN RUN FFT

1.6 miles (2.6 kilometers)   (PATC map No. 10: I-7)

A yellow post marks the start of the Thorofare Mtn. FFT at a point on the Old Rag Fire Rd. 1.8m. east of the Skyline Drive.

SDMP 43.0. The trail leads down to a sag, then up toward Thorofare Mtn. (The Thorofare Mtn. School was once located on this old road.)

Just before reaching the present end of the Thorofare Mtn. FFT, the Corbin Mtn. FFT leads right from it, also following an old road. This FFT is distinct here but is very poorly blazed and gives out completely in about one mile, never reaching Corbin Mtn.

To reach the Indian Run FFT one must continue straight ahead on the Thorofare Mtn. FFT for 100 ft. beyond the Corbin Mtn. FFT junction. The Indian Run FFT leads sharply left from the Thorofare Mtn. FFT. There is a metal post, up the Indian Run FFT a few feet, marking the trail, but it may be hidden by bushes so care is needed to find it. (The Thorofare FFT is not blazed beyond this junction.) The Indian Run FFT passes through a sag between Thorofare Mtn. and Stony Man Mtn. before descending along Indian Run to intersect the Nicholson Hollow Trail at a point about 0.1m. above the Corbin Cabin and 1.7m. from the Skyline Drive. These fire foot trails are recommended only for the experienced hiker. Such hikers do use the Indian Run and Thorofare Mtn. FFTs along with the Nicholson Hollow Tr., the *A T* and the Old Rag Fire Road for a circuit hike.

CORBIN HOLLOW FFT

2.0 miles (3.2 kilometers)   (PATC map No. 10: J-7)

This trail is not hard to follow. Its upper end is on the Old Rag Fire Rd. at a point 2.3m. from the Skyline Drive, SDMP 43.0, and 2.7m. on the fire road from the Weakley Hollow Fire Rd. The lower end is on the Weakley Hollow Fire Rd. 1.3m. on that road NE of its junction with the Old Rag Fire Rd. and 1.2m. SW of the parking area at the Park boundary. The trail follows Brokenback Run through Corbin Hollow. This area was formerly the location of a very primitive and poverty-stricken mountain community.

ROBERTSON MTN. FFT

2.4 miles (3.9 kilometers)   (PATC map No. 10: J-7)

This trail can be recommended for hikers as it is not hard to follow and offers some excellent views of Corbin Hollow and Old Rag Mtn. Its upper end is on the Old Rag Fire Rd. at a point 2.4m. east of the Skyline Drive, SDMP 43.0, via the fire road, and 2.6m. northwest of the Weakley Hollow Fire Rd. via the road. The lower end is on the Weakley Hollow Fire Rd. at a point 1.3m. up the road from Va. Sec. 600 at the Park boundary (and parking area) and 1.2m. down the road from its junction with the Old Rag Fire Rd. The upper ends of the Robertson Mtn. FFT and Corbin Hollow FFT are about 0.1m. apart; so are their lower ends.

From the Old Rag Fire Rd. the Robertson Mtn. FFT, starting at an elevation of about 2800 ft., climbs for 0.8m., with many switchbacks, to the top of Robertson Mtn., el. 3296 ft. From the summit it descends eastward, again with many switchbacks. Where it joins the Weakley Hollow Rd. the elevation is only 1532 ft.

WHITEOAK FIRE ROAD

1.8 miles (2.9 kilometers)   (PATC map No. 10: I-9)

The chief use of this road, for hikers, is as a link to complete the circuit when descending Cedar Run Trail and ascending Whiteoak Canyon as far as the Upper Falls. The Skyland-Big Meadows Horse Trail also utilizes this road, following it from Whiteoak Run to just short of the Skyline Drive. The lower end of this road is at the Whiteoak Run, just above the Upper Falls at the site of G. F. Pollock's Middle Bridge. (Via the Whiteoak Canyon Trail it is 2.3m. to the Skyline Drive, SDMP 42.5) The upper end is on the Skyline Drive, SDMP 45.0, about 0.6m. "north" of Hawksbill Gap and the upper end of the Cedar Run Trail.

OLD RAG MTN. CIRCUIT:

7.1 miles (11.4 kilometers)   (PATC map No. 10: L-6)

(Includes the Ridge Trail, 2.7m., the Saddle Trail, 1.9m. and Weakley Hollow Fire Rd., 2.5m.)

To hikers Old Rag Mountain has a very special character. The only other mountains in the East that can compete with it are Mt. Katahdin in Maine and Grandfather Mountain in North Carolina. And of the three, Old Rag has the advantage, or disadvantage, of being the most accessible. Old Rag is the favorite hike of many youth organizations of the Washington area, so that every weekend finds one or more large groups of youngsters camping or hiking on the mountain, as well as family groups, novice hikers, and veteran walkers. Those who survive the steep climb up the Ridge Trail are rewarded by the fascinating walk over and around the tremendous rocks and by the outstanding views, first one direction, then another.

Old Rag stands apart from the main Blue Ridge, separated from it by the narrow Old Rag Valley. It consists of a long, rocky ridge composed primarily of granite. However, long ago, lava welled up in cracks in the granite and formed a series of basaltic dykes, varying in thickness from a few feet to fifty. This basaltic material has weathered more rapidly than the surrounding granite, creating some of the rock features that give the mountain its ragged appearance. At one place on the Ridge Trail there is a regular staircase, with high vertical walls of granite and "steps" formed by the characteristic weathering of columnar basalt in blocks.

In wintertime, when snow and ice make the trails on Old Rag too difficult and dangerous for most hikers, there is still a special breed of walker who enjoys the challenge this mountain has to offer. He comes equipped with proper clothing for exposure to cold and wind, and uses crampons when travelling over icy spots.

It is advisable to carry water when hiking up Old Rag. The spring near the top is often dry, especially during the summer, and there is no water at Byrd's Nest #1 which is situated in the saddle, about 0.4m. from the summit along the Saddle Trail. The other shelter, Old Rag Shelter, is much lower down on the Saddle

Trail and water is available here. (Shelters may be used for camping only in inclement weather.)

Access:

The Ridge Trail starts at the parking area on the Weakley Hollow Fire Rd. To reach the lower end of the Saddle Trail, one must walk the 2.5m. up the Weakley Hollow Fire Rd. to its junction with the Berry Hollow Fire Rd. and Old Rag Fire Rd. The automobile approach to the Weakley Hollow Parking area is as follows: From Va. St. Rt. 231 south of Sperryville, turn west on Va. Sec. 602 at a point just south of the bridge over the Hughes River. Follow up the south side of the river, first on Rt. 602, then 707, then 600, for about 5 miles. The Weakley Hollow Rd. is the continuation of Rt. 600 within the Park. The parking lot is just inside the Park boundary. If it should be filled, there is some parking space available 0.3m. down Rt. 600, where the road makes a sharp turn; also there is an "Overflow" parking area 0.5m. farther down.

Detailed trail data:

Circuit described in a clockwise direction, starting with the Ridge Trail.

0.0-7.1 From the Old Rag Parking area on the Weakley Hollow Fire Rd. just inside the Park boundary, el. 1080 ft., the Ridge Trail heads due south.

0.5-6.6 Spring is 100 ft. to right of trail, under walnut trees. This the last sure water on the Ridge Trail.

1.3-5.8 Pass a wet weather spring, to right of trail, close under steep side of the ridge.

1.4-5.7 Reach crest of ridge in broad wooded saddle and turn sharply to the right.

1.6-5.5 Emerge from woods onto rocks.

2.3-4.8 Spur trail leads left 300 ft. downhill to wet-weather spring.

2.6-4.5 A second spur trail leads downhill to the spring

2.7-4.4 End of the Ridge Trail. To right are the projecting rocks forming the summit of Old Rag, el. 3291 ft. The trail, now the Saddle Trail, descends south along the ridge crest.

2.8-4.3 Path leads right 300 ft. to site of former fire tower.

2.9-4.2 Spur trail leads right 300 ft. to cave formed by huge sloping rocks. Saddle Trail descends.

3.1-4.0 Reach the "Saddle" where blue blazes end. Here the shelter, Byrd's Nest #1, is located. There are inside and outside fireplaces but no water. Shelters may be used for camping only in inclement weather. (Beyond the shelter the Ragged Run Rd. descends to the south. This road is *closed to hikers* outside the Park boundary.) Trail turns sharp right, leaving the ridge, and descends steadily by switchbacks along the northwest slopes of the mountain.

4.2-2.9 The Old Rag Shelter is 100 ft. ahead here. Trail turns right onto dirt road and continues to descend.

4.6-2.5 Reach junction of the 3 fire roads—Weakley Hollow, Berry Hollow, and Old Rag—at the site of the former Old Rag Post Office, turn right on Weakley Hollow Fire Rd. and descend. (From the fire road junction it is 5.0m. to the Skyline Drive, SDMP 43.0, via the Old Rag Fire Rd. and 1.6m. left, via the Berry Hollow Fire Rd. to the foot of the Whiteoak Canyon Trail.)

7.1-0.0 Reach the Old Rag Parking Area and Va. Sec. 600 just beyond.

SKYLAND-BIG MEADOWS HORSE TRAIL

11.2 miles (18.0 kilometers)   (PATC map No. 10: H-8)

From the stables at Skyland this trail leads across the Drive and over to the Old Rag Fire Rd. which it follows down to Comer's Deadening. Here it turns right and enters Whiteoak Canyon. It crosses Whiteoak Run just above the Upper Falls, then follows the Whiteoak Fire Rd. almost to its junction with the Skyline Drive, SDMP 45.0. From here it parallels the Drive until beyond the Upper Hawksbill Parking area; it then descends along the southwest slope of Spitler Hill and circles the head of the Rose River Canyon. It again crosses the Drive just south of Fishers Gap and then parallels the Drive to reach the Big Meadows stables. The trail has posts marking the half-miles.

The section of horse trail between Whiteoak Fire Rd. and Fishers Gap gets very little horse traffic so is pleasant walking. That part near the Rose River is quite scenic. Hikers should remember to yield the right-of-way to the horse party should they meet.

Detailed description:

Skyland to Big Meadows

0.0-11.2 Trail leads from Skyland stables, crossing the *AT*. It then passes through much mountain laurel as it angles toward the Skyline Drive.

0.2-11.0 Cross to the east side of the Skyline Drive. Trail now parallels the Drive.

0.6-10.6 Come into the Old Rag Fire Rd. and follow it to the left. (A parking area is 200 ft. to the right along the road. The Skyline Drive is 0.1m. farther.)

1.5-9.7 Horse trail turns sharply right away from the fire road at a signpost and heads toward Whiteoak Canyon. This area is known as Comer's Deadening. Horse trail now follows old road that was once a part of the Whiteoak Fire Road.

2.7-8.5 Ford Whiteoak Run just above the Upper Falls. From here the horse trail follows the Whiteoak Fire Rd.

4.3-6.9 At a point on the Whiteoak Fire Road a little over 0.1m. from the Skyline Drive the horse trail turns left and parallels the Drive.

4.8-6.4 Intersection with Cedar Falls Trail and a trail to Hawksbill Shelter. (To the right, via the Cedar Falls Trail it is only a few feet to the Skyline Drive at Hawksbill Gap.)

6.2-5.0 Horse trail comes into old farm road at a point near the summit of Spitler Hill and follows the road to the left. (To the right the old road leads to the Skyline Drive coming in at a point just south of the Upper Hawksbill Parking Area, SDMP 46.7.) Ladies'-Tresses, a type of orchid, may be found here, blooming in Sept. and Oct. For over a half mile the trail passes through old fields, now quite overgrown. Old road gradually narrows into trail.

8.0-3.2 Cross stream, a branch of the Rose River.

8.5-2.7 Cross a second branch of the Rose River.

9.1-2.1 The Copper Mine Loop Trail enters from the left and follows the horse trail.

9.6-1.6 Cross the Dark Hollow Fire Rd. at a point just east of Fishers Gap, SDMP 49.3. 0.1m. farther cross to the right (west) of the Skyline Drive. The horse trail swings out-of-sight of the Drive, then turns to parallel it.

11.0-0.2 Intersection with the Dark Hollow Falls Trail at a point on that trail a few feet east from its start on the Swamp Nature Trail.

11.2-0.0 Big Meadows stables, SDMP 51.2. See PATC map #10: Big Meadows Inset.

CRESCENT ROCK TRAIL

1.1m. (1.8 km.)   (PATC map No. 10: I-9)

This short trail runs from the Skyline Drive, SDMP 44.4, across from the Crescent Rock Overlook (look for cement signpost just south of the north entrance) down to the Limberlost Trail, with a gentle downgrade all the way. A pleasant half-day circuit hike (4½m.) can be made by following this trail from the Overlook, turning right onto the Limberlost Trail and following it for 0.4m., then ascending the Whiteoak Canyon Trail to the Skyline Drive. Cross the Drive and a few yards up the road toward the Skyland stables, turn left onto the *AT* and follow it for two miles. There a short spur trail, marked by a cement post, leads to the north end of the Crescent Rock Overlook.

BETTYS ROCK TRAIL

0.3 miles (0.5 kilometers)   (PATC map No. 10: I-9)

From the Crescent Rock Parking Overlook, SDMP 44.4, this short trail leads due north to a rocky outcrop known as Bettys Rock which affords excellent views west. In the rock crannies grow the tiny flowers of the three-toothed cinquefoil, a primarily Canadian plant, which is found in the southern mountains only at high elevations in exposed situations such as this one.

HAWKSBILL MTN. TRAIL

1.8 miles (2.9 kilometers)   (PATC map No. 10: Hawksbill Inset)

NAKEDTOP TRAIL

1.1 miles (1.8 kilometers)   (PATC map No. 10: Hawksbill Inset)

SERVICE RD. TO BYRD'S NEST #2

0.9 miles (1.4 kn.)   (PATC map No. 10: Hawksbill Inset)

Hawksbill Mtn. is the highest mountain in the Shenandoah Park. Native spruce and balsam are found on its upper slopes. An observation platform at the summit, el. 4050 ft., provides excellent views of Timber Hollow to the north and of Page Valley and the Massanuttens to the west. The hiker has the choice of four routes up the mountain. From its northern end at Hawksbill Gap, SDMP 45.6, a trail leads 0.8m. to the summit, then descends along the service road for about 0.4m. from where it forks left and descends 0.6m. farther to the Upper Hawksbill Parking Area, SDMP 46.7. A third route up Hawksbill is via the service road to the Byrd's Nest #2. It leaves the Drive at SDMP 47.1. and reaches the shelter, just below the summit in 0.9m. The fourth route is via the Nakedtop Trail. This trail, which intersects the *AT*, has one end at the summit of Hawksbill Mtn., the other on Nakedtop, a wooded peak of the western shoulder of Hawksbill Mtn. From the summit this trail leads down 0.7m. to the *AT*, follows the *AT* right for 100 ft., then turns left off it and continues 0.4m. to Nakedtop. The trail loops around Nakedtop offering several nice views. A circuit route over Hawksbill could include the Hawksbill Tr. from Hawksbill Gap to the summit, 0.8m., the Nakedtop Tr. down to the *AT*, 0.7m. and the *AT* back to Hawksbill Gap, 1.0m. See back of PATC Map #10.

Byrd's Nest #2, an open-faced shelter, is situated just below the summit of Hawksbill Mtn. It can be used for camping only in inclement weather. See Chap. 6 "Shelters and Cabins." Water is not available here but there is a spring 0.8m. downhill.

BURACKER HOLLOW FFT

approx. 2 miles (3 kilometers)   (PATC map No. 10: I-10)

This fire foot trail follows an old road from the Skyline Drive at Hawksbill Gap, SDMP 45.6, down through Timber Hollow to the Park boundary. The trail continues outside the Park into Buracker Hollow but the land is posted.

TRAILS IN THE BIG MEADOWS-HOOVER CAMP AREA

The Big Meadows Developed Area includes the Harry F. Byrd, Sr. Visitor Center, a wayside, lodge, cabins, restaurant, camp store, stables, gift shop, picnic grounds and the largest campgrounds in the Park. The campgrounds is the only one in the Park kept open during the entire year.

Big Meadows is located on a very broad, flat area of the Blue Ridge. Many geologists believe that this area is the remnant of an old, high peneplain. Because of its surprising flatness water does not run off easily and some of the area is quite boggy. The Swamp Nature Trail was constructed to show some of the interesting features of the area. A network of trails and fire roads provide the camper with many miles of good walking. There are a number of circuit hikes possible in the area, some quite short, others which can provide a full day of hiking. Hikers using trails maintained primarily for horses should yield the right-of-way.

Hoover Camp, situated within the Park on the Rapidan River, was originally built for a presidential hide-away by Herbert Hoover while he was in office. Later he donated the camp to the U.S. Government for use by future presidents and their guests. The Park Service administers the property and welcomes visitors—hikers and horseback riders—on the grounds of the camp. Only three of the original buildings—the President's Cabin, the Prime Minister's Cabin and "The Creel" remain today. However, historical markers have been placed at the sites of the former buildings explaining how and by whom they were used.

Access to Camp Hoover from the east is via the Rapidan Fire Road and Va. Sec. 649. Refer to write-up for this road. To reach the camp from the Skyline Drive one can (1) follow the Rapidan Fire Rd. from Big Meadows, SDMP 51.3, (2) descend the Mill Prong Trail from Milam Gap, SDMP 52.8, or (3) follow the *AT* north from Bootens Gap, SDMP 55.1, to reach the Laurel Prong Trail and descend the latter.

RED GATE FIRE ROAD

4.8 miles (7.8 kilometers)   (PATC map No. 10: G-11)

This road, gated at both ends, leads from the base of the mountains 4 mi. east of Stanley to the Skyline Drive at Fishers Gap, SDMP 49.3. (This road is the western portion of the old Gordonsville Pike. It continues on the east slope of the Blue Ridge as the Dark Hollow Falls Fire Road and, below Hogcamp Branch, as the Rose River Fire Road.) The Red Gate Fire Rd. climbs with a gentle grade and has many switchbacks to gain 1500 ft. of elevation. It offers a pleasant walk except that one does have to beware of cars as Park and Concessionaire personnel use this road to reach Big Meadows.

To reach the lower end of the Red Gate Rd. turn east in Stanley (from U.S. 340) on either Va. Sec. 624 or 689. Beyond the junction of these roads, follow Rt. 689 eastward for about 1 mile, then continue straight on Va. Sec. 611 where Rt. 689 turns sharply left. Continue on Rt. 611 to the Park boundary where road becomes the Red Gate Rd. and is gated.

SWAMP NATURE TRAIL (BIG MEADOWS)

2.0 miles (3.2 km.)   (PATC map No. 10: Big Meadows Inset)

A portion of the Big Meadows area is quite swampy. As the altitude is unusually high for a swamp, plants are found here that are quite rare elsewhere in the Park. One section of the Swamp Nature Trail follows along the edge of this swamp and some of these plants are identified with help from the self-guiding tour pamphlet. For the nature walk, follow the trail in a clockwise direction, starting at the signpost on the east end of the Amphitheatre Parking area.

If the Swamp Trail is to be used as one link in the Dark Hollow Falls-Copper Mine Loop circuit, one usually follows it "in reverse" by finding the "end" of the Swamp Trail across the road from the west end of the parking lot and a few hundred feet south. Follow the trail counterclockwise as far as the junction with the Dark Hollow Falls Trail.

Detailed description:

(Clockwise)

0.0-2.0 Amphitheatre Parking Area, Big Meadows. Sign marks start of trail which leads northwest from the start.

0.1-1.9 Turn right onto the *A T* and follow it "north".

0.6-1.4 At trail junction the Swamp Trail continues straight ahead, while the *A T* turns sharply left.

1.4-0.6 Post marks junction with Dark Hollow Trail which begins here. Dark Hollow Trail is to the left; the nature trail continues straight ahead.

1.8-0.2 At junction marked by post the Swamp Trail follows left fork. (Right fork, straight ahead, leads to campground.)

1.9-0.1 Cross paved path and paved Big Meadows Road.

2.0-0.0 Official end of Nature Trail but path continues. About 250 ft. farther a spur trail leads left to Big Meadows lodge. In another 100 ft., the path comes into road leading from the Amphitheatre Parking area.

DARK HOLLOW FALLS-COPPER MINE LOOP TRAIL

3.7 miles (6.0 kilometers)   (PATC map No. 10: H-13)

The Dark Hollow Falls Trail is the most popular one in the Park. It leads to a very lovely cascading waterfall on the Hogcamp Branch of the Rose River. For a very short trip park at the Dark Hollow Falls Parking Area on the Skyline Drive, SDMP 50.7. For a slightly longer trip park at the Amphitheatre Parking Area of Big Meadows (follow road signs) and take the Swamp Nature Trail to reach the start of the Dark Hollow Falls Trail. From the Amphitheatre Parking Area it is 1.4m. to the

Dark Hollow Falls trailhead if following the Swamp Trail clockwise, or about 0.7m. if following the Swamp Trail counterclockwise or "in reverse".

For a more extended hike a circuit trip of about 6 miles can be made from the Amphitheatre Parking Area using the Swamp Trail, then descending the Dark Hollow Falls Trail, continuing along the Cooper Mine Loop Trail (which is very scenic and passes a falls on the Rose River) to Fishers Gap, then returning to Big Meadows via the *AT*. (Refer to PATC map #10 and to PATC publication, *Circuit Hikes in the SNP.*)

Detailed description:

Described from Big Meadows Swamp Nature Trail to Fishers Gap

0.0-3.7 Upper end of Dark Hollow Falls Trail on Swamp Nature Trail

0.2-3.5 Cross Skyline Drive, SDMP 50.7, at north end of Dark Hollow Falls Parking Area. From here trail descends steadily with stream on its right.

0.8-2.9 Reach top of Dark Hollow Falls, a series of terraced cascades. From here trail descends very steeply.

1.0-2.7 Reach old road, now the Dark Hollow Falls Fire Rd. It is a portion of the pre-park Gordonsville Pike. (To the left, road leads 1.1m. to Fishers Gap.) Turn right onto the road and cross bridge over Hogcamp Branch. Fifty feet beyond the bridge, at trail sign, turn left off the road, (below here the road is called the Rose River Fire Rd.), and follow the Copper Mine Loop Trail down the creek.

1.9-1.8 At junction marked by cement post turn sharply left and cross Hogcamp Branch. (Trail to right leads 0.3m. to the Rose River Fire Rd. (or old Gordonsville Pike)). In 250 ft. cross a small stream. Fifty feet beyond, it passes the site of an old copper mine to the left of the trail. The trail soon approaches the main branch of the Rose River, turns left at a sign pointing to Rose River Falls and climbs along the west bank of the river.

2.5-1.2 Pass waterfall.

2.8-0.9 Turn left, uphill, onto an old road, now the route of the Big Meadows-Skyland Horse Trail.

3.7-0.0 Turn right onto the Dark Hollow Falls Fire Rd. and in a few feet reach the Skyline Drive, SDMP 49.3, at Fishers Gap. (To complete the circuit hike cross the Drive and follow the Red Gate Fire Rd. a few feet to reach the *AT*. Turn left onto the *AT* and follow it 1.0m. to its junction with the Swamp Nature Trail. Continue on *AT* and the Swamp Trail "in reverse" for another 0.5m. Turn left at post and follow Swamp Trail 0.1m. to the Amphitheatre Parking Area.)

DARK HOLLOW FALLS FIRE RD.-ROSE RIVER FIRE RD. (OLD GORDONSVILLE PIKE)

6.5 miles (10.5 kilometers)   (PATC map No. 10: H-12)

From Fishers Gap, SDMP 49.3, this old road winds its way down to Va. Sec. 670 west of Syria. In pre-Park days it was known as the Gordonsville Pike and many hikers still refer to it by this name. However, from Fishers Gap to Hogcamp Branch below Dark Hollow Falls it is now the Dark Hollow Falls Fire Road, while below the bridge over Hogcamp Branch it is now the Rose River Fire Rd. (West of the Skyline Drive, the road continues as the Red Gate Fire Rd.)

The upper portion, the Dark Hollow Falls Fire Rd., can be used for circuit hikes either in combination with the Dark Hollow Falls Tr. and *AT* or with the Copper Mine Loop Trail. The lower portion is used for a circuit hike that involves ascending the Rose River either by scrambling over the rocks or following a "fisherman's trail" upcreek along the southwest bank, then following the Copper Mine Loop Trail left to the fire road, and finally descending the latter. (Refer to PATC publication: *Circuit Hikes in the SNP.*)

Access:

From Va. Rt. 231 at a point about 16 miles south of U.S. 522 near Sperryville and 5 m. north of Madison, turn west onto Va. Sec. 670. Follow Rt. 670 through Criglersville and Syria and continue on Rt. 670 to the Park boundary. Parking space near the end of Rt. 670 is very limited. From the boundary continue up road on foot, with river to right of the road in deep gorge. (At about the spot where the road bends to the left away from the river a path leads right, through an overgrown field, to the river

and up it along the southwest bank. If you wish to find this trail
and have continued up the road too far you will find on the left of
the road a yellow metal post marking the Dark Hollow FFT; if
so, backtrack about 0.1m!)

Detailed Description:
    From Fishers Gap to Va. Sec. 670
    0.0-6.5 Skyline Drive at Fishers Gap, SDMP 49.3
    1.1-5.4 To the right the Dark Hollow Falls Tr., marked by
post, leads uphill 0.8m. to Skyline Drive. Just beyond this trail
junction road crosses Hogcamp Branch. Fifty feet farther a post
marks the Copper Mine Loop Trail which leads left down
Hogcamp Branch.
    2.0-4.5 Stony Mtn. FFT leads right for 1.1m. to Rapidan Fire
Road.
    2.5-4.0 To left a spur trail leads 0.3m. to Copper Mine Loop
Trail.
    5.2-1.3 Post on right marks Dark Hollow FFT. (This fire foot
trail leads 2.2m. to the Rapidan Rd. at Broyles Gap.)
    6.5-0.0 Park boundary.

STONY MTN. FFT

1.1 mile (1.8 kilometers)   (PATC map No. 10: I-12)

This trail is well blazed but may be weedy in summer. It follows
an old road and is useful as it connects the Rose River Fire Road
(Gordonsville Pike) and the Rapidan Fire Road. Its northern
end is 2.0m down the Dark Hollow Falls-Rose River Fire Rd.
from the Skyline Drive. The southern end is 2.9m. down the
Rapidan Fire Rd. from the Drive.

DARK HOLLOW FFT
UPPER DARK HOLLOW FFT

2.2 miles (3.5 kilometers)   (PATC map No. 10: J-12)

This trail route connects the Rose River Fire Rd.
(Gordonsville Pike) and the Rapidan Fire Rd. Its lower end is
about 1.3m. up the Rose River Fire Rd. from the Park Boundary

(at end of Va. Rt. 670.) The trail route involves a climb of about 1250 ft. to reach its upper end on the Rapidan Fire Rd. at Broyles Gap. The lower portion of trail, the Dark Hollow FFT, has only a narrow footway but has recently (1976) been recleared and freshly blazed; it passes through a beautiful hemlock forest. Where it joins the Upper Dark Hollow FFT the latter is a road. As it ascends toward the Rapidan Fire Rd. the Upper Dark Hollow FFT gradually narrows but has a broad footway all the way. This upper portion of the trail route is used by horseback riders as well as hikers.

Experienced hikers should find this trail useful as part of a circuit hike. Starting at the lower end of the Rose River Fire Rd., walk up the road for about 4m. to reach the Stony Mtn. FFT, then follow this fire foot trail about 1m. over to the Rapidan Fire Rd. Descend the Rapidan Rd. for about 1m. to Broyles Gap, then descend the Upper Dark Hollow and Dark Hollow FFTs back to the Rose River Fire Rd. and descend road to the car. (See PATC map #10.) Total circuit is about 9#m. in length.

RAPIDAN FIRE ROAD—VIRGINIA SECONDARY RT. 649

9.8 miles (15.8 kilometers)   (PATC map No. 10: H-13)

This fire road is gated at the Skyline Drive (at Big Meadows) and at the "first" Park boundary, just below the junction with the Hoover Camp Road. This upper portion of the road is used as a horse trail and also by hikers. It is useful as one segment of a circuit hike which also includes the Mill Prong Trail and AT. (See PATC publication, *Circuit Hikes in the SNP.*) The road continues east of the gate through a Virginia Wildlife Area and descends along the Rapidan River. It then reenters the SNP. After another mile along the river the road climbs to the top of the Chapman Mountain ridge before reaching the easternmost Park boundary. Although there is some traffic on this part of the road it is light and the road is not unpleasant for walking. This portion of the road can be used along with the Doubletop Mtn. Trail (non-maintained but with a good footway) for a circuit. There is a

good swimming hole on the river at the junction of this road and
Va. Sec. 662, the road up the Rapidan from Graves Mill.

Access:

The upper end is on the Skyline Drive, SDMP 51.3, across
from the Big Meadows Wayside where there is ample parking.

To reach the road from the east, turn west off Va. 231 onto Va.
Sec. 670 at a point about 16 miles south of U.S. 522 near
Sperryville and 5 miles north of Madison. Follow Rt. 670 for
about 1m. beyond Criglersville. Here turn left onto Va. 649,
crossing the Rose River and following up a side stream toward
Chapman Mtn. Road is narrow but drivable over Chapman
Mtn. and on beyond the junction with Va. Sec. 662 on the
Rapidan River to just below the Camp Hoover Access Road
where it reenters the SNP. Here it is gated.

Detailed Description:

From Skyline Drive to most eastward Park boundary. All
mileages given below are estimated.)

0.0-10.0 Junction with Skyline Drive, SDMP 51.3, across
from Big Meadows Wayside.

1.2-8.8 To right of the road the Mill Prong Horse Trail leads
1.8m. to Hoover Camp.

2.9-7.1 The Stony Mtn. FFT leads left to the Rose River Fire
Rd. (Gordonsville Pike).

3.8-6.2 Upper Dark Hollow FFT leads left to Rose River
Fire Rd. (Gordonsville Pike).

5.4-4.6 At road junction fire road continues straight ahead.
The road to the right leads up the Rapidan River for about 3/4
miles to Camp Hoover.

5.8-4.2 Reach Park boundary where road is gated and enter
Virginia Wildlife Area where road becomes Va. Sec. 649 and is
open to automobile traffic.

7.5-2.5 At road fork, Rt. 649 continues straight ahead
descending along the Rapidan River. (Road to the right, the
Fork Mtn. Rd., goes in and out of the SNP as it climbs to the
radio tower on Fork Mtn. This road is rough and not
recommended for automobile use.)

7.6-2.4 Reenter SNP.

8.8-1.2 At road junction take left fork and climb, leaving the river. (Right fork is Va. Sec. 662 which follows on down the Rapidan River reaching the Park boundary in about 1.7 m.)

9.4-0.6 At road junction on top of ridge (of Chapman Mtn.) continue straight ahead. (To right a Va. Forest Rd. leads out Blakey Ridge past the Utz Hightop Lookout Tower. Gated road to left is an access road to private land. The Doubletop Trail starts from about 0.2m. up this road.)

10.0-0.0 Road leaves the Park. (From here it is 3.0m. to Va. Rt. 670, the road through Criglersville.)

MILL PRONG TRAIL

1.8 miles (2.9 kilometers)   (PATC map No. 10: H-15)

This trail leads from the *AT* in Milam Gap east to Hoover Camp. The first mile, from Milam Gap to the junction with the Mill Prong Horse Trail, is blue-blazed. The trail can be used along with the Laurel Prong Trail and *AT* for one good circuit hike, 7.0m., or it can be used along with the Rapidan Fire Road, the road into Hoover Camp, and the *AT* for another good circuit trip, 12m. (See PATC publication, *Circuit Hikes in the SNP.*)

Access:

From Milam Gap, SDMP 52.8, follow the *AT* south a few feet to signpost marking start of the Mill Prong Trail.

To reach the lower end of the trail, follow directions for getting to Hoover Camp from the east. The Mill Prong trailhead is on the Hoover Camp access road, 100 ft. west of the bridge over Mill Prong.

Detailed Description:

Milam Gap to Hoover Camp

0.0-1.8 Junction with the *AT,* a few feet south of the Skyline Drive crossing at Milam Gap, SDMP 52.8. Trail descends gently through an old field and orchard, now overgrown.

0.6-1.2 Cross main branch of Mill Prong. Trail now descends through tall trees and fern-covered forest floor.

1.0-0.8 Cross another branch of Mill Prong and bear right, reaching junction with the Mill Prong Horse Trail which comes in from the left. (Via the Mill Prong Horse Tr. it is 1.0m. north to the Rapidan Fire Rd. and 1.2m. farther along the fire road to the Skyline Drive at Big Meadows Wayside.) Trail now descends along the creek.

1.5-0.3 Cross to right of creek just below Big Rock Falls. *Crossing is easy to miss.*

1.8-0.0 Junction with access road to Hoover Camp at a point on the road 100 ft. west of the bridge over Mill Prong.

MILL PRONG HORSE TRAIL (OR MILL PRONG SPUR TRAIL)

1.8 miles (2.9 kilometers)   (PATC map No. 10: I-13)

This trail leads from the Rapidan Fire Road to Hoover Camp. Its lower part is coincident with the Mill Prong Trail described above. The upper end of this trail is on the Rapidan Fire Foad at a point 1.2m. from the Skyline Drive at Big Meadows. The lower end is at Hoover Camp just west of the road bridge over Mill Prong. It is about 1.2m. from the Rapidan Fire Rd. to the junction with the blue-blazed Mill Prong Tr. and another 0.8m. on to Hoover Camp.

Hikers may use this trail, along with the Mill Prong Trail and the *AT*, for a shorter circuit hike to Hoover Camp (about 8m.) than the Rapidan Fire Rd.—Hoover Camp Rd.—Mill Prong Tr.—*AT* circuit. (See PATC map No. 10 and PATC publication, *Circuit Hikes in the SNP.*)

LAUREL PRONG TRAIL

2.8 miles (4.5 kilometers)   PATC map No. 10: I-16)

This trail starts from the *AT* near Bootens Gap, descends very gently along the south slope of Hazeltop Mtn. to Laurel Gap, then descends more steeply through an area of much mountain laurel (kalmia). For the final mile it leads through the valley of Laurel Prong. To the right of the trail, in several locations along the creek, one can find the great laurel or rosebay rhododendron which blooms here in late June or early July. Near its end at Hoover Camp the trail passes through much large hemlock. In some places a carpet of false lily of the valley, blooming in late

May, carpets the ground; in other places running cedar, a type of club moss, acts as a ground cover.

Access:

From Bootens Gap, SDMP 55.1, follow the *AT* north for 0.6m. A cement post marks the Laurel Prong trailhead.

To reach the lower end of the trail, follow directions for getting to Hoover Camp from the east. The Laurel Prong trailhead is near the end of the access road to Hoover Camp, about 300 ft. west of the bridge over Mill Prong.

Detailed description:

From the *AT* to Hoover Camp

0.0-2.8 Junction with the *AT* at a point 0.6m. north of Bootens Gap.

1.0-1.8 Reach Laurel Gap. Cement Post marks start of an overgrown trail leading up to Cat Knob where it connects with the present Jones Mtn. Tr. Laurel Prong Tr. turns left here and continues to descend.

2.2-0.6 Cement Post marks the Fork Mtn. Trail, blue-blazed, which leads right for about 1½ miles to "The Sag" and the Fork Mtn. Fire Rd. (The upper end of the Fork Mtn. Tr. also connects with the Staunton River Tr. and the Jones Mtn. Tr., both blue blazed.)

2.8-0.0 Reach Hoover Camp. To reach Mill Prong Trail follow access road left for 250 ft.

DOUBLETOP MOUNTAIN TRAIL

approx. 4 miles (or 6.5 kilometers)   (PATC map No. 10: N-14)

Hiking begins on Va. Sec. 649 (Rapidan Fire Rd.) at the top of the Chapman Mtn. Ridge. Turn onto gated road leading north along the ridge and follow for about 0.2m. to where the Doubletop Trail goes left from the road and continues along the ridge crest. At first the trail is dim and hard to follow and a map and compass are helpful. However, when about a mile from Rt. 649, the trail gets much better and is shored up along the side of the mountain by stonework of the type built by the CCC's. From here there are good views of Fork Mountain with its tower and of Jones Mountain to the southwest and, to the southeast, the

mountain vistas of the Southern Section of the SNP. The trail
continues on around the sides of the first top and into a slight sag.
Here, in winter, one can see Old Rag Mtn. to the north. After
skirting the second top (Doubletop has three tops!) the trail turns
down the mountain and comes into a dirt road. Follow this road
to the right, come to the Rapidan River and follow on upstream
for a short distance to a bridge and the Rapidan Fire Rd. Follow
the fire road (Rt. 649) left to return to the start of the hike.
Circuit hike is about 6.5m. long.

VA. SEC. RT. 622 (within The Park)

Enter the SNP about 1.3m. north of Graves Mill. (Graves Mill
is about 5½m. up Va. Sec. 622 from Wolftown on Va. 230.)
Within the park the road continues up the Rapidan to its junction with Va. Sec. 649 (or Rapidan Fire Rd.). It is open to automobile traffic its entire length and serves as an access road to the
Hoover Camp area and to the Staunton River Trail. The
Rapidan River along this road offers a number of spots suitable
for swimming.

FORK MTN. ROAD

approx. 4½ miles   (PATC map No. 10: L-14)

This road is not gated but is too rough for most cars. It leads
from the Rapidan Fire Rd. about 2m. southeast of Hoover Camp
up the eastern and southern slopes of Fork Mtn., winding in and
out of the SNP. It reaches "The Sag", the divide between the
Staunton River drainage area and that of Laurel Prong, then
climbs to the tower on the top of Fork Mtn., el. 3840 ft. Where
the road crosses the upper reaches of the Staunton River the
Staunton River Tr. enters from the left. 0.2m. farther the
Jones Mtn. FFT enters from the left. At "The Sag" the Fork
Mtn. Tr. leads west 1.3m. to Laurel Prong Tr. and the Jones
Mtn. Tr. leads south to Cat Knob and then descends the
Jones Mtn. ridge to end of the Staunton River Tr.

STAUNTON RIVER TRAIL

approx. 4.3 miles (6.9km.)   (PATC Map. No. 10:N-15)

This trail follows up the Staunton River from VA Sec. 662 at the junction of the Staunton and Rapidan Rivers all the way to its source and continues on to "The Sag" where it connects with the upper ends of the Jones Mtn. Tr. and the Fork Mtn. Tr., both blue-blazed. The last 0.8m. of the trail is along the Fork Mtn. Fire Rd. which continues beyond "The Sag" to the summit of Fork Mtn.

Jones Mtn. cabin users can make a nice circuit hike of about 7½ miles by ascending the Jones Mtn. Tr. and returning via the Staunton River Tr. (and including the McDaniel Hollow Tr. if so desired.)

Access:

To reach the lower end of this trail follow Va. Rt. 230 west from U.S. 29 south of Madison for 4 miles to Wolftown (or follow Rt. 230 northeast from U.S. 33 in Stanardsville). Turn north onto Va. Sec. 662 and continue on paved road as far as Graves Mill, 5.5m. At road junction, take the right fork, still Rt. 662, which crosses Kinsey Run and follows up the Rapidan River soon entering the SNP. At 2.0m. beyond Graves Mill reach junction of the Staunton and Rapidan Rivers. There is room for a few cars on Rt. 662 and also a few feet up the old Staunton River Rd. One small parking area is reserved for cabin users. Do not block either road.

Detailed description:

0.0-4.3 Junction with VA Sec. 662 at the junction of the Staunton and Rapidan Rivers. The trail follows an old road along the southwest side of the Staunton River.

2.0-2.3 Junction with the Jones Mtn. Tr. which leads left, uphill. (Jones Mtn. Tr. leads 4.8m. passing Bear Church Rock, then along the ridge of Jones Mtn. to Cat Knob and then down to its upper end at "The Sag." Jones Mtn. Cabin is reached by following this trail for 0.8m. from the Staunton River Tr. junction, then following the side trail 0.2m.

2.4-1.9 Junction with the McDaniel Hollow Tr., blue-blazed, which leads southeast to join the Jones Mtn. Tr. in 0.5m.

3.5-0.8 Turn left onto the Fork Mtn. Fire Rd. and continue to climb.

4.3-0.0 Reach "The Sag." Here the Staunton River Tr., the Fork Mtn. Tr. and the upper end of the Jones Mtn. Tr. meet. (The Fork Mtn. Fire Rd. continues to the summit of Fork Mtn.)

FORK MTN. TRAIL

approx. 1.4 miles (2.2km.)					(PATC Map No. 10:J-15)

This very lovely trail has recently been recleared and blue-blazed. Its lower end is on the Laurel Prong Tr. 0.6m. from Hoover Camp. The Fork Mtn. Tr. crosses Laurel Prong in an area of much rosebay rhododendron and hemlock. As it gradually climbs Fork Mtn. the rhododendron is replaced by mountain laurel. The route of the trail follows an old farm road as it switchbacks up the mountain to reach a junction with the Fork Mtn. Fire Rd. at "The Sag." At this junction it connects with the blue-blazed Jones Mtn. Tr. and blue-blazed Staunton River Tr.

LEWIS SPRING FALLS TRAIL

1.8 miles (2.9 kilometers)					(PATC map No. 10:G-13)

This trail leads from the *AT* at a point immediately below Big Meadows Lodge to Lewis Spring Falls and on to the *AT* at Lewis Spring, used with the *AT* it offers a pleasant circuit trip of only 3.1m.

To reach the start of this trail find the path between the Amphitheatre Parking Area and the Big Meadows Lodge and follow it north about 0.1m. to the *AT* intersection marked by a signpost. The Lewis Spring Falls Trail will be directly across here. (To the left the *AT* leads "south". The southern end of the Lewis Spring Falls Trail is 0.9m. from here via the *AT*. To the right the *AT* leads "north" circling the Big Meadows Campground and reaching Fishers Gap in 1.6m.) Lewis Spring Falls Tr. descends. At 1.1m. a spur trail leads right steeply downhill for 0.2m. to the base of the falls. At 1.2 m. a trail leads right 150 ft. to an overlook at the head of the falls. Trail now ascends steeply, reaching Lewis Spring Service Rd. at 1.7m. Reach the *AT* at 1.8m. (To complete the circuit hike, turn left on the *AT* and follow it back to Big Meadows.)

JONES MOUNTAIN TRAIL

approx. 4.8 miles (7.7km.)   (PATC Map No. 10:L-15)

The lower end of this blue-blazed trail is on the Staunton River Trail two miles from its junction with VA Sec. 622. The trail's upper end is at "The Sag" on Fork Mtn. Access to Jones Mtn. Cabin, a mountain cabin restored by the PATC and available for use by campers, is via this trail. Reservations for the use of the cabin must be made at PATC Headquarters. See Chap. VI: "Shelters and Cabins." The trail passes over Bear Church Rock which offers an excellent view of the Staunton River valley and eastward.

Detailed description: Staunton River Tr. to "The Sag"

0.0-4.8 Junction with the Staunton River Trail at a point 2.0m. west of VA Sec. 662. (Staunton River Tr. follows up the river and reaches "The Sag" in 2.3m. from this junction.)

0.5-4.3 Junction with the blue-blazed McDaniel Hollow Trail, which leads right for 0.5m. to end of the Staunton River Trail.

0.8-4.0 Jones Mtn. Cabin Trail leads left (east) for 0.2m. to the cabin.

1.3-3.5 Reach Bear Church Rock which offers an excellent view to the north and east. The trail now follows the ridge of Jones Mtn.

2.2-2.6 Where the ridge from Bear Church Rock and Bluff Mtn. join, the trail turns northwestward.

3.4-1.4 Reach a slight sag between Jones Mtn. and Cat Knob. Here Jones Mtn. fire foot trail leads to the right for 0.6m. to join the Fork Mtn. Fire Rd. It is blazed and followable.

4.0-0.8 Reach the summit of Cat Knob. Trail swings sharply to the northeast here.

4.8-0.0 Reach "The Sag" and the junction with the Fork Mtn. Fire Rd. and the upper ends of the Fork Mtn. Tr. and the Staunton River Tr., both blue-blazed. (It is 2.3m. down the

Staunton River Tr. to the lower end of the Jones Mtn. Tr., thus offering a 7½ mile circuit hike to users of Jones Mtn. cabin.)

McDANIEL HOLLOW TRAIL

approx. 0.5 miles (0.8km.)   (PATC Map No. 10:L-16)

This short blue-blazed trail has one end on the Jones Mtn. Tr. its other end on the Staunton River Tr. It follows the route of an old mountain road across McDaniel Hollow and affords a short cut for hikers making a circuit using the Staunton River and Jones Mtn. Trails.

TANNERS RIDGE HORSE TRAIL

2.5 miles (4.0 kilometers)   (PATC map No. 10: H-13)

This is a loop trail that leads from the Big Meadows stables out along Tanners Ridge and back, crossing the A T twice.

TANNERS RIDGE ROAD

1.4 miles within the SNP (2.2 km.)   (PATC map No. 10: H-14)

This road, gated at the Drive and at the Park boundary, leads west from the Skyline Drive, SDMP 51.6, for 1.4m. to the Park boundary where it becomes Va. Sec. 682. (about 6 mile from Stanley). There is a cemetery, still being used for burials, at the junction of this road with the A T. the A T junction is 0.3m. from the Drive.

POWELL MTN. FFT

2.9 miles (4.6 kilometers)   (PATC map No. 10: I-16)

At present this trail is for bushwhackers only. The trail is overgrown and its blazing is faint and otherwise inadequate. The route is entirely within Park boundaries. It leads from the Skyline Drive just south of the Hazeltop Ridge Overlook, SDMP 54.4, down to Va. Sec. 759. If this trail is reblazed it could be used along with the upper stretch of Rt. 759, the Meadow School Fire Rd. and the A T for a circuit trip of under 10 miles.

FULTZ RUN FFT
HARRIS COVE FFT
CHAPMAN-DOVELL FFT
STONY RUN FFT
WEST NAKED CREEK FIRE RD.

These trails, on the west side of the Skyline Drive and south of Tanners Ridge Rd. pass through an arm of the Shenandoah Park extending a considerable distance west from the bulk of the Park. They are difficult to get to as many of them extend onto private land. They are not recommended for the regular hiker.

MEADOW SCHOOL FIRE RD.

approx. 1.5m. (2.4 kilometers)   (PATC map No. 10: I-18)

This road, gated at the Skyline Drive and at the Park boundary, descends the west slope of the Blue Ridge. Its upper end is on the Skyline Drive at a point, SDMP 56.8, directly opposite the Slaughter Fire Rd. which leads past Bearfence Mtn. Shelter. Outside the Park the Meadow School Fire Rd. becomes Va. Sec. 759. (From the lower end of the fire road it is about 10m., via Rt. 759, to Elkton.) (Fire Road not shown on 12th edition of map No. 10).

LEWIS MTN. FFT

4.1 miles (6.6km.)   (PATC map No. 10: J-19)

The upper end of this fire trail is on the *A T* at the south edge of the Lewis Mtn. Campground. The first 1.0m., over the highest peak of the mountain, can be followed with no difficulty but beyond here the trail is impossible to follow. The lower end, near the Conway River, is marked but the trail soon gives out.

CONWAY RIVER FIRE RD.

1.4 miles within the Park (2.3km.)   (PATC map No. 10: I-17)

This road, gated at the top and at the Park boundary, leads from the Skyline Drive, SDMP 55.1, to the edge of the park, about 1.4m., then continues through land set aside as a Virginia Wildlife Area for another 2-3/4m.; then, as Va. Sec. 615, it continues on down to the valley as far as Graves Mill on the Rapidan River.

BEARFENCE MTN. LOOPS

0.3m. and 0.3m. (.5km. and 0.5km.)   (PATC map No. 10: I-18)

A very short but very scenic trail leads from the *A T* up over the rocky ridgetop of Bearfence Mtn., then back down to the *A T*. In addition, a very rough trail—more a rock scramble than a real trail—continues north along the ridgetop for another 0.2m., then swings downhill, crossing the *A T* and continuing on for another 0.1m. to the Bearfence Mtn. Parking Area on the Skyline Drive, SDMP 56.4. The Bearfence Mtn. loops and *A T* together make a rough figure eight. The Park Service conducts nature hikes here during the summer. The southernmost junction of the loop trails with the *A T* is 0.6m. north of the access road to Bearfence Mtn. Shelter via the *A T*. The northernmost junction is 0.4m. farther north along the *A T*.

OLD SLAUGHTER ROAD

3.7 miles (6.0 kilometers)   (PATC map No. 10: I-18)

This road's upper end is on the Skyline Drive, SDMP 568, and is just across the Drive from the Meadow School Fire Rd. Its lower end is near the Conway River on an upward extension of Va. Sec. 667. The first 0.3m. of this old road serves as the service road for Bearfence Mtn. Shelter. (Reminder: no camping at the shelter except in extremely inclement weather.) Below the shelter the road has deteriorated into a foot trail. The first 1.5m. is pleasant walking and should be particularly lovely in early June as there is much mountain laurel along the trail as it descends along the Devils Ditch. Farther down the mountain the road is crisscrossed by other old roads and it is difficult to know which road is the Slaughter Road as there are no **blazes and no signs to** help. For this reason the lower 2 miles of the road are recommended only for the experienced hiker prepared to bushwhack.

POCOSIN FIRE RD.

2.5 miles (4.0 kilometers)   (PATC map No. 10:J-21)

From the Skyline Drive, SDMP 59.5, this road leads Southeastward passing Pocosin Cabin, a locked structure available for use of hikers and campers. (Reservations must be made in advance at PATC Headquarters. See Chap. 6: "Shelters and Cabins".) The road can be used along with the Pocosin Horse Trail, South River Fire Rd. and *A T* for an excellent circuit hike of about 7½m. A somewhat longer circuit hike would also include the South River Falls Trail. The fire road becomes Va. Sec. 637 outside the Park. It is gated at the Skyline Drive and at the Park Boundary.

Detailed description:
   0.0-2.5 Skyline Drive, SDMP 59.5
   0.2-2.3 Intersection with the *AT.* (Via the *AT* it is 2.8m. south to the South River Fire Rd. and 0.5m farther to the South River Falls Trail.)
   0.3-2.2 Pocosin Cabin to right of the road.
   1.1-1.4 From the road the Pocosin Horse Trail leads 1.3m. to the South River Fire Rd. (Via the South River Fire Rd. it is 1.2m. to the junction with the South River Falls Tr. and 0.8m. farther to the *AT.*) Just beyond this junction and to the right of the road are the interesting ruins of the former Upper Pocosin Mission.
   1.3-1.2 To the left, the Pocosin Hollow FFT leads north. (The fire trail is poorly blazed and exceedingly difficult to follow down Pocosin Hollow.)
   2.5-0.0 Park boundary. Road continues outside the Park. It becomes Va. Sec. 637 farther east.

POCOSIN TRAIL (POCOSIN HORSE TRAIL)

1.3 miles (2.1 kilometers)   (PATC map No. 10: K-21)

   This trail connects the Pocosin Fire Road and the South River Fire Rd. and can be used with them for a good hike. At the junction of the trail with the Pocosin Fire Rd. one can examine the ruins of the old Upper Pocosin Mission. On the trail above 0.1m. from its end on the South River Fire Rd. a side road leads east passing the interesting, periwinkle-covered South River Cemetery in 0.1m.

POCOSIN HOLLOW FFT

2.6 miles (4.2 kilometers)   (PATC map No. 10: K-21)

   This trail is no good now except for those hikers willing to bushwhack as it is poorly marked and almost impossible to follow down through the hollow. However, the area which once was highly populated is an interesting one to explore and the fire trail passes one surprisingly large old cemetery with all the graves marked only with field stones.

SOUTH RIVER FALLS TRAIL

1.8 miles (3.0 kilometers)   (PATC map No. 10: J-23)

This scenic trail leads from the South River Picnic Grounds, SDMP 62.8, down into the deep wooded gorge of the South River. It continues as far as the foot of the very lovely South River Falls. From top to bottom the trail loses 1000 ft. of elevation. The cascading falls are about 70 ft. high.

Detailed description:

0.0 Trailhead is on the road that loops through the South River Picnic Grounds at a point where the road is farthest to the east.

0.1 Intersection with the *A T*. (Via the *A T* it is 3.0m. south to Swift Run Gap and 3.3m. north to Pocosin Cabin.)

1.0 Pass observation point near the top of the falls.

1.2 At juncton with an old road turn right, downhill. (to the left, the old road leads to the South River Fire Rd.)

1.8 Reach the South River about 500 ft. below the falls. Go upstream on foot-trail.

1.9 Base of falls. For a circuit hike and an easier return to the picnic grounds, backtrack for the first 0.7m. Where the South River Falls Tr. turns left off the old road, continue straight for another 0.4m. to reach the South River Fire Rd. Follow the fire road uphill about 0.8m. to the *A T* intersection. Turn left onto the *A T* and follow it 0.5m. to the South River Falls Trail.

SOUTH RIVER FIRE ROAD

2.3m. described (3.7 Km.)   (PATC map No. 10: J-23)

This road leads east from the Skyline Drive, SDMP 62.7, just north of the South River Overlook. It can be used as a link in several possible circuit trips in combination with the South River Falls Trail, the *A T*, the Pocosin Horse Trail, and the Pocosin

Fire Rd. To the east the road eventually becomes Va. Sec. 642 which comes into paved Va. Sec. 637 about 5m. north of Stanardsville. The road is gated at the Drive and at the Park boundary.

Detailed description:

From Skyline Drive eastward.

0.0 Skyline Drive, SDMP 62.7, just north of the South River Overlook.

0.3 Intersection with the *AT*. (From here via the *AT* it is 0.5m. south to the South River Falls Trail and 2.8 north to Pocosin Cabin.)

1.1 Junction with an old road, a branch of the South River Falls Trail.

1.5 Cross gate.

2.0 An old road leads uphill on the left.,

2.3 Junction with the Pocosin Horse Trail. (Horse trail leads left for 1.3m. to the Pocosin Fire Rd. The horse trail, a road here, is gated.) From this junction the fire road continues on down into the valley, becoming Va. Sec. 642.

SADDLEBACK MTN. FFT—SOUTH RIVER SHELTER FFT

2.7 miles (4.3km)   (PATC map No. 10: J-24)

The trail shown on the PATC map as the South River Shelter FFT but on the USGS Swift Run Gap 15 min. quad as the Saddleback Mtn. FFT can be followed with care from the South River Shelter to the *AT* (where it is marked as the Saddleback FFT). The southern part of this trail is not blazed and is badly overgrown but is visible as it follows an old road. The fire trail which is shown on the maps as running east-west along the southern slopes of Saddleback Mtn. is overgrown and should not be attempted except by those willing to bushwhack.

BIG BEND FIRE RD.

4.2 miles (6.1 kilometers)   (PATC map No. 10: J-26)

For the hiker who wants to walk with no climbing, this old road is ideal as there is no more than 500 ft. change in elevation in its entire length. The road leads north from U.S. 33 at a point on the highway 1.3m. east of Swift Run Gap. The fire road is gated.

ALLEN HOLLOW FFT

approx. 1.5 miles to Park boundary   (PATC map No. 10: I-19)

From where it starts on the Skyline Drive this trail is cleared and well blazed. Its lower end has not been checked out for this Guide Book. The trail starts from the Drive at a point just across from the Lewis Mtn. Campground entrance, SDMP 47.5, and is marked as the Allen Hollow FFT by a metal post (but is shown on the PATC map No. 10: 12th edition, as the Lewis Mtn. West FFT.)

DRY RUN FALLS FIRE RD.

2.8 miles (4.5 kilometers)   (PATC map No. 10: J-23)

This fire road, gated at the Skyline Drive and near the Park boundary, leads from the Drive, SDMP 62.6, down the west side of the Blue Ridge. The former trail to Cedar Falls, now completely overgrown, started from this road. Farther down the road, a faint trace of an old road leads left to Dry Run a few hundred feet upcreek from Dry Run Falls. These falls are well worth seeing after a period of wet weather.

The lower end of the fire road is on Va. Sec. 625. From this point it is 0.3m. west to the upper end of the Big Ugly Run FFT and 2.8m. farther to Va. Sec. 759. From the junction with Rt. 759 it is 2.6m. via Rt. 759 to U.S. 340 in Elkton.

BIG UGLY RUN FFT

1.2 miles (1.9 kilometers)   (PATC map No. 10: H-22)

This short trail is marked by posts at each end. Though not blazed it is easy to follow as steady use of the trail keeps it open. Big Ugly Run is neither big nor ugly; the trail along it a pleasant one. A small orchid, Rattlesnake Plantain, is plentiful here. Its July bloom, though unimposing, is always a pleasure to wild flower enthusiasts. The upper end of the trail is on Va. Sec. 625 at a point on the road about 0.3m. west of the lower end of the Dry Run Fire Rd. The lower end is on Va. Sec. 606 which parallels the South Branch of Naked Creek. The junction of trail with road is about 0.4m. north of the junction of Va. Sec. 606 with Va. Sec. 607.

HENSLEY HOLLOW FFT

(1.2 miles within the Park)   (PATC map No. 10: I-25)

HENSLEY CHURCH FFT

2.2 miles (3.5 kilometers)   (PATC map No. 10: J-21)

The Hensley Hollow FFT is closed to hikers beyond the Park boundary so is not recommended. The Hensley Church FFT is badly overgrown but could be used by bushwhackers. Its upper end is on the Skyline Drive a few hundred feet north of the Pocosin Fire Rd. junction, SDMP 59.5. The lower end is at the Hensley Church on Va. Sec. 625. (To reach the lower end follow Va. Sec. 759 from Elkton to its junction with Va. Sec. 625. Turn right onto Rt. 625 and follow it almost to its end; the church is about a mile beyond the lower end of Dry Run Fire Rd.) The trail, marked by a yellow post, follows a jeep road from behind the church for over a mile to reach a high meadow. It enters the Park along a badly overgrown, former wood road, difficult to find, near the highest point of the meadow. Look for faint yellow blazes.

SOUTHERN SECTION

HIGHTOP SHELTER FFT

0.5 miles (0.8 kilometers)   (PATC map No. 11: J-3)

This short trail leads south from the Skyline Drive, starting at a point just across from the east or "north" end of the Swift Run Overlook SDMP 67.2. It climbs steadily to end on a trail leading from the Hightop shelter to the spring just below it.

HIGHTOP SHELTER RD.

0.7 mile (1.1 kilometers)   (PATC map No. 11: J-4)

This road leads from the Smith Roach Gap Fire Road, at a point on the fire road about 3/4 m. from the Skyline Drive, SDMP 68.6, and continues to the Hightop Shelter, crossing the *AT* 0.2m. before reaching it. For a short circuit hike one can follow the *AT* from Smith Roach Gap to the summit of Hightop, then descend by backtracking as far as the Hightop Shelter Rd., following the latter to the Smith Roach Gap Fire Rd. and following the fire road back to Smith Roach Gap.

SMITH ROACH GAP FIRE ROAD

1.0 miles (1.6 km.) within the Park   (PATC map No. 11: J-4)

This road leads southeastward from the Skyline Drive at Smith Roach Gap, SDMP 68.6, to the Park boundary. The access road to Hightop Shelter leads left from the fire road at a point on the latter about 3/4 m. from the Drive. A short way beyond the Park boundary the road divides: the left fork, Va. Sec. 626. descends gradually, skirting the head of White Oak Spring Branch, then descending a ridge extending from Hightop Mtn., and finally coming into Va. Sec. 630 at a point very near Va. Sec. 810. The right fork leads south over private land, following a long ridge toward Slaters Mountain, eventually coming into Va. Sec. 631. Both road branches are of interest to hikers.

SIMMONS GAP FIRE ROAD

1.0 miles (1.6 kilometers) east of Skyline Drive and
1.5 miles (2.4 kilometers) west of Skyline Drive within the Park
(PATC map No. 11: H-7)

This road, which crosses the Skyline Drive at Simmons Gap,
leads from the Park boundary in Beldor Hollow as a
continuation of Va. Sec. 628 to the eastern boundary of the Park
where it becomes Va. Sec. 628 again. The road is gated at both
Park boundaries and on both sides of the Drive. Hikers
sometimes use the western portion of this road along with the
Rocky Mount Trail and the old Gap Run Road (trail) for a loop
hike. See PATC Map No. 11.

FLATTOP MTN. FFT

0.7 miles (1.1 kilometer)   (PATC map No. 11: I-7)

This trail follows an old roadbed from the Ranger Station at
Simmons Gap up a hollow toward Flattop Mtn. and ends at the
Park boundary. Along much of the way the *AT* closely parallels
the old roadbed. The fire fire foot trail is not blazed nor marked
with the customary posts.

ROCKY MOUNT TRAIL

5.4 miles (8.7 kilometers)   (PATC map No. 11: H-8)

In the southern section of the Park there is a Rocky Mount, a
Rocky Mountain and a Rockytop. Rocky Mount is the most
northern of these. The blue-blazed Rocky Mount Trail starts at
the Skyline Drive, SDMP 76.1, and is marked by a cement sign
post. It leads along a northward-bearing side ridge reaching the
peak, Rocky Mount, el. 2741 ft., in 3.4m. From the peak it
descends steeply to Gap Run.

There are several interesting circuit hikes which include this
trail. One of these involves descending the Rocky Mount Trail,
turning right and following the old road up Gap Run, then
ascending the Gap Run Trail to its upper end on the Rocky

Mount Trail and returning to the start via the latter trail; total distance about 10 miles.

The lower end of the Rocky Mount Trail may be reached via the Gap Run Road Trail.

Detailed description:

0.0-5.4 Skyline Drive, SDMP 76.1. (This point can be reached from the *AT* by following a short unmarked spur trail from the *AT* to the Drive near the Two-Mile Run Overlook and walking north along the Drive for about 0.3m.) The Rocky Mount Tr. follows along a ridge which extends northward. Many good views are offered.

2.2-3.2 Reach trail junction. To the right the blue-blazed Gap Run Trail leads down along Gap Run to join the old Gap Run Road, now just a trail.

3.4-2.0 Reach the summit of Rocky Mount, el. 2741 ft. From here the trail descends rather steeply. In about a mile the trail turns right off the ridge, descends to a creek, and follows down the creek.

5.4-0.0 Junction with Gap Run Rd. Trail. To the left along the old road (yellow blazed) it is about 0.7m. to the Park boundary. To the right, along the road, the junction with the Beldor Ridge FFT is 0.2m., the lower end of the Gap Run Trail (and the Park boundary) is 0.8m. and its end on Va. Sec. 628 is 1.2m. (Via Rt. 628, to the right, it is 1.5m. farther to where the road enters the Park and becomes the Simmons Gap Fire Rd.)

GAP RUN TRAIL

1.5 miles (2.3 kilometers)   (PATC map No. 11:G-7)

This blue-blazed trail starts from the Rocky Mount Trail at a point 2.2m. from the Skyline Drive and leads down along Gap Run to the Gap Run Road Trial, joining it at a point 0.4m. NW of Va. Sec. 628 via the old road and 0.8m. south of the lower end of the Rocky Mount Trail. The Gap Run Trail is often used along with the Rocky Mount Trail for a circuit hike. Access to the lower end of the Gap Run Tr. is from Gap Run Rd. Trail.

GAP RUN ROAD TRAIL

1.9 miles (3.1 kilometers)   (PATC map No. 11: G-6)

This old road follows Gap Run as it bisects a thin western arm of the Park, separated from the main ridge by the valley of Hawksbill Creek. The southeastern end of the old road can be reached from U.S. 33 by turning south on Va. Sec. 628 at a point on Rt. 33 about 2 1/4 miles west of Swift Run Gap, just at the edge of the Park. Follow Rt. 628 up the valley of Hawksbill Creek for 3.8 m. (Parking space is very limited.) The Gap Run Rd. leads right, uphill and somewhat back. The first 0.4m. is on private land.

To reach the northwest end of this trail follow U.S. 340 south from Elkton to a point about 1/2m. south of the highway bridge over Hawksbill Creek and turn east onto Va. Sec. 754. Follow Rt. 754 for 0.4m., then turn left onto Va. Sec. 630 and follow it for 1.0m. Here turn left onto the more southern of two dirt roads leading toward the Park. This road ends at a house in about ½m. It is advisable to ask permission to park along the road and to cross on foot through the meadow to reach the Gap Run Road Trail beyond.

Detailed description:

Va. Sec. 628 toward the northwest.

0.0 Junction with Va. Sec. 628. (From this point via Rt. 628 it is 3.8m. north to U.S. 33 and 1.5m. south to the lower end of the Simmons Gap Fire Road which is the continuation of Rt. 628 within the Park.) Trail, a jeep road here, passes through private land, soon following along the Park boundary.

0.4 To the left the Gap Run Trail leads 1.5m. up Gap Run to join the Rocky Mount Trail. Gap Run Road Trail enters Park at this junction. The next 0.8m. of this road is marked with blue blazes.

1.0 Beldor Ridge FFT leads right from the old road.

1.2 To the left the Rocky Mount Trail leads 5.4m. to the Skyline Drive, SDMP 76.1. Beyond this junction the Gap Run Road Trail is marked with yellow blazes as far as the Park boundary. Red lobelia (cardinal flower) grows along the old road here, blooming in August.

1.9 Reach Park boundary near a fence corner. Road continues along the fence but is no longer in the Park. In 0.2m., where road enters field, it is gated. Beyond the field the road is drivable (but still private property) and leads to Va. Sec. 630.

BELDOR RIDGE FFT

3.9 miles (6.3 kilometers)   (PATC map No. 11: G-5)

HANSE MTN. FFT

1.5 miles (2.5 kilometers)   (PATC map No. 11: G-2)

The Beldor Ridge FFT leads along Beldor Ridge from the Gap Run Road to Hawksbill Creek and on to U.S. 33. It is occasionally cleared and blazed and is followable at present. It is recommended for experienced hikers only. Whether the stretch of trail between the Park boundary and U.S. 33 is open is not known. The junction of the Beldor Ridge FFT and Hanse Mtn. FFT is right at the Park boundary. (See PATC Map No. 11)

The Hanse Mtn. FFT leads from the Beldor Ridge FFT over Hanse Mtn. to Sapling Ridge Rd., Va. Sec. 634. This trail is blazed but badly overgrown. Its end on Rt. 634 is marked by a yellow post. This trailhead is at a point on Rt. 634 (where the Park boundary touches the road) about 0.2m. from U.S. 33.

TWO-MILE RIDGE FFT

2.2 miles (3.5 kilometers)   (PATC map No. 11: H-8)

This fire foot trail leads north from the Skyline Drive following the narrow Two-Mile Ridge which separates Two-Mile Run and One-Mile Run. The trail ends at an interesting rock outcrop about a tenth mile short of the peak, el. 2408 ft., at the end of the ridge. (No view from the peak itself) There are views from the rocks, especially in winter.

To reach the start of this trail park at the Two-Mile Run Overlook), SDMP 76.2, and walk south along the Drive for about 0.1m. Trailhead is marked by yellow metal signpost. (The *AT* comes within 100 ft. of the east side of the Drive 100 ft. south of here. Look for unmarked path.) The trail may be overgrown but is blazed well and can be followed with care. In 1.0m., in a sag, the trail forks. The left fork, which leads downhill, is the One-Mile Run Trail. To continue along the ridge trail take the right fork. Reach rock outcrop in another 1.2m.

ONE-MILE RUN FFT

3.5 miles (5.6 kilometers)   (PATC map No. 11: G-8)

This fire foot trail runs from the Two-Mile Ridge FFT down to One-Mile Run, then on down the run for nearly two miles. Then it swings north and continues on to Two-Mile Run. It ends on a private road just north of Two-Mile Run. One can then follow the dirt road 0.8m. to reach the highway junction of Va. Sec. 754 and 649.

To reach the upper end of the One-Mile Run FFT from the Skyline Drive follow the Two-Mile Ridge Trail for 1.0m. and, at the trail junction, take the left fork leading downhill. (No metal post here but a metal marker, on a tree, is labeled One-Mile Run FFT.)

To reach this trail from U.S. 340 follow either Va. Sec. 754 or 649 east to where they join. (The U.S. 340-Rt. 649 junction is 5.3m. south of Elkton at Island Ford: the U.S. 340-Rt. 754 junction is 6.3m. south of Elkton at Rocky Bar.) Park cars along the public road near the road junction. Proceed on foot up the dirt road (private) leading SE toward the Park. Continue for 0.8m., avoiding a road branch leading left. A yellow metal post marks the start of the fire foot trail which follows an old wood road to the right here. For the first 0.3m. along the trail avoid all left forks as these old roads lead to old mine pits. Beyond the first 0.3m. take the left fork at each road junction. About 3/4 mile from its start the fire foot trail enters the Park. Within the Park the trail is well blazed (yellow) and following it presents no problem.

IVY CREEK SHELTER SERVICE ROAD

0.4 miles (0.6 kilometers)   (PATC map No. 11: I-11)

This short road, which runs from the Skyline Drive, SDMP 79.4 to the Ivy Creek Shelter, can be used by hikers as part of a short circuit hike which would include a climb up to the Loft Mtn. ridge via the Deadening Nature Trail, SDMP 79.5, then the stretch of *AT* between the Nature Trail and the Ivy Creek Shelter, and the return to the Skyline Drive via the service road and, finally, a 0.1m. walk along the Drive for a total circuit distance of 2.1m.

DEADENING NATURE TRAIL

1.3 mile circuit (2.1 kilometers)   (PATC map No. 11: I-11)

This is a short but very interesting Park Service Selfguiding trail. (See Loft Mtn. Developed Area map inset, back of PATC map No. 11). It involves a fairly steep climb from the Skyline Drive to the *AT* on Loft Mtn. and an equally steep descent. The trail starts on the east side of the Drive, right at the entrance to the Loft Mtn. Developed Area, SDMP 79.5. It climbs 0.6m. to the *AT*, turns left and follows the *AT* for 0.1m., then descends 0.6m. to its starting point.

THE FALLS TRAIL

4.7 miles (7.5 kilometers)   (PATC map No. 11: H-12)

This is a lovely trail. There are beautiful waterfalls on both the Doyle River and Jones Run. Enormous trees growing near the creeks add interest. The Falls Trail, combined with a short section of the *AT*, forms an 8 mile loop ideal for a circuit hike.

This graded trail was constructed by the CCC in 1936-37. It involves a steep descent along one water course and a steep climb along the other. The northern terminus is at the Doyle River Cabin Parking Area on the Skyline Drive, SDMP 81.1, el. 2800 ft.; the southern terminus, also on the Drive, is at the Falls Trail Parking Area, SDMP 83.8, el. 2790 ft. The elevation of the trail at the junction of Doyle River and Jones Run is only 1500 ft. The FallsTrail and the *AT* intersect just below the Doyle River Parking Area at a point on the *AT* 2.2m. north of Browns Gap and again just below the Falls Trail Parking Area at a point on the *AT* 1.2m. south of Browns Gap. (Distance along the *AT* between the trail intersections 3.4m.)

The Doyle River Cabin, a locked structure, is located near the Falls Trail, 0.4 from its northern terminus. For use of this cabin, reservations must be obtained in advance from PATC Headquarters. (See Chap. 6: "Shelters and Cabins")

The old Browns Gap Fire Road, leads down the mountain from Browns Gap to Browns Cove, intersecting the Falls Trail a short distance above the upper falls on the Doyle River. A shorter loop hike, 6½ miles in length, can be made by descending Jones Run along the Falls Trail, ascending Doyle River past the upper falls, then following the Browns Gap Fire Rd. to the *AT*, and finally proceeding south along the *AT* to the Falls Trail intersection.

Detailed description:

South (where there is ample parking space) to north

0.0-4.7 Southern terminus, Falls Trail Parking Area, Skyline Drive, SDMP 83.8, el. 2700 ft. Trail crosses the *AT* in 100 ft., then continues eastward, descending.

0.6-4.1 Trail crosses Jones Run.

1.5-3.2 Trail returns to the run and follows down along its south bank.

1.6-3.1 Reach base of a sloping falls.

1.7-3.0 Reach top of the Upper Falls. A short side trail affords good view of the falls.

1.9-2.7 Reach top of Lower Falls.

2.5-2.2 Reach "half-way" point, the junction of Jones Run and Doyle River. Trail ascends from here.

3.2-1.5 Reach top of the Lower Falls of Doyle River, a two-step cascade between high rock cliffs.

3.5-1.2 Reach top of the Upper Falls. This is a three-step cascade in a lovely canyon.

3.8-0.9 Cross Browns Gap Fire Rd. (Road leads west uphill for 1.7m. to intersect the *AT* at Browns Gap. To the east the road leads down into Browns Cove becoming Va. Sec. 810 at a point about 18m. from Stanardsville. and 11m. from Crozet.)

4.4-0.3 Pass spring on right of trail. Here a spur trail on the right leads 0.1m. steeply up to Doyle River Cabin.

4.7-0.0 Cross the *AT*. (Via the *AT* from this junction it is 10.0m. north to Simmons Gap 2.2m. south to Browns Gap, and 3.4m. to the southern terminus of the Falls Trail.) In 200 ft. reach Skyline Drive at Doyle River Cabin Parking Area, SDMP 81.1, el. 2800 ft.

BROWNS GAP FIRE RD.

3.5 miles within the Park (5.2 km.)   (PATC map No. 11: G-13)

This old road, the eastern extension of the Madison Run Rd., leads from the Skyline Drive at Browns Gap, SDMP 82.9, down the east slopes of the Blue Ridge to Browns Cove, crossing the Falls Trail and the Doyle River in 1.8m. The old road continues beyond the Park boundary for another 1.0m. where it becomes Va. Sec. 629. The start of Rt. 629 is at a point 0.8m. above the highway bridge over the Doyle River and 1.2m, from Va. Sec. 810. One should park along or near Va. 810 as Rt. 629 is only a one-track road above the bridge and there is almost no place to pull off the road.

The Browns Gap Rd. was used by Stonewall Jackson and his men during the Civil War. About 0.4m. down from the Skyline Drive, to the left of the road, a short footpath leads to the grave of William H. Howard, Co. F, 44 Va. Inf., C.S.A. Father down the road but above the Doyle River is a tulip tree of tremendous girth. The stretch of the old road between the Falls Tr. intersection and the Park boundary is quite lovely. There are many large trees including hemlock, and the road itself clings along the edge of a steep hillside with the river far below.

BIG RUN FIRE ROAD

4.4 miles (7.1 kilometer)   (PATC map No. 11: E-10)

This is the valley route through the canyon of Big Run, which flows from south to north. Big Run and its tributaries form the largest watershed area in the Park. The grade of the fire road is very gentle all the way from the Park boundary to its upper end on the Big Run Trail at the shelter. It is a very pleasant walk and makes one leg of a circuit hike with the other leg being either the Rockytop Trail or the Rocky Mtn.-Brown Mtn. Trail. The cliffs, talus slopes and gorge at "The Portal" just below the fire road's bridge over Big Run are very spectacular.

Access:

The upper 'end can be reached from the Big Run Trail, following it "south" from Big Run Parking Overlook SDMP 81.2, for 2.2m. to just beyond the Big Run Shelter or following the Big Run Trail north from its intersection with the *AT* at a point 0.6m. north of Browns Gap, SDMP 82.9.

To reach the lower end of the Big Run Fire Rd. turn west from Rt. U.S. 340 at a point about 6½ miles north of Grottoes and 9 miles south of Elkton onto the fire road which is unmarked. The Shenandoah Park extends all the way to Rt. 340 here; see PATC map No. 11. Park within the SNP in any suitable spot, being careful not to block the fire road. On foot follow the fire road east, soon leaving the Park and crossing through private property for about one mile before re-entering the Park. (Landowner has put chains across the road in addition to the Park Service's gate where road reenters the Park. Trail description starts at the Park Service gate.)

Detailed description:

From lower end toward the shelter:

0.0-4.4 Gate on road at Park boundary.

0.2-4.2 Junction with Rockytop Trail which enters from the right. (To the left here one can bushwhack down to Big Run at "The Portal".) Road descends from here to reach the run.

0.7-3.7 Cross bridge over Big Run. Rocky Mountain-Brown Mtn. Trail comes in on left at far end of bridge. Trailhead is marked by cement post. Continue up the run. There are nine fords on the road, seven of Big Run, the other two of side streams. When the run is full the fording may be difficult.

1.7-2.7 There is a deep pool here. To the left the area is flat and shrubby where once there was a field. Slightly above the pool are the third and fourth fords.

2.1-2.3 At a fork, continue ahead crossing Rocky Mtn. Run, a side stream, immediately after. (Left fork is the Rocky Mtn. Run FFT which connects with the Rocky Mtn.-Brown Mtn. Tr. in 2.7m.) 250 yds. farther the Patterson Ridge FFT enters road from the left.

3.0-1.4 Road crosses to west bank here, recrosses in 0.3m. and again in another 0.2m.

3.7-0.7 The ninth ford, this time of a side creek entering from the right.

4.4-0.0 Road ends at junction with the Big Run Trail at a point just west of Big Run Shelter.

ROCKY MTN. RUN FFT

2.7 miles (4.3 kilometers)   (PATC map No. 11: F-10)

This fire trail is marked by yellow posts at each end and is fairly well blazed but is often overgrown. It can be followed with caution, by experienced hikers. It runs from the Big Run Fire Rd. up to the Rocky Mtn.-Brown Mtn. Trail and is used with them for a circuit hike.

PATTERSON RIDGE FFT

3.1 miles (5.0 kilometers)   (PATC map No. 11: I-11)

This fire foot trail leads from the Skyline Drive, SDMP 79.4, at a point opposite the service road leading to Ivy Creek Shelter, descending westward along Patterson Ridge. It comes into the Big Run Fire Rd. at a point 0.1m. above the lower end of the Rocky Mtn. Run FFT and 1.5m. above the lower end of the Rocky Mtn.-Brown Mtn. Trail. It can be used by experienced hikers for circuit hikes.

BIG RUN TRAIL

4.2 miles (6.7 kilometers)   (PATC map No. 11: H-12)

This trail affords access to the upper end of Big Run. The Big Run Shelter, available for use by campers only in inclement weather, is located at the lowest point of this trail. The shelter is only 150 ft. from the junction of the Big Run Fire Rd. and the Big Run Tr. The Big Run Tr. together with the Big Run Fire Rd. affords access to the lower ends of the Rockytop Tr. and the Rocky Mtn.-Brown Mtn. Tr. as well as the Rocky Mtn Run FFT and the Patterson Ridge FFT. The Big Run Trail, at its south end, links the *AT* with the Rockytop Trail.

An excellent short circuit hike of 5.8m, can be made by using the *AT* in one direction and the Big Run Trail in the other.

Access:
The northern end of this trail is at Big Run Parking Overlook on the Skyline Drive, SDMP 81.2. (250 ft. north along the Drive from here is the northern end of the Falls Tr. which crosses the *AT* in 200 ft.)

The southern end of this trail is on the *AT* at a point 0.6m. north of Browns Gap.

Detailed description:
North to South
0.0-4.2 Big Run Parking Overlook. Trail descends steeply by switchbacks.

0.7-3.5 From here trail follows crest of a ridge between branches of Big Run, then swings left down into the main hollow.

2.2-2.0 Reach Big Run Shelter, el. 1750 ft. (Available for use overnight only in case of inclement weather.) There is water available from stream near shelter. 150 ft. beyond the shelter the Big Run Tr. reaches the junction with the Big Run Fire Rd. which enters from the right. Beyond the junction the trail ascends steadily following above a branch of Big Run.

3.0-1.2 Turn sharply right, away from the ravine.

3.5-0.7 At trail junction the Big Run Tr. turns left. To the right the Rockytop Tr. leads 5.7m. down the ridge to the Big Run Fire Rd. Straight ahead is the Big Run FFT which descends

0.3m. to Madison Run Rd. entering it at a point on that road about 0.8m. from Browns Gap.

4.2-0.0 Junction with the *AT* at a point on the latter 0.6m. north of Browns Gap, SDMP 82.9 and 0.3m. south of the Skyline Drive, crossing, SDMP 82.2.

ROCKY MOUNTAIN-BROWN MOUNTAIN TRAIL

5.3 miles (8.5 kilometers)   (PATC map No. 11: H-9)

Rocky Mtn. and Brown Mtn. comprise the ridge extending west from the main Blue Ridge along the north side of Big Run. To the north of this ridge is the lower Two-Mile Ridge with Rocky Mount in the background. To the south is the high imposing ridge along which the Rockytop Trail runs.

From the Brown Mtn. Parking Overlook on the Skyline Drive, SDMP 76.9, this blue-blazed trail leads west along the ridge, first crossing the twin summits of Rocky Mountain, then over Brown Mtn. before dropping steeply to the Big Run Fire Rd. A popular loop hike is made by descending this trail and ascending the Big Run Fire Rd. to the Big Run Shelter, then following left along the Big Run Trail to the Big Run Overlook. (11 m.) To make a complete circuit one should cross the Drive and walk north to the Falls Trail junction, walk down to the *AT*, then follow the *AT* north as far as the Ivy Creek Overlook, then walk along the Drive the remaining distance to Brown Mtn. Overlook. Circuit hike distance about 18m.

A shorter circuit hike can be made by descending the Rocky Mtn.-Brown Mtn. Trail, following up the Big Run Fire Rd. for 1.3m., then turning left onto the Rocky Mtn. Run FFT and climbing along this trail for 2.7m. to its junction with the Rocky Mtn.-Brown Mtn. Trail. Then return to the Skyline Drive via the latter trail. Circuit distance 10 miles.

Access to the lower end of the RockyMtn.-Brown Mtn. Tr. is via the Big Run Fire Rd.

Detailed description:
   Skyline Drive to Big Run Fire Rd.
   0.0-5.3 Brown Mtn. Overlook, Skyline Drive, SDMP 76.9.

0.7-4.6 To left the Rocky Mtn. FFT leads down steeply to Big Run Fire Rd.

1.6-3.7 Reach crest of the peak of Rocky Mtn., el. 2800 ft. Here are striking views of the Massanutten range. The footing is rough along the trail beyond this point.

2.2-3.1 Pass to the right of the second peak of Rocky Mtn., el. 2864 ft. Along the trail from here to the summit of Brown Mtn. there is much turkeybeard (xerophyllum asphodeloides) a grasslike member of the lily family blooming in early June. Turkeybeard is a close relative of western beargrass.

3.1-2.2 Reach summit of Brown Mtn., el. 2560 ft. The Brown Mtn. ridge, like Rockytop to the southwest, consists of a sandstone streaked with fossil wormholes. The trail now descends along a ridge crest with magnificent views of Rockytop, the Shenandoah Valley and the south end of the Massanutten Range. It then descends steeply toward Big Run.

5.3-0.0 Junction with Big Run Fire Road at east end of the bridge over Big Run. "The Portal" of Big Run is a short distance down creek from here. Via the fire road it is 1.4m. uphill to the lower end of the Rocky Mountain Run FFT and 3.7m. to its end on the Big Run Trail. It is 0.5m. to the right along the fire road to the lower end of the Rockytop Trail and 0.2m. to the gate at the Park boundary.

ROCKYTOP TRAIL

5.7 miles (9.2 kilometers)   (PATC map No. 11: G-13)

This trail extends along the crest of the ridge which forms the sheer southwest wall of Big Run Canyon. It takes its name from its outstanding feature, Rockytop. (Hikers prefer to call the more northern peak, el. 2856 ft, the "real" Rockytop, rather than the one marked on the maps.) Where the trail skirts the western face of this highest peak it offers a superb view of the peaks to the southwest and of the Shenandoah Valley. In addition, the rocks of this part of the ridge are quite fascinating. An examination of them will show they contain long slender cylindrical markings, perhaps an eighth inch in diameter. It is believed that these are fossils of wormholes now 500 million years old! (See Chap. 3: Geology of the SNP.) For the wild flower enthusiast the Rockytop Trail also offers an abundance of the turkeybeard, our eastern version of the West's beargrass. You'll find it in bloom in early June.

This trail, blue-blazed, has a rather narrow footway and is rough underfoot. However its advantages far outweigh its disadvantages. It offers excellent views, access to the Austin Mtn. FFT, the Lewis Mtn. FFT and the Lewis Peak Tr. and can be used with either the Lewis Peak Trail or the Big Run Fire Rd. for a circuit hike.

Access:

The upper end of the Rockytop Trail is on the Big Run Tr. To reach it from the Skyline Drive follow the *AT* north from Browns Gap, SDMP 82.9, for 0.6m., turn left onto the Big Run Tr. and follow it for 0.7m. to its junction with the Rockytop Trail which is marked by a cement sign post.

The lower end of the Rockytop Trail is on the Big Run Fire Rd., 0.2m. east of the gate at the Park boundary.

Detailed description:

Big Run Tr. to Big Run Fire Rd.

0.0-5.7 Junction of the Big Run Trail, the Rockytop Trail, and Big Run FFT. Trailhead is marked by a cement sign post. (The Big Run FFT leads a short distance, 0.3m., to Madison Run Rd.) From the junction the Rockytop Tr. ascends.

0.4-5.3 Take right fork here. (Left fork is Austin Mtn. FFT which leads 3.2m. down Austin Mtn. ridge and comes into Madison Run Rd. near the Park boundary.) Trail now skirts the right side of the ridge for 0.6m., then swings over to the left side, crossing a talus slope with views of Austin and Lewis Mtns.

1.3-4.4 In sag the Lewis Mtn. FFT leads left. (Fire foot trail deadends on Lewis Mtn.)

2.2-3.5 Junction with Lewis Peak Trail, blue-blazed, is marked by cement post. Rockytop Tr. is right fork.

3.0-2.7 Reach sag at base of the hikers' "Rockytop", the highest peak of the ridge, and ascend along its left side.

3.5-2.2 Cross talus slope with outstanding views of Austin Mtn., Lewis Mtn., and Lewis Peak to the southwest and the Shenandoah Valley and Massanutten range farther north. Many of the rocks here and on the smaller rock slopes beyond this point are full of the "wormhole" fossils giving the rocks a striated appearance.

3.6-2.1 Bear right and ascend by switchbacks over the crest of a ridge bearing northwest here and descend along the northbearing ridge. (Hangman Run splits the main ridge here.)

5.7-0.0 Reach Big Run Fire Rd. Junction is marked with singpost. To left on the Fire Rd., the Park boundary where road is gated is 0.2m. To the right the road passes the junction with the Rocky Mtn.-Brown Mtn. Tr. in 0.5m. and continues to Big Run Shelter, 4.2m. (From the shelter it is 1.3m. via the Big Run Tr. back to its intersection with the Rockytop Trail. Round trip from Browns Gap is 13.4m.)

AUSTIN MTN FFT

3.2 miles (5.1 kilometers)   (PATC map No. 11: F-13)

This trail runs from the Rockytop Trail across Austin Mtn. and on down to Madison Run Fire Rd. The Austin Mtn. FFT is the most southern of the three parallel routes that lead westward from the high ridge of the Rockytop Tr. to outlying conical peaks. The upper (eastern) end of the Austin Mtn. FFT begins on the Rockytop Trail near the upper end of the latter. It follows a side ridge between Deep Run and Madison Run to just short of the top of Austin Mtn. Here a side trail leads to the top, which affords excellent views over Deep Run to Lewis Mtn. and of Rockytop. The main trail slabs the south side of the mountain, then descends steeply to Madison Run Fire Rd. Sections of this trail are rocky, steep and poorly graded. Heavy-duty foot gear is recommended.

Access:

To reach the upper end of this trail follow the *AT* for 0.6m. north from Browns Gap, SDMP 82.9. Turn left onto the Big Run Trail and follow it for 0.7m. to its junction with the Rockytop

Trail. Then follow the Rockytop Trail (straight ahead at the junction) for 0.4m. to the Austin Mtn. FFT trailhead.

The lower end of the Austin Mtn. FFT is on Madison Run Fire Rd. at a point on the road 4.4m. from the Skyline Drive at Browns Gap, SDMP 82.9. To reach the trail from U.S. 340 follow Va. Sec. 663 from Grottoes (or Va. Sec. 629 from just north of Grottoes) and continue on Rt. 663 beyond the junction with Rt. 629 to the junction of Rt. 663 and Rt. 708, a point about 2.5m. from U.S. 340. Continue up Rt. 663 another 0.2m. to where road is gated. There is some room for parking here. On foot follow up fire road for 0.7m. to trailhead marked by a metal post.

Detailed description:

Rockytop Tr. to Madison Run Rd.

0.0-3.2 Junction with Rockytop Trail.

1.8-1.4 At trail junction the right fork is a side trail leading to the summit of Austin Mountain. This side trail offers excellent views. Main trail follows left fork and slabs along the south slope of Austin Mtn.

2.1-1.1 Here the trail descends steeply across rock slopes and under cliffs.

2.7-0.5 Sharp turn in the trail. Steep descent continues.

3.2-0.0 Reach Madison Run Rd. To the left, via the road, it is 4.4m. to the Skyline Drive at Browns Gap. To the right it is 0.6m. to the lower end of the Furnace Mtn. FFT and 0.1m. farther to where the road is gated and becomes Va. Sec. 663. Circuit hike from Browns Gap using the *AT*, Big Run Tr., Rockytop Tr., Austin Mtn. FFT and Madison Run Fire Rd. is about 9½m.

LEWIS MTN. FFT

1.5 miles (2.4 kilometers)   (PATC map No. 11: F-12)

This trail is the central of the three parallel routes leading west from the Rockytop Trail. It is a yellow-blazed trail with a narrow tread and is apt to be overgrown in places. The view from Lewis Mtn. is limited to that of Lewis Peak and Rockytop.

The eastern end of this trail is on the Rockytop Trail at a point 1.3m. from its upper end. The trail follows the ridge which separates Upper Lewis Run and Deep Run. It reaches a sag at the base of Lewis Mtn. in 1.2m. From here a 0.3m. climb leads to the summit of Lewis Mtn., 2554 ft. The trail terminates at the summit.

LEWIS PEAK TRAIL

2.6 miles (4.2 kilometers)   (PATC map No. 11: F-12)

This blue-blazed trail is the most northern of the three parallel routes leading west from the Rockytop Trail. It continues beyond Lewis Peak, descending to the Park boundary and on a short distance farther to a dirt road in the valley. Lewis Peak itself is reached by a 0.3m. side trail. From the peak there is a panoramic view of the Shenandoah Valley and the Massanutten range to the northwest and west and the surrounding peaks of the Blue Ridge on the north, east, and south.

Access:

The upper end is reached via the Rockytop Trail. The trailhead is 2.2m. from the upper end of the Rockytop Trail, and 3.5m. from its lower end on Big Run Fire Rd.

To reach the lower end of the Lewis Peak Tr. turn off U.S. 340 onto a dirt road leading into the Shenandoah Park, where the Park extends to the highway, a point about 6½ miles north of Grottoes and nine miles south of Elkton. See PATC map #11. Park wherever a suitable spot is available but do not block the fire road. On foot take right fork of the fire road (which is badly washed in spots) and follow it south leaving the Park in about 1 mile. Continue on road, private property, another mile. Lewis Peak trailhead is just beyond the ford of Upper Lewis Run.

Detailed description:

Rockytop Tr. to Shenandoah Valley

0.0-2.6 Junction with the Rockytop Trail. (From this point via the Rockytop Tr. it is 1.0m. south to the junction with the Lewis Mtn. FFT, 1.9m. to the junction with Austin Mtn. FFT, and 2.3m. to its upper end on Big Run Tr. To the north via the Rockytop Trail it is 3.4m. to the Big Run Fire Rd. and, via the fire road, another 0.2m to the Park boundary.) From the junction Lewis Peak Tr. follows the crest of a ridge extending west between the two branches of Lewis Run.

0.7-1.9 Reach sag.

0.9-1.7 At junction main trail goes left. Right fork is a 0.3m. spur trail leading to the summit of Lewis Peak, el. 2760 ft. From Lewis Peak there is a panoramic view of the Shenandoah Valley, the Massanutten range and the surrounding peaks of the Blue Ridge. Main trail now descends toward the west and northwest along a ridge paralleling Upper Lewis Run.

2.4-0.2 Cross Upper Lewis Run. Fifty feet beyond turn right onto well-worn road, passing by a cabin.

2.6-0.0 Come into (private) Lewis Run Fire Rd. where trail ends. Follow road to the right for about 2 miles to reach U.S. 340.

BIG RUN FFT

0.3 miles (0.5 kilometers)   (PATC map No. 11: G-13)

This short trail runs from the junction of the Big Run Trail and Rockytop Trail down to the Madison Run Fire Road, entering it at a point 0.8m. west of the Skyline Drive at Browns Gap. The fire foot trail is blazed, cleared, and both ends are marked.

MADISON RUN FIRE ROAD

5.1 miles (8.2 kilometers)   (PATC map No. 11: G-13)

This road, gated at each end, runs from Browns Gap down the west side of the Blue Ridge, becoming Va. Sec. 663 outside the Park. It can be used with either Austin Mtn. FFT or Furnace Mtn. FFT for a circuit hike. The upper end of this road starts at Browns Gap, SDMP 82.9, el. 2599 ft. The lower end of this road can be reached by following Rt. 663 east to where it becomes the fire road, a distance of about 2¾m. from U.S. 340 in Grottoes. Elevation at the Park boundary is 1360 ft.

Detailed description:

Browns Gap to Va. Sec. 663

0.0-5.1 Browns Gap, SDMP 82.9

0.8-4.3 Big Run FFT leads right, uphill. (The fire foot trail ends at the junction of the Rockytop and Big Run Trails in 0.3m.)

4.4-0.7 Austin Mtn. FFT leads right, reaching the Rockytop Trail in 3.2m.

5.0-0.1 Furnace Mtn. FFT leads left 3.4m. to the Trayfoot Mtn. Fire Road.

5.1-0.0 Road is gated. Beyond it becomes Va. Sec. 663.

LEWIS RUN FIRE ROAD

approx. 3 miles (5 kilometers)   (PATC map No. 11: D-10)

This road leads southwest from the Big Run Fire Rd. near its start on U.S. 340 to the Park boundary. It continues outside the Park, through private lands, for another 2 miles to its junction with Va. Sec. 708 at a point 1½m. via Rt. 708 from U.S. 340. The lower end of the Lewis Peak Trail is on this road. As landowners may object to parking along this road outside the Park it is recommended that cars should enter the Park where the Big Run Fire Rd. starts (about 6 miles north of Grottoes and 9 miles south of Elkton) and then should be parked near the junction of the fire roads being careful not to block either road.

CRIMORA FIRE ROAD

approx. 8 miles (13 kilometers)   (PATC map No. 11: C-13)

This old road runs from Va. Sec. 663 east of Grottoes south to Va. Sec. 661 near Paine Run and from Va. Sec. 614 just south of Paine Run on to Va. Sec. 612 east of Crimora. It winds in and out of the Park with little change in elevation. Some of the sections outside the Park are now closed to hikers. A two mile stretch, from Rt. 663 south, is entirely within the Park but no foot trails intersect it so its use is limited primarily to bushwhackers. The southernmost section is used to reach the Riprap Shelter Service Road.

TRAYFOOT MTN. FIRE ROAD

1.6 miles (2.6 kilometers)   (PATC map No. 11: G-15)

This fire road, gated near the Drive, leads from the Skyline Drive, SDMP 84.7, to the tower on Trayfoot Mtn. The fire road offers the shortest route to Blackrock from the Drive. There is parking space for several cars on the road, a few hundred feet from the Drive. The Trayfoot Mtn. FFT and Furnace Mtn. FFT both have their upper ends on this road.

Detailed description:
  0.0-1.6 Skyline Drive, SDMP 84.7. Road leads west, soon almost touching, but not crossing, the *A T.* Road and Trail run parallel for about 0.1m. Then the road passes to the south of Blackrock whereas the *A T* circles the Blackrock area.
  0.4-1.2 Intersection with the *A T,* just south of Blackrock.
  0.5-1.1 A road to the left here leads down a southwestward extending ridge, paralleling the *A T.* (It serves as the service road to Blackrock Shelter.) Trayfoot Fire Road continues straight ahead.
  0.9-0.7 Where road reaches the ridge crest a spur trail leads right and back along the ridge for 0.1m. to the *A T* at Blackrock.
  1.4-0.2 Where road turns sharply to the left, the Furnace Mtn. FFT leads north (straight ahead) reaching the Madison Run Fire Rd. in 3.4m.
  1.6-0.0 Reach summit of Trayfoot Mtn. and tower. A few hundred feet short of the tower the Trayfoot Mtn. FFT leads right and follows the ridge crest that descends southwest. It reaches the Paine Run Fire Rd. in 3.8m.

FURNACE MTN. FFT

3.4 miles (5.5 kilometers)   (PATC map No. 11: F-16)

This trail, which has its upper end on the Trayfoot Mtn. Fire Road, leads down the long northwest-bearing ridge of Trayfoot Mtn. toward the peak of Furnace Mtn. From a sag at the base of this peak, the main trail descends along the west slopes of the mountain while a spur trail leads right 0.5m. over the summit.

The lower end of the trail is on the Madison Run Fire Road a tenth of a mile east of the Park boundary (and gate). It is recommended for experienced hikers only.

Access:

To reach the lower end of the trail follow Va. Sec. 663 east from U.S. 340 in Grottoes (or follow Va. Sec. 629 from a point on U.S. 340 north of Grottoes to Rt. 663, then continue left on Rt. 663) and continue up road to Park boundary where road is gated. Continue up road (Madison Run Fire Road) on foot. Lower end of Furnace Mtn. Trail is 0.1m. up the road, on the south side. It is marked by a yellow metal post. Trail, though blazed, is somewhat vague at this end. It crosses Madison Run, then heads *downstream* for a hundred feet or so before starting to climb.

To reach the upper end of this trail follow the Trayfoot Mtn. Fire Rd. from the Drive, SDMP 84.7, for 1.4 m. to where the road makes a sharp bend to the left before ascending toward the tower. The trailhead is right at the bend, to the right of the road. One may also reach the trailhead by following the *AT* 1.1m. from where it crosses the Skyline Drive, SDMP 84.3, to Blackrock. From here take the unmarked trail leading out along the ridge and follow it 0.1m. to where it joins the Trayfoot Mtn. Fire Rd. Continue out the ridge on the road for 0.6m. to the sharp bend described above.

Detailed description:

Trayfoot Mtn. Fire Rd. to Madison Run Fire Rd.

0.0-3.4 Junction with the Trayfoot Mtn. Fire Rd. Trail follows ridge leading north-northwest.

0.7-2.7 At trail junction turn sharply right. (The trail straight ahead leads out Abbott Ridge for about 1 mile. The trail on the left leads for about 1m. along Hall Mtn.)

1.8-1.6 Take left fork at trail junction. (Trail to the right leads for 0.5m. to beyond the summit of Furnace Mtn.; it ends on a ledge with an excellent view over Madison Run.)

3.4-0.0 Reach Madison Run Fire Rd. (Lower end of Austin Mtn. FFT is 0.6m. to the right, up the fire road. To the left in 0.1m. the road is gated at the Park boundary. From the gate where it becomes Va. Sec. 663 it is about 2.5m. to U.S. 340 in Grottoes.)

ABBOTT RIDGE FFT

1.0 miles (1.6 km.)   (PATC map No. 11: F-15)

HALL MTN. FFT

1.3 miles (2.1 km.)   (PATC map No. 11: F-15)

These trails are ideal for the adventurous, experienced hiker as they are hard to reach and therefore seldom travelled. Each of them follows a side ridge leading west from the northeast end of Trayfoot Mtn. Both trails start from the Furnace Mtn. FFT at the same point, 0.7m. down that trail from the Trayfoot Mtn. Fire Rd. (and 1.4m. from the *AT* at Blackrock) and 2.7m. up from Madison Run Fire Road. (See description of Furnace Mtn. FFT. for access.)

The Abbott Ridge FFT is clear except in a few spots. Most of the trail route is along the ridge crest. Views from the trail are not exceptional.

The Hall Mtn. FFT is followable but somewhat overgrown. For the first half mile the trail slabs along the side of the ridge and here the footway is very narrow. As the trail climbs Hall Mtn. it passes along rock slopes and the views are excellent.

TRAYFOOT MTN. FFT

3.8 miles (6.1 kilometers)   (PATC map No. 11: F-16)

This trail, recommended for experienced hikers only, traverses one of the outstanding side ridges in the southern part of the Park. Trayfoot Mtn. is a long ridge which leads southwest from the main Blue Ridge. It forms the divide between Paine Run and Stull Run. Along the route are some outstanding rock formations offering excellent views. The trail starts from the Trayfoot Mtn. Fire Rd. just below the tower, el. 3380 ft. The trail's lower end, on the Paine Run Fire Rd., is about 1440 ft. elevation. This trail, used in conjunction with the Paine Run Fire

Rd. and Trayfoot Mtn. Fire Rd., makes a good loop trip of about 9m. (A complete circuit would include the stretch of *AT* between Blackrock Gap and Trayfoot Mtn. Fire Rd. for a total distance of about 10m.)

To reach the trail from U.S. 340 turn east about 4½m. south of Grottoes onto Va. Sec. 614 at a point just south of the highway bridge over Paine Run. Follow Rt. 614 and continue beyond state maintenance. Continue pass an open gate a short distance and park, to the right of the road, on Park property at a small turnaround and parking area. (Note: Road is open for hikers only through the courtesy of the landowners and only during the day. Please cooperate by helping them keep both road and parking area free of trash. Old Crimora Fire Rd. leads south here. Do not block it.) Continue up private road on foot to Paine Run. The Paine Run Fire Rd., blocked at its lower end by large rocks, is just north of the run. Follow it up the run for 0.3m. to the start of the Trayfoot Mtn. FFT which is marked here by a yellow metal post.

Detailed description:

Trayfoot Mtn. Fire Rd. to Paine Run Fire Rd.

0.0-3.8 Junction with the Trayfoot Mtn. Fire Rd. just below the tower. (From this point it is 0.9m. to the *AT* at Blackrock and 1.6m. to the Skyline Drive, SDMP 84.7.) Trail leads southwest along the crest of Trayfoot Mtn. ridge. Descend gradually, crossing numerous knobs. There are frequent views on both sides of the trail.

3.2-0.6 Turn sharply left (east). Excellent view of Buzzard Rock peak across Paine Run from here.

3.5-0.3 Turn sharply right.

3.8-0.0 Junction with Paine Run Rd. To left the road crosses the creek coming out of Lefthand Hollow in a few feet. The road continues for 3.4m. to the Skyline Drive at Blackrock Gap. To the right the road reaches the Park boundary in 0.3m. and comes into private road leading left. This road, at present open to hikers on foot, becomes in 0.8m. Va. Sec. 614. It is about 2m. farther to U.S. 340.

PAINE RUN FIRE ROAD

3.7 miles (6.0 kilometers)   (PATC map No. 11: G-17)

This road leads west from the Skyline Drive at Black Rock Gap, SDMP 87.4. In about one mile it passes near the Blackrock Springs, the site of a former hotel. Below the springs the road descends along Paine Run, finally passing through a narrow gorge between the SE end of the Trayfoot Mtn. ridge and a sharp peak, Buzzard Rock. The road, now permanently closed to vehicles at its lower end, comes into a privately owned road which leads due west for 0.8m. before becoming Va. Sec. 614.

To reach this road from U.S. 340, turn east onto Va. Sec. 614 at a point just south of the highway bridge over Paine Run. Continue beyond the state maintenance to where the road is gated. Landowners are allowing daytime hikers to drive beyond the gate a short distance to reach a small turn around and parking area on SNP property (where the old Crimora Fire Rd. leads south.) Continue along the private road on foot to reach Paine Run. Find the Paine Run Fire Road, blocked by boulders, on the north side of the creek.

At a point about 0.3m. up from the lower end of the fire road the Trayfoot Mtn. FFT heads north for 3.8m. to end on the Trayfoot Mtn. Fire Rd. a short distance below the tower. A 9½m. circuit hike can be made from Blackrock Gap by following the *AT* north to Blackrock, then the short cut-off trail that leads along the ridge from Blackrock to the Trayfoot Fire Road, then follow the Trayfoot Mtn. Fire Rd. west to the upper end of the Trayfoot Mtn. FFT, descend along the fire foot trail to Paine Run Rd. and ascend the fire road back to Blackrock Gap.

RIPRAP TRAIL

6.3 miles (10.2 kilometers)   (PATC map No. 11: G-18)

This is a very picturesque route. From its northernmost end on the *AT* it swings west and climbs along Calvary Rocks, where excellent views are to be had, and continues on by

Chimney Rock with more views. It descends Cold Spring Hollow and on into Riprap Hollow passing by the beautifully located Riprap Shelter. This is one of the few areas of the Park where one can find the Catawba rhododendron (blooming in late May), a very common shrub farther south. Below the shelter the trail route follows the Riprap Shelter Service Road for over half a mile, then turns up a side creek, climbs to Wildcat Ridge and ascends along this ridge to cross the *AT* and reach the Skyline Drive. Just south of the trail along Wildcat Ridge is beautiful Crimora Lake which may be barely visible from the trail.

An excellent circuit hike of about 9½m. can be made using the Riprap Trail in one direction and the *AT* in the other.

Access:

To reach the northern end of the Riprap Trail park at the Calvary Rocks Parking Area, SDMP 90.0, take the spur trail to the *AT* and turn right. Follow the *AT* north for 0.4m. to the start of the Riprap Trail.

The southern end of the trail is on the Skyline Drive at the Wildcat Ridge Parking Area, SDMP 92.1, about 0.1m. south of the Moormans River Overlook.

Detailed description:

North to south

0.0-6.3 Junction with the *AT* at a point on the *AT* 0.4m. north of the short spur trail leading to Calvary Rocks Parking Area, SDMP 90.0. (and 2.9m. south of Blackrock Gap via the *AT*.)

1.0-5.3 Spur trail leads left for 75 ft. to the projecting cliffs of Calvary Rocks.

1.2-5.1 Trail turns sharply left here. A spur trail leads right for 75 ft. to edge of cliffs, Chimney Rock, with fine views north.

1.8-4.5 Turn sharply left from the ridge down into Cold Spring Hollow. (Trail to the right here is the Rocks Mtn. FFT which leads along the crest of Rocks Mtn. for about 3m., then descends Davis Mtn. to reach the Riprap Shelter Service Road near its lower end.)

2.8-3.5 Trail crosses Riprap Run where the streams from the Cold Spring Hollow and Riprap Hollow join. Below, the trail descends steeply through a rocky chasm. Route here is very spectacular.

3.0-3.3 Cross to east bank of stream.

3.1-3.2 Trail crosses to west bank of stream. Spur trail leads right to Riprap Shelter. Shelter is attractively situated, facing east toward the creek and a high ridge behind it. There is a deep pool at the base of sloping falls here which makes an excellent swimming hole. (Note: Shelter may be used for sleeping only during inclement weather.) There is a considerable amount of pink (Catawba) rhododendron near the creek and shelter.

3.6-2.7 Turn sharply left on trail whereas the Riprap Shelter Access Road continues ahead down the creek, Meadow Run. (Shelter and trail can be reached from below by climbing up this road from the Park boundary. From the trail junction it is 0.9m. down this road to the Crimora Fire Road just beyond the Park boundary. Note: This access to the Park is through private land and may be closed to hikers. The Riprap Shelter Service Road is gated about 0.3m. inside the Park.) Trail crosses the run and climbs along a side stream up Wildcat Hollow.

3.7-2.6 To left, across the run, is a conspicuous cave at base of cliffs. A short spur trail leads across the run to the cave.

4.2-2.1 Turn sharply right from the old trail and cross run in 100 ft. Climb steeply toward Wildcat Ridge.

4.5-1.8 Reach crest of Wildcat Ridge in a sag and turn sharply left along it. (To the right here the Wildcat Ridge FFT, badly overgrown, leads down the ridge to the Riprap Shelter Service Rd. entering it near the Park boundary.) Ascend, skirting the north side of a knob.

4.8-1.5 Come into a sag. Trail now ascends along the south slope of another knob. There are occasional fine views south. In winter one may be able to glimpse Crimora Lake in Dorsey Hangar Hollow below the trail. Trail now switchbacks to the left.

5.3-1.0 Cross over knob, el. 2514 ft., and continue to ascend along the ridge.

6.2-0.0 Intersection with the *AT*. (To left, via the *AT* it is 2.8m. to the Calvary Rocks Parking Area, and 3.1m. to the northern end of the Riprap Trail. To the right it is 0.3m. to the

next *AT* crossing of the Skyline Drive and 2.3m. to Turk Gap.)
Continue straight ahead, ascending slightly.

6.3-0.0 Junction with the Skyline Drive at Wildcat Ridge
Parking Area, SDMP 92.1.

WILDCAT RIDGE FFT

1.6 miles (2.5 kilometers)   (PATC map No. 11: F-21)

This fire foot trail, which continues down Wildcat Ridge,
where the Wildcat Ridge-Riprap Trail turns north from it to
descend toward Riprap Hollow, is badly overgrown and should
not be attempted except by experienced hikers. Where the ridge
ends the trail descends steeply with switchbacks; it then levels off
before reaching the Riprap Shelter Service Road. The trail-road
junction is 50 ft. east of the Park boundary and 0.1m. east of the
Crimora Fire Road. To the right, via the road, it is 0.8m to where
the Riprap Trail comes into the road and 0.6. farther to the
Riprap Shelter.

ROCKS RIDGE FFT

approx. 3 miles (5 kilometers)   (PATC map No. 11: F-19)

This trail is suitable for experienced hikers only. It has its
upper end on the Riprap Trail, at a point 1.8m. from the *AT*. It
descends southeastward along a long, narrow ridge which ends
at Davis Mtn. The trail swings counterclockwise around Davis
Mtn. as it descends, and joins the Service Road to Riprap
Shelter at a point 0.2m below the point where the Riprap Trail
leaves the road, and 0.7m. above the road's junction with the
Crimora Fire Road.

RIPRAP SHELTER SERVICE ROAD

1.3 miles (2.1 kilometers)   (PATC map No. 11: F-21)

This road runs from the Crimora Fire Rd. (outside the Park
here) up to Riprap Shelter. To reach this road from U.S. 340 turn
east onto Va. Sec. 612 at Crimora and drive about 1.7m, nearly to

the end of state maintenance, then follow the Crimora Fire Rd.
left to its junction with the service road, a distance of about 1 mile.
Turn right and in a few feet enter the Park.

Detailed description:

0.0-1.3 Park boundary. A foot trail leads southeast here up
Dorsey Hanger Hollow to lovely Crimora Lake. A mining road
on the south side of the lake connects this lake with the mine
lakes to the south and the Turk Gap Trail, a former fire road. A
few feet farther up the service road the Wildcat Ridge FFT,
badly overgrown, leads right, up Wildcat Ridge.

0.3-1.0 Here road is gated.

0.7-0.6 Rocks Ridge FFT leads left to climb Davis Mtn. and
continues up the ridge for 3m. to join the Riprap Trail.

0.9-0.4 Riprap Tr. leads right 2.7m. to Skyline Drive.

1.3-0.0 End of road a little below the Riprap shelter.

TURK GAP TRAIL

1.6 miles (2.6 kilometers)   (PATC map No. 11:I-22)

This old road is gated at the Drive and at the Park boundary.
From Turk Gap, SDMP 94.1, it leads down the west side of the
Blue Ridge reaching the Park boundary just above the muddy
ponds of the old Crimora mine. (The Crimora Manganese Mine
was one of the largest manganese mining operations in the Blue
Ridge. The operations commenced in 1867 and extended,
through various mining methods, periodically to 1947;
operations were resumed in 1949, but the mines are now closed.
The manganese was mined out of clay deposits in a syncline of
Cambrian quartzite. Visitors will find this area more interesting
if they have read the detailed history of the mines, "The Crimora
Manganese Mine" by Samuel V. Moore, in the October 1947
PATC bulletin.)

To use Turk Gap Trail for a loop or circuit hike, descend this
trail and continue down to the ponds. Here one can follow an
old mine road north to lovely Crimora Lake in Dorsey Hanger
Hollow. (Crimora Lake, an artificial lake, formerly furnished
water power for mining operations.) From Crimora Lake
follow the foot trail that follows the outlet stream from below

the dam. This trail ends on the Riprap Shelter Service Road at a point on the road just inside the Park boundary. Continue up the service road for about 0.9m. Then turn right onto the Riprap Trail and ascend this trail all the way to the Drive for the loop trip of about 7½ miles, or turn right onto the *AT* 0.1m. before reaching the Drive and continue along the *AT* back to Turk Gap, a circuit of about 9½ miles.

TURK MTN. FFT

1.1 mile (1.8 kilometers)   (PATC map No. 11: I-22)

SAWMILL RIDGE FFT

2.4 miles (3.9 kilometers)   (PATC map No. 11: I-22)

These two trails, which are coincident for the first 0.6m., are well blazed and are highly recommended. They start at a point on the Skyline Drive, SDMP 94.2, just south of Turk Gap, and head west. In 100 ft. the fire trail(s) comes into the *AT* and follows it south (left) for about 0.2m. Here, at a junction marked by yellow posts, the fire trail(s) head west along a side ridge. Four-tenths mile farther the fire trails separate, the Sawmill Ridge FFT forks to the left while the Turk Mtn. FFT continues straight ahead.

From the junction the Turk Mtn. FFT climbs 0.5m. to the summit of Turk Mtn., el. 2981 ft., where the trail ends. The view from Turk Mtn. is outstanding. As on several of the other peaks of the Park which are west of the main Blue Ridge crest, the rock is a type of sandstone full of fossil wormholes, giving the rock a distinctive striated appearance.

The Sawmill Ridge FFT slabs along the side of Turk Mtn. for some distance, then reaches the ridge crest of Sawmill Ridge and follows the ridge out to a small knob, el. 2582 ft., a distance of 1.8m. from the trail fork. Much of the rock along this fire trail is like that on top of Turk Mtn. There are views from along Sawmill Ridge. Turkeybeard, a member of the lily family, is found growing here, blooming time early June.

MOORMANS RIVER FIRE ROAD

9.5 miles (15.3 kilometers)   (PATC map No. 11: G-17)

This was the original route of the Appalachian Trail between Blackrock Gap and Jarman Gap. From Blackrock Gap the road leads southeast, then south, following down the North Fork of the Moormans River to Va. Sec. 614. From here the fire road fords the North Fork at a point a short distance above the Charlottesville Reservoir. It then climbs southwestward to Jarman Gap following up the South Fork of the Moormans River. The fire road is gated at both ends and at the Park boundaries.

A rather long circuit hike, 21m., can be made by following the fire road in one direction and the *AT* in the other. For shorter circuits a portion of the fire road can be used along with the Turk Branch FFT and *AT*. From Blackrock Gap a circuit using the fire road, the fire foot trail and the *AT* is about 18m. long; from Jarman Gap a circuit using the southern portion of the fire road, the fire foot trail and the *AT* is only 8m. in length.

To reach the fire road from the valley follow Va. Sec. 810 from Crozet to White Hall (about 4½ m.) Then follow Va. Sec. 614 west for 5¾m. to its end just beyond the Charlottesville Reservoir. The junction with the fire road is here.

Detailed description:

North to south

0.0-9.5 From the Skyline Drive at Blackrock Gap, SDMP 87.4, el. 2321 ft., the road leads southeast, immediately crossing the *AT*.

1.4-8.1 Take right fork and cross stream. (Old road to the left leads up the valley through overgrown fields to Via Gap.) Continue downstream, heading almost due south.

1.6-7.9 To the left an old road leads uphill to Pasture Fence Mtn.

3.7-5.8 To the right a side trail leads 0.1m. up Big Branch to a series of cascades, the highest of which has a free fall of about 50 ft.

5.5-4.0 Cross Va. Sec. 614 at the end of that road. (Rt. 614

leads 5¾m. to White Hall on Va. Sec. 810.) In 0.1m. ford the North Fork of the Moormans River. The ford, el. 1000ft., is a few hundred feet below the former highway bridge, the foundations of which are still visible, and a few hundred feet upriver from the Charlottesville Reservoir. The fire road continues south to reach the South Fork of the Moormans River, then climbs along it, crossing the stream a number of times.
times.

7.6-1.9 To the right the Turk Branch FFT leads up the mountain to the Skyline Drive, joining it at a point about 0.3m. south of Turk Gap, SDMP 94.1.

9.3-0.2 Intersection with the *AT* at a point on the *AT* 0.2m. north of the Bucks Elbow Mt. Fire Rd.

9.5-0.0 Junction with Skyline Drive and Bucks Elbow Mtn. Fire Rd. at Jarman Gap, SDMP 96.7, el. 2173 ft. (The *AT* is 0.1m. east here via the Bucks Elbow Mtn. Fire Rd.)

TURK BRANCH FFT

2.1 miles (3.4 kilometers)   (PATC map No. 11: I-22)

This is a pretty trail and not a difficult one to follow. From the Skyline Drive about 0.3m. south of Turk Gap, SDMP 94.1, el. 2600′, the trail follows an old road down the east side of the Blue Ridge. Its lower end is on the Moormans River Fire Road, el. 1440′ at a point on the fire road 1.9m. north of Jarman Gap. By descending the Turk Branch FFT to the fire road, following up the fire road (south) to the *AT* just below Jarman Gap, and then taking the *AT* north to Turk Gap, a circuit hike of about 7½m. can be made. (Starting the circuit at Jarman Gap the hike would be a quarter mile longer as one would first have to hike down the Moormans River Fire Rd. to its intersection with the *AT*; then, after the circuit, retrace that distance along the fire road back to the Drive.) A much longer circuit can be made by descending the Turk Branch FFT, then following the fire road north to Blackrock Gap, and returning to Turk Gap via the *AT* (circuit about 18m.).

BUCKS ELBOW MTN. FIRE ROAD

0.6 miles within the Park   (PATC map No. 11: J-24)

JARMAN GAP FIRE ROAD

1.8 miles within the Park   (PATC map No. 11: J-24)

GAS LINE ROAD

2.0 miles   (PATC map No. 11: J-23)

From the Skyline Drive and its junction with the Moormans River Fire Road at Jarman Gap, SDMP 96.7, the Bucks Elbow Mtn. Fire Rd. leads east, uphill, winding its way up to the top of Bucks Elbow Mtn. (outside the Park) to a FAA installation. The road intersects the *AT* at a point 0.1m. from the Drive.

On the west side of the Drive the Jarman Gap Fire Road, a continuation of the Bucks Elbow Mtn. Fire Rd., leads down to the valley. As this road does not connect with other trails it is little used by hikers.

From the Skyline Drive, SDMP 96.2, the Gas Line Road also leads down the west slopes of the Blue Ridge. It comes into the Jarman Gap Fire Rd. near the Park boundary. It was constructed to give access to the gas pipeline and is of little interest to hikers at present. Like the fire roads it is gated at the Skyline Drive.

CHAPTER 6

SHELTERS AND CABINS

Shelters

The 20 open-faced shelters of the Park, 16 of them located near the Appalachian Trail, are regrettably no longer available for camping except in extremely inclement weather. In recent years (1965-1974) the shelters had been very much over-used and the areas surrounding them were suffering. The shelters were all too often filled by non-hiking campers or weekend hikers so that backpackers trying to travel considerable distances along the *AT* (The shelters were constructed primarily for the long-distance hiker) would find them full and could not count on using them. The Park Service Administration has reasoned that the lightweight tents now available could be carried by the backpacker, so that his need for Park shelters is much less now than in the past; hence the "No Camping" regulation at shelters.

The shelters do have stone fireplaces and hikers may still use them for cooking but then must move on to camp for the night. (Reminder: camping permit required.) Water is available at all but one (Byrd's Nest #1) of the shelters.

Chart below gives the distances along the *AT* between each shelter near the Trail in the Park. (The distance from the *AT* to each shelter is given in parenthesis.)

Shelters are listed in order from north to south

U.S. 522 to Indian Run Shelter (0.4m.)	**5.2**
Indian Run (0.4m.) to Gravel Springs (0.2m.)	**7.8**
Gravel Springs (0.2m.) to Elkwallow (0.0m.)	**6.1**
Elkwallow (0.0m.) to Byrd's Nest #4 (0.0m.)	**4.3**
Byrd's Nest #4 (0.0m.) to Pass Mountain (0.2m.)	**2.7**
Pass Mountain (0.2m.) to Byrd's Nest #3(0.0m.)	**4.2**
Byrd's Nest #3 (0.0m.) to Shaver Hollow (0.3m.)	**3.2**
Shaver Hollow (0.3m.) to Hawksbill Gap (0.3m.) ...	**6.3**
Shaver Hollow (0.3m.) to Byrd's Nest #2 (0.9m.)	**6.3**
Hawkbill Gap (0.3m.) to Bearfence Mtn. (0.2m.) ...	**12.7**

Byrd's Nest 2 (0.9m. via Nakedtop Tr. to
  summit of Hawksbill) to Bearfence Mtn. (0.2m.)**11.7**
Bearfence Mountain (0.2m.) to South River (0.3m.)**6.6**
SouthRiver (0.3m.) to Hightop (0.1m.) **5.9**
Hightop (0.1m.) to Pinefield (0.1m.) **8.3**
Pinefield (0.1m.) to Ivy Creek (0.1m.) **3.7**
Ivy Creek (0.1m.) to Blackrock (0.2m.) **9.4**
Blackrock (0.2m) to Sawmill Run (0.3m.) **10.0**
Sawmill Run (0.3m.) to Rockfish Gap **9.5**

Location of Shelters not near the *AT*

Old Rag Shelter (Central Section, PATC map No. 10: K-8)
located on the Saddle Trail up Old Rag Mtn. 0.4m. up the
trail from the junction of the Weakley Hollow, Berry Hollow
and Old Rag Fire Roads.

Byrd's Nest #1 (Central Section, PATC map No. 10: L-8)
located on the Saddle Trail up Old Rag Mtn. 1.5m. up the
mountain from the junction of the Weakley Hollow, Berry
Hollow and Old Rag Fire Roads.

Big Run Shelter (Southern Section, PATC map No. 11: G-12)
located on the Big Run Trail about midway between its
northern and southern termini. See Big Run Trail
description.

Riprap Shelter (Southern Section, PATC map No. 11: G-20)
located on the Riprap Trail, about halfway between its
northern and southern termini. See Riprap Trail
description.

Cabins

The PATC operates six locked cabins in the SNP. These
cabins are the property of the National Park Service and are
operated by the PATC under permit. Each cabin is attractively
located in the center of good hiking country. Four of them are
located near both the *AT* and Skyline Drive.

The cabins are designed for either overnight or longer use and
make excellent bases for stays of several days while exploring the
surrounding country.

A moderate fee is charged for use of the cabins. Details are available from the Potomac Appalachian Trail Club Headquarters, 1718 N St., N. W., Washington, D. C. 20036, open from 7pm. to 10pm. Mondays through Fridays: not open Saturdays, Sundays or holidays. Cabin reservations must be made in advance for their occupancy; keys are obtained from PATC Headquarters. The cabins are available both to members and to responsible non-members. Members may make reservations one month in advance, once per year; they otherwise follow the three-week-ahead limitation imposed on non-members. Non-members making a reservation for the first time must be properly identified and will be required to fill out a responsibility statement and to purchase the PA Cabins issue.

The cabins are equipped with all necessary items except food, personal bedding, flashlight, and firewood. There is an inside wood stove and fireplace (some inside, some outside) for cooking, plus all necessary pots and pans, plates, cutlery, cups, saucers, glasses, etc. Also provided are bunks, mattresses, and blankets (one per occupant) up to the stated capacity of the cabin. It is advisable to bring one's own sleeping bag. Broom, ax, saw, first-aid kit, kerosene and lanterns, and other items necessary for good housekeeping are provided. There is a latrine near each cabin.

Soap, toilet paper, tea, coffee, sugar, salt and pepper are sometimes available at the cabins. Users may add to the stock of these items if they have any of their own supply left over; they should be placed in the proper containers. No "strike anywhere" matches are to be left at the cabins. (Rodents may gnaw on them.) No unused food other than the items already mentioned should be left in the cabins and campers should take such items back to town with them. Remnants, including buried food, attract vermin to the cabin areas.

The number of occupants of a cabin may not exceed the stated capacity of the cabin. The maximum stay by one party at one or a succession of cabins is 10 days, including only one weekend. Because of the popularity of the cabins, only one reservation may be in process at one time. The cabin reservation period runs from 4 pm. of the first date stated to 4 pm. of the day succeeding the last date. If a reservation is to be cancelled it must be cancelled for the entire period and a new application filed if reservation for a shorter period is desired.

Range View Cabin is located in the northern section of the Park; Corbin, Rock Spring, Pocosin and Jones Mtn. Cabins in the central section; and Doyle River Cabin in the southern section. All are shown, along with their trail and road approaches, on the appropriate PATC maps.

Detailed Description of Cabins

Range View Cabin

This is a one-room stone cabin built in 1933 by members of the PATC. It is equipped with four double-decked, single-width bunks, an inside cooking stove and an outside fireplace under eaves of the cabin. The cabin looks out across an area cleared of trees and tall brush toward farms in the valley below. Campers from Matthews Arm Campground and hikers along the *AT* often visit the cabin area, especially on weekends, so it is somewhat lacking in privacy.

Parking for this cabin is at the Rattlesnake Point Overlook on the Skyline Drive, SDMP 21.9. From Washington, D. C. the shortest driving route is via Front Royal. To reach the cabin from the parking area follow the *AT*, which crosses the Drive just south of the overlook, south for 0.7m., then turn left onto the spur trail that leads 0.1m. to the cabin.

Corbin Cabin

This is an old mountaineer's cabin, restored by PATC volunteers in the early 1950s. (See Alvin Peterson's article in the July-September 1954 PATC Bulletin.) It is a solidly built, two story cabin with sleeping quarters on both floors. There is a fireplace in the living room, wood stove in the kitchen, and an outside fireplace.

The cabin is located in Nicholson (Free State) Hollow beside the Hughes River, a pleasant mountain stream. Water is obtained from this stream.

SUMMARY OF CABIN INFORMATION

Cabin	Capacity	Recommended for families with small children	Driving distance from D.C. to parking area (mi.)	Hike-in distance from parking area (mi.)	Hike-in distance from AT (mi.)	SDMP at or near parking area	PATC map coordinate
Range View	8	Yes	93	0.8	0.1	21.9	9: F-13
Corbin	8	No	93	1.4	1.5	37.9	10: I-6
Rock Spring	12	No	103	0.8	0.2	48.1	10: H-11
Jones Mtn.	10	No	106	3.0	—	—	10: M-15
Pocosin	12	Yes	114	0.2	0.1	59.5	10: J-21
Doyle River	12	No	129	0.3	0.3	81.1	11: H-12

One may approach the cabin either from the east (for a shorter driving distance but a much longer hike-in) or from the Skyline Drive. Most cabin users prefer to drive to the Shaver Hollow Parking Area on the Skyline Drive, SDMP 37.8. They then follow the rather steep Corbin Cabin Cut-off Trail for 1.4m. to reach the cabin. This route is also the shortest approach from the *AT*. (There is a short spur trail connecting the *AT* and Parking Area.) Some cabin users prefer to park at the Hughes River Gap Parking Overlook, SMP 38.6, and hike down the Nicholson Hollow trail 1.9m. to the cabin.

To reach the cabin from the Piedmont, turn west from Va. Rt. 231 at a point (about 10m. south of Sperryville) just south of the highway ridge over the Hughes River onto Va. Sec. 602. Continue up the south side of the river on paved road (It will first be Rt. 602, then 707, and then 600.) In 4.3m. from Rt. 231 where road turns sharply to the left, park car and follow up the Nicholson Hollow Trail on foot for 4.0m. to reach the cabin.

Rock Spring Cabin

This cabin, built of squared logs, looks out across the valley to the Massanutten range behind. The view from the cabin is excellent during the day but at night the twinkling lights of Stanley and Luray add a magical touch to the landscape. The cabin is equipped with enough bunks to sleep 12 persons, an inside wood stove and outside fireplace. It can be kept cozily warm in winter. There is a spring 50 yds. north of the cabin.

Warning: There is an extremely sharp drop-off in front of the cabin which can be dangerous for small children.

Parking for this cabin is just north of the Spitler Knoll Overlook on the Skyline Drive, SDMP 48.1. A short spur trail leads from the Rock Spring Parking Area to the *AT*. Follow the *AT* north for 0.6m., then turn left onto the spur trail leading 0.2m. to the cabin.

Jones Mountain Cabin

This cabin was originally the home of mountaineer

moonshiner Harvey Nicholson. It was unoccupied from the 1930s when the SNP was established until recently and was falling into ruins. Then members of the PATC, with the Park Service Administration's permission, restored the cabin making every effort to retain those parts of the original structure that were still serviceable and to replace damaged material with handcrafted replacements. In 1975 the restored cabin, which now presents a fine example of early cabin workmanship, became available for campers. A person may not reserve the Jones Mountain Cabin, however, unless he has previously held and used cabin reservations elsewhere without evidence of cabin abuse.

To reach the Cabin from Skyline Drive is difficult. The shortest route (about 5 miles) would be to start at Bootens Gap, follow the *AT* north for 0.6m., then descend the Laurel Prong Tr. to Laurel Gap. Bushwhack about a half mile to Cat Knob; there pick up the Jones Mtn. Tr. and follow it out to Bear Church Rock; then descend to the cabin.

To reach the cabin from the Piedmont, turn west onto VA Rt. 230 from US 29 just south of Madison. Follow Rt. 230 for 4 miles to Wolftown, then turn right onto VA Sec. 662. Continue on Rt. 662 taking the right fork, still Rt. 662 but a dirt road, at Graves Mill and continuing up the Rapidan River, soon entering the SNP. At 2.0m. beyond Graves Mill reach the junction of the Staunton River with the Rapidan. A few feet up the old road to the left of Rt. 662 there is a special parkng area for cabin users. From this parking area it is 3.0m. by foot to the cabin, following the Staunton River Tr. for 2.0m., then the Jones Mtn. Tr. for 0.8m., and finally the short trail to the cabin.

The cabin is equipped with mattresses to sleep 10, a wood stove for heating, and both inside and outside fireplaces. There is a spring about 75 ft. from the cabin. There is a large front porch high above the ground. *Warning:* While double railings have been built along the edges of the front porch and, inside the cabin, along the edge of the open-ended loft used for sleeping quarters, this cabin is not recommended for families with small children; the long hike-in is also difficult for such families.

Pocosin Cabin

This cabin is a one-room squared log structure located in a pleasant area with a good view toward the Piedmont. There are a number of excellent hiking possibilities in the area for both the experienced and novice hiker. The cabin is furnished with three double-deck double-width bunks with foam mattresses. A wood stove is provided for cooking and heating inside and there is also a fireplace outside under the cabin eaves.

Parking for this cabin is about 0.1m. along the Pocosin Fire Road from the Skyline Drive, SDMP 59.5. The hike-in is another 0.2m. along the fire road. A short (0.1m.) connecting trail leads between the cabin and the *AT*. This cabin is recommended for families with small children as there are no hazards near the cabin such as steep embankments; also the hike-in is short and easy.

Doyle River Cabin

This cabin, constructed of squared logs, sits above a cliff near the head of the Doyle River. It overlooks a picturesque valley with views of Cedar Mtn. and Via Gap. Sunsets are often spectacular as viewed from the cabin. There are bunks enough to sleep 12 persons. An inside wood stove and outside fireplace are available. The spring is 350 ft. downhill from the cabin.

Warning: Because of the cliff face in front of the cabin, it is not recommended for families with small children.

Parking space is provided at the north end of the Falls Trail on the east side of the Skyline Drive, SDMP 81.1. Hike-in distance (via the Falls Trail) is 0.4m.

INDEX
of Place Names Along the Trails